IMAGES
of America

GRAND RIVER

On the Cover: This unobstructed view of Grand Haven is seen from Dewey Hill looking south across the channel where the Grand River flows into Lake Michigan. The city has seen significant growth on both sides of the channel, but one thing has not changed: Dewey Hill is still a good vantage point. (Courtesy of the Loutit District Library, Grand Haven.)

IMAGES
of America

GRAND RIVER

Norma Lewis
Introduction by Michael Gutowsky

ARCADIA
PUBLISHING

ISBN 978-1-4671-1350-2

Published by Arcadia Publishing
Charleston, South Carolina

Printed in the United States of America

Library of Congress Control Number: 2015930410

For all general information, please contact Arcadia Publishing:
Telephone 843-853-2070
Fax 843-853-0044
E-mail sales@arcadiapublishing.com
For customer service and orders:
Toll-Free 1-888-313-2665

Visit us on the Internet at www.arcadiapublishing.com

For my multitalented granddaughter, Shelby Lynne Ayers, with deep appreciation for all her hard work assisting with this book
And in loving memory of Jay De Vries

Contents

ACKNOWLEDGMENTS

My first thank-you is to Shelby Ayers, without whose computer skills I could not have done this. She also took some of the photographs, went with me on historic-image explorations, scanned and rescanned, and helped with fact-checking and the other miscellaneous tasks involved in putting together this kind of book. My gratitude also goes to Jillian Berry for the maps. Beautiful job, Jill.

With heartfelt appreciation, I thank Michael Gutowsky for his informative introduction, and all the people at the various libraries, museums, and historical societies who generously shared their knowledge and their treasures: Jeanette McDonald, Jackson Public Library; Rachel Veramay, Ella Sharp Museum, Jackson; Deb Malewski, Eaton Rapids Area Historical Society; Heidi Butler, Capital Area District Library, Lansing; Jennie Russell, Michigan State University Library; Suzanne Schramski, Grand Ledge Area Historical Society; Malgosia Myc, Bentley Historical Library, University of Michigan; Margaret Sheffer, Portland Area Historical Society; Sue Houseman, Lyons-Muir Historical Museum; Pat Raimer, Boston-Saranac Historical Society Museum; Kathleen Cook, Ionia County Historical Society; Luanne Kaeb, Lowell Museum; Richard Harms, Hekman Library, Calvin College; Tim Gleisner and his always helpful staff, especially Melissa A. Fox, Grand Rapids Public Library; Gary Buyker Library, Hudsonville; Jim Budzynski, Coopersville Area Historical Society Museum; Nancy Richards, Grand Valley State University Library; Jeanette Weiden, Loutit District Library, Grand Haven; and Jane Ladley and Meredith Meyer, Tri-Cities Museum, Grand Haven. Kudos to all of you for keeping this area's history alive and accessible.

Last but not least, I am indebted to Jesse Darland and all the great people at Arcadia Publishing who make publishing with them a joy.

Introduction

Let us pick more than 200 years ago as the starting point for when the Grand River began impacting people. That is when the Native Americans known as the Three Fires settled along its banks. One of those groups, the Ottawa, discovered the rapids of the river and named the area Owashtanong, meaning an ideal place to live. These rapids are now synonymous with the name of Michigan's second-largest city, Grand Rapids.

Michigan's history can be traced by following the meandering route of the Grand River. The river traverses north and west from its start in the Irish Hills below Jackson to its end at Grand Haven. At 265 miles, it is Michigan's longest river. The Red Cedar, which flows through the campus of Michigan State University, and the Looking Glass, Maple, Flat, Thornapple, and Rogue Rivers comprise the main tributaries that feed into the Grand River. It flows through seven counties before emptying into Lake Michigan.

The Grand River watershed is the second-largest in Michigan, draining water from parts of the 15 southern and western counties. The watershed serves to connect primarily agricultural communities such as Olivet, Eaton Rapids, Portland, Ionia, Lake Odessa, and Saranac, along with urban areas like Lansing and Grand Rapids. The wetlands, marshes, and bogs filter out pollutants, in turn supporting a unique biodiversity both in the water and on land. As 13 percent of the Lake Michigan watershed, the Grand River is a critical component of the health of the lake itself.

Grand Rapids, Grand River Avenue, Grand Ledge, the Grand Valley, Grand Valley State University, many businesses—in fact, almost every name in Michigan that starts with Grand was inspired by the river. Red Flannel Day in Cedar Springs harks back to the latter part of the 19th century, when lumberjacks poled logs from the nearby pine and oak forests down the Grand River. Every decade, the river is celebrated with a two-week expedition along its entire length that puts a spotlight on its challenges and opportunities. People from all walks of life, students, professors, business leaders, government officials, scientists, and historians come together to paddle from Liberty Center near Jackson to Grand Haven.

It is an opportunity to celebrate the river's story, much of it marked by decades of abuse going back to the mid-1800s. The development of southern Michigan cities linked by railroads generated increased human and industrial waste. Clearing of white pine forests clogged the Grand River with sawdust. Logging brought more sediment into the river. In the late 1880s, one Grand Rapids resident described the river as an open sewer "covered with a green odiferous scum mixed with oil from the gas works." In 1905, the *Grand Rapids Evening Press* predicted that in a century the Grand River would be more sewer than river.

By the 1950s and 1960s, the plight of the United States' rivers gained attention when the Cuyahoga River in the Cleveland, Ohio, area began randomly catching fire. The Clean Water Act passed in 1972 limits the amounts of pollutants that may be discharged, thus allowing rivers and lakes to reclaim their water quality, along with providing incalculable benefits to the nation's health and that of all living organisms. Beginning in the 1990s, Grand Rapids spent over $200 million to improve its sewer system and reduce the overflow of sewage waste into the river by 99 percent. Fishing has come back to the Grand, and the river now supports nearly 100 species of fish.

There is still work to be done. More than 10 dams along the Grand River and approximately 200 more on its tributaries no longer serve a purpose and collect runoff water in impoundments. The runoff water is a mix of dirt, oil, and debris along with sediment containing dangerous herbicides, fertilizer, and insecticides. Development also causes problems resulting in fewer wetlands to filter those pollutants. These stresses to the Grand River are exacerbated by flooding.

April 2013 tested Grand Rapids' preparedness for flooding, and the city barely passed. Day after day of rain caused widespread flooding when the water rose to a record high. In harm's way were downtown buildings and neighborhoods, including the city's wastewater treatment plant. Residents were called upon to fill sandbags in an attempt to hold off the expected water rise and floating, untreated sewage that would accompany it. Fortunately, the three to four inches of rain forecast never came, and the floodwalls held.

But with warming temperatures, more winter and spring precipitation, and extreme weather projected by the West Michigan Environmental Action Council, will the floodwalls be adequate to protect the city from future flooding? That is a particularly salient question in view of Grand Rapids' plans for sufficient development to accommodate another 10,000 downtown residents in the coming years.

The news is not all bad. Community leaders, government officials, environmental groups, and volunteers are now working together to restore the river to more closely resemble its once pristine self. Over 200 bird species may be seen, along with about 50 species of mammals. People swim, paddle, and float again in the river.

There are riverboats on the Grand River to entertain passengers in Lansing and Grand Rapids. Couples romance under the summer moonlit sky on carriage rides that span the river in Grand Rapids. Much of the route for both the Fifth Third Riverbank Run and the Grand Rapids Marathon is along the river.

The river attracts us. It make us get out of our houses and cars to look and to think. Its calm waters soothe our minds. Canoeists like that. Faster stretches of the river excite our imaginations. Kayakers like that. Fishermen throw out their lines and catch everything from bass to trout to walleye. Many people just find a park bench, open a lawn chair, or spread a blanket on the soft grass.

Grand Ledge is the exception. Instead of grass, the banks are ancient sandstone and quartz outcroppings rising up to 50 feet for approximately one mile. On the north side of river at Oak Park, rock climbers practice their sport in a natural setting. The sandstone rock contains traces of iron, giving it an orange hue. Slivers of coal are visible along the hiking path, a reminder of the coal mining in days past. Also visible are remnants of caves that according to legend once harbored fugitive slaves and stolen horses. Chief Okemos and other Native Americans tapped trees for maple sugar annually at this place, which they called "Big Rocks." Fossils possibly date back 300 million years ago to a time when some believe that Grand Ledge was a saltwater sea.

All of us who spend any time on or near the Grand River have a relationship with it. Any good relationship, like any good marriage, should be cultivated and cared for.

—Mike Gutowsky
Instructor of Geography with Grand Valley State University,
Western Michigan University, Muskegon Community College

One

Jackson to Lansing

The Grand River begins virtually unnoticed at Liberty, Michigan, just south of Jackson. Liberty itself is easily overlooked and prides itself on being "conveniently located in the middle of nowhere." Other than being a mecca for bird-watchers, there is not much going on until the river reaches Jackson.

Jackson was founded in 1829 by Horace Blackman and Alexander Laverty, who named it Jacksonopolis, for Andrew Jackson. The name was changed to Jacksonburgh, then dropped to simply Jackson. Today, Detroit is known as Motor City, but in the early days of Michigan's automotive industry, anyone with a garage to tinker in tried building a car. Jackson soon had more than 20 companies cranking out vehicles. In 1854, the Republican Party was founded "under the oaks" of a grove on Morgan's Forty. In 1860, the party nominated a self-educated lawyer from Illinois named Abraham Lincoln, who became president and changed the course of history. Jackson is also home to the state's first prison, which had a tremendous impact on the city's economy by providing a ready pool of reliable labor.

From Jackson, the river flows north and west toward Lansing. Along the way, it courses through smaller townships and villages, including the city of Eaton Rapids. Settlers were drawn to the town as early as 1835 by the abundant timber and the power the river could provide. Eaton Rapids became known around the country and beyond when E.B. Frost discovered mineral water and called Eaton Rapids the "Saratoga of the West." The city rallied, building new hotels, restaurants, and other establishment to serve the tourists who were arriving in two trains every day. Other early industries included sawmills and woolen mills.

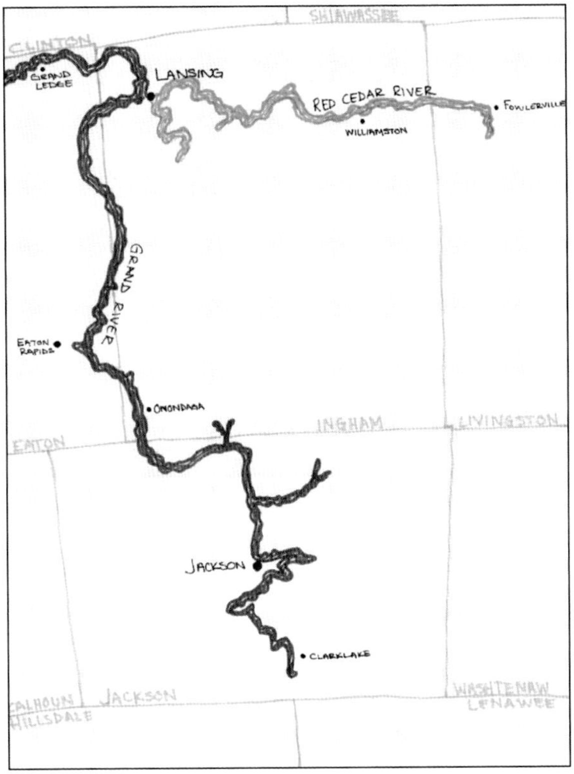

From its humble beginning just south of Jackson, the Grand River flows through Jackson, Ingham, and Eaton Counties on the way to Lansing. (Map by Jillian Berry.)

Though the river begins here, it can easily be overlooked and assumed to be a series of lakes and ponds. A little farther downstream, there is a rock bearing the following inscription: "Grand River Headwaters. Here at Liberty Mills is the first dam on the Grand River originating in nearby hills, the river flows nearly 300 miles north and west to where it joins Lake Michigan at Grand Haven. The Grand is Michigan's longest river." (Courtesy of the Ella Sharp Museum, Jackson.)

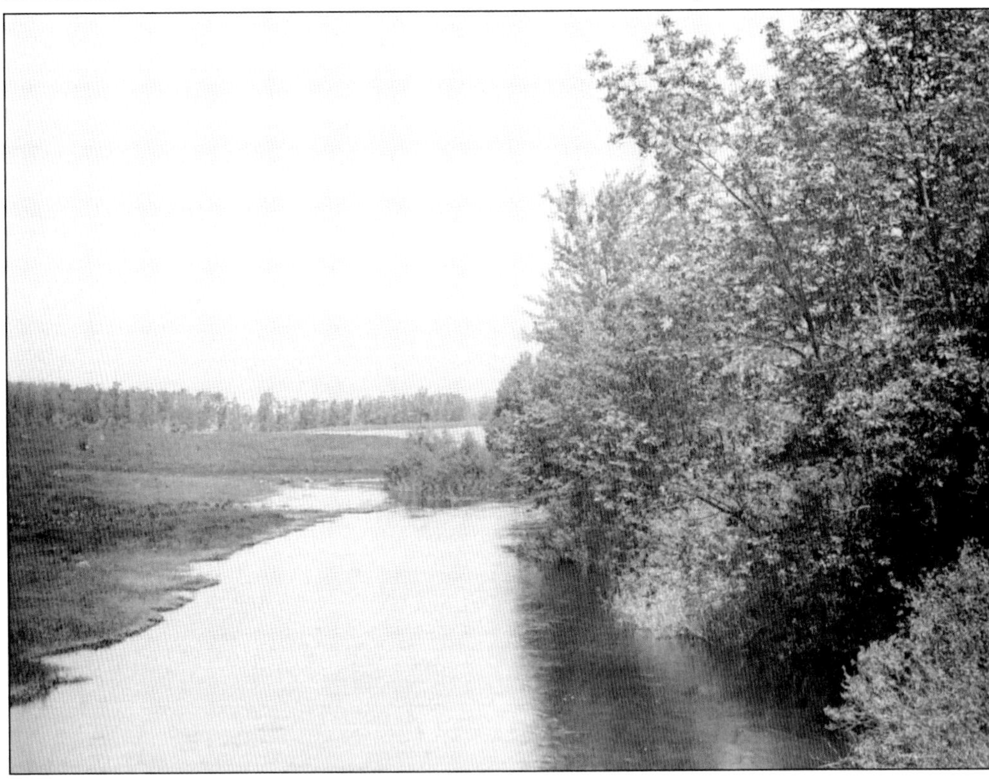

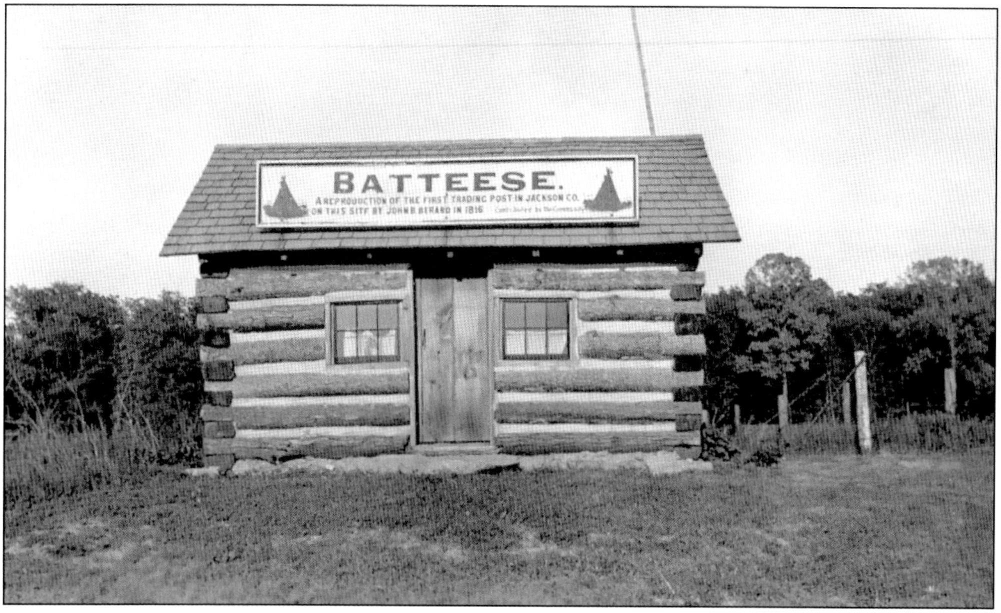

Like most of the towns and cities along the river, Jackson County started with a trading post. This is a replica of the one established in 1816 by John Baptiste Berard. "Batteese" is a corruption of Baptiste, the name by which he was usually called. Batteese Creek and Batteese Lake are both named for him. (Courtesy of the Bentley Historical Library, University of Michigan.)

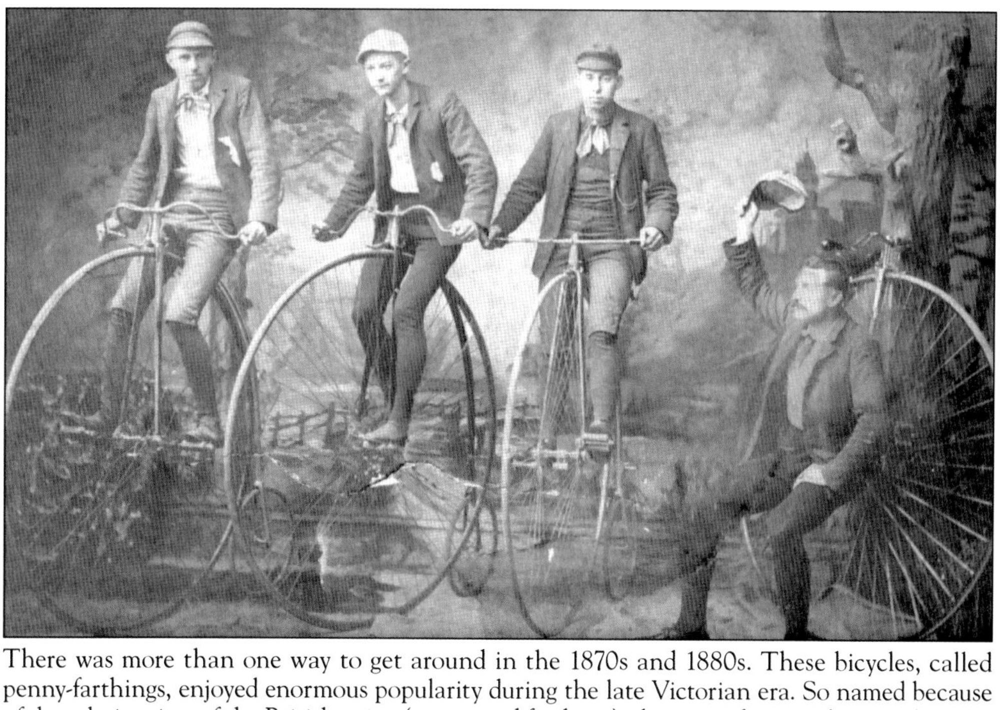

There was more than one way to get around in the 1870s and 1880s. These bicycles, called penny-farthings, enjoyed enormous popularity during the late Victorian era. So named because of the relative sizes of the British coins (penny and farthing), they were fun to ride once the rider mastered the art of mounting them. (Courtesy of the Jackson Public Library.)

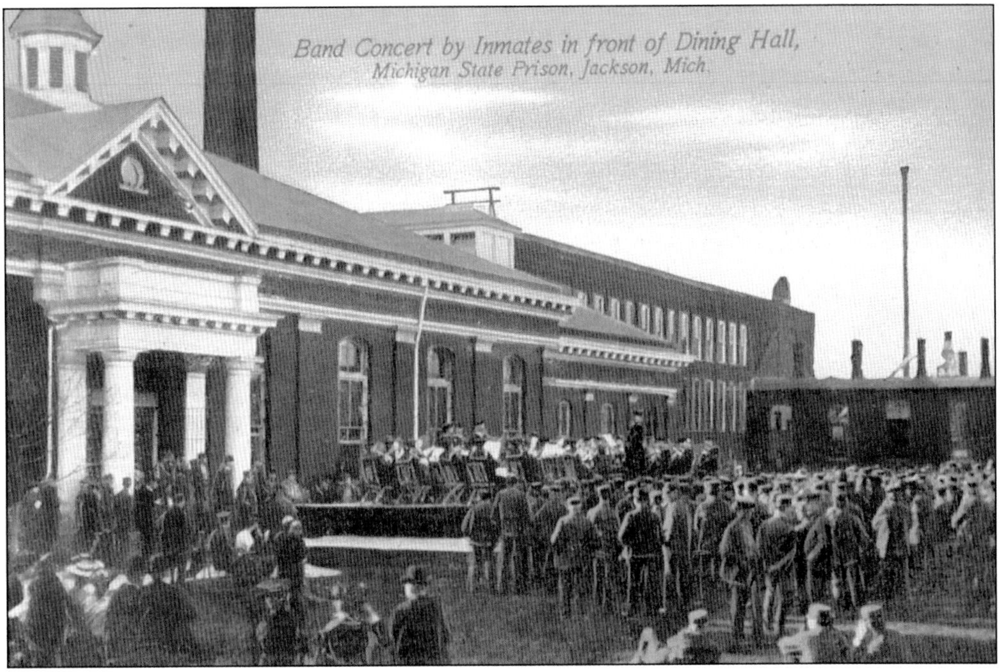

Jackson benefited greatly when the state's first prison opened there in 1839. Just four years later, it meant inexpensive labor for the businesses that were sprouting all over town. All work was done by contract within the prison walls, and inmates produced harnesses, farm equipment, steam engines, and even shoes. The photograph above shows a large number of musically inclined inmates giving a band concert to which the public was invited. Below, inmates assist with food preparation in the facility's bakery. (Both, courtesy of the Jackson Public Library.)

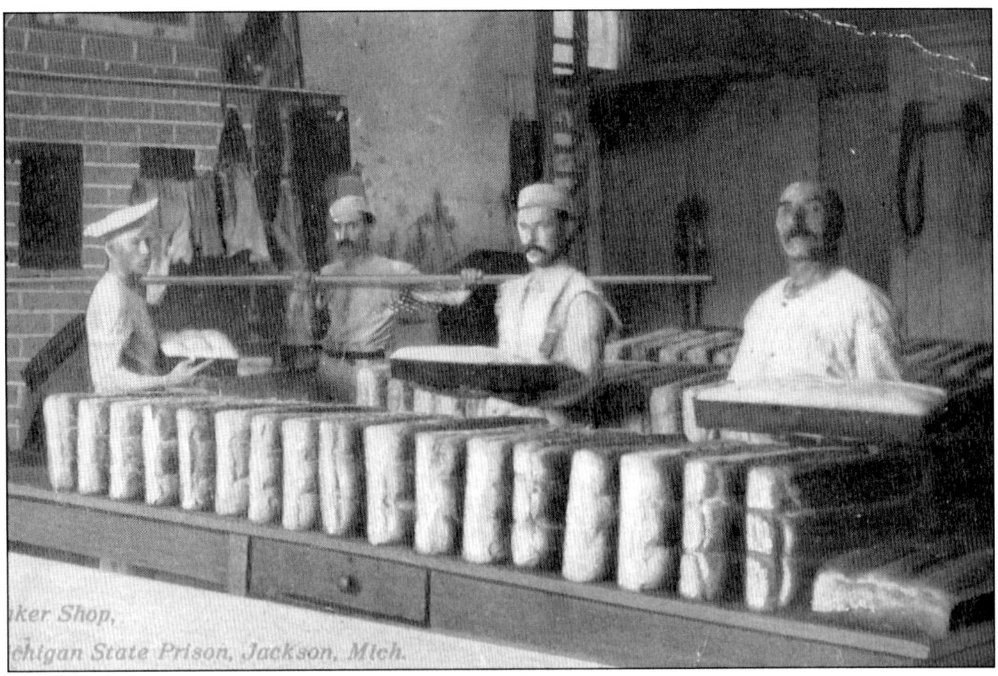

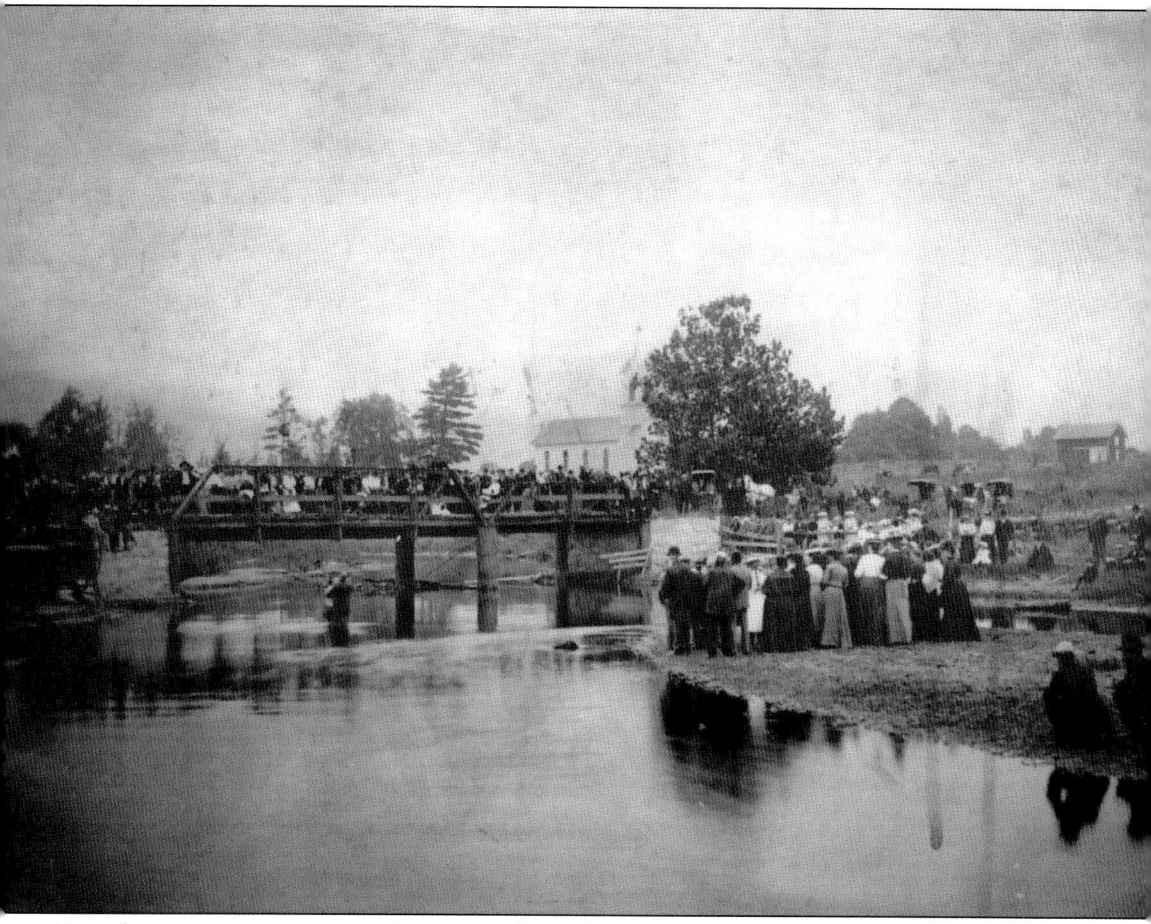

River baptisms were major social events in the early communities. They were often followed by picnics and hymn sings lasting most of the day, right up until it was time to go back inside for the evening service. Early settlers worked hard and turned to their churches for some well-deserved downtime. (Courtesy of the Bentley Historical Library, University of Michigan.)

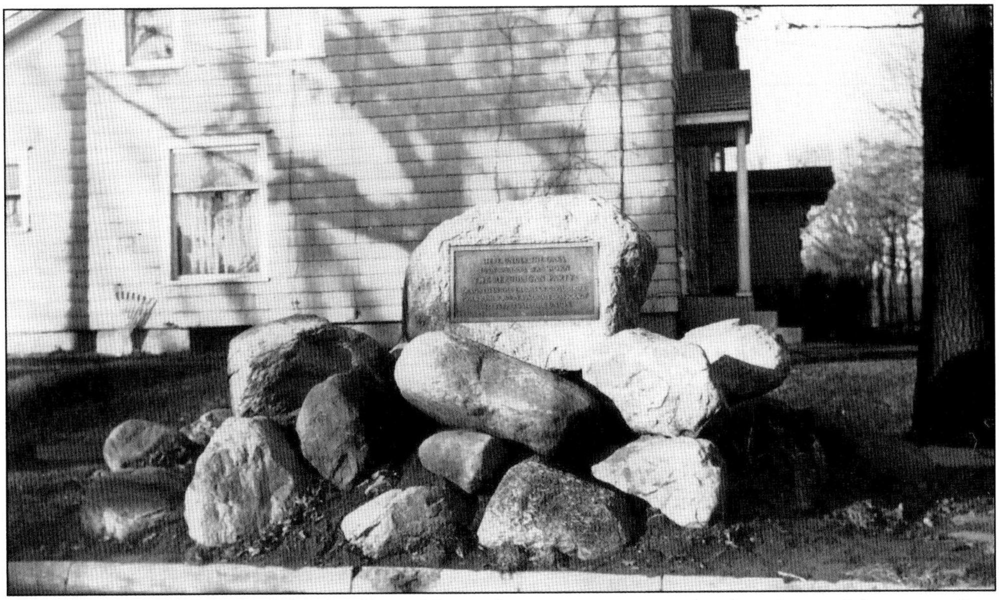

Bronson Hall is the site of the first Republican Party convention, the founding of the party that nominated Abraham Lincoln for the presidency a few years later. There were so many attendees, they had to adjourn to an outdoor venue. The party was formed because the Whig Party was being weakened by other antislavery parties, including the Abolitionists and the Free-Soilers. (Courtesy of the Bentley Historical Library, University of Michigan.)

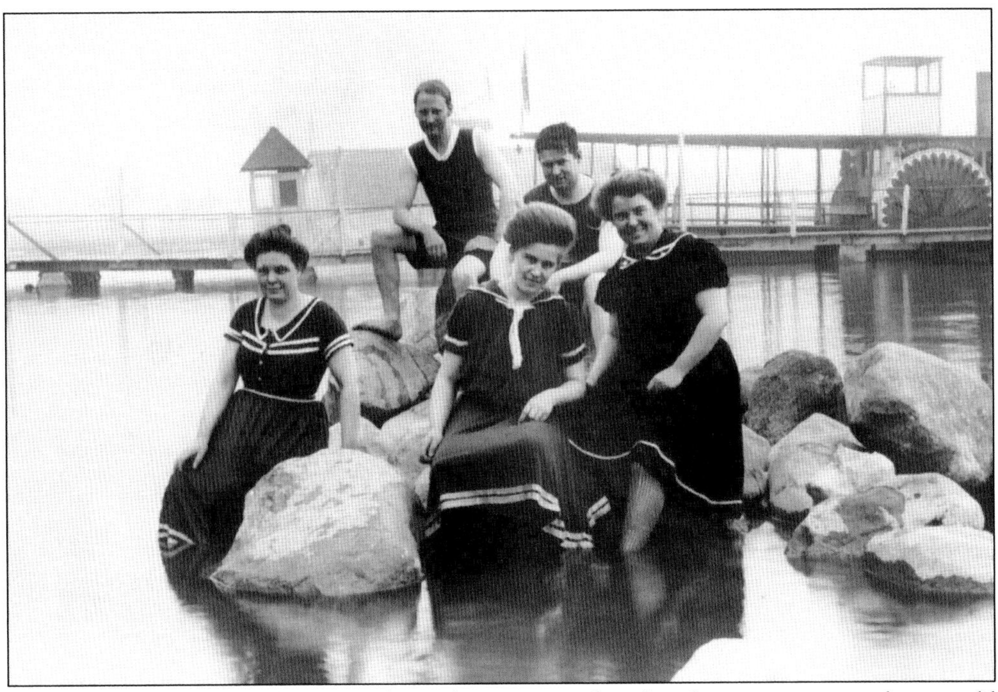

Jackson may have been a thriving industrial community, but that does not mean residents could not make time for a day of leisure. Those days often meant spending time on the water. (Courtesy of the Jackson Public Library.)

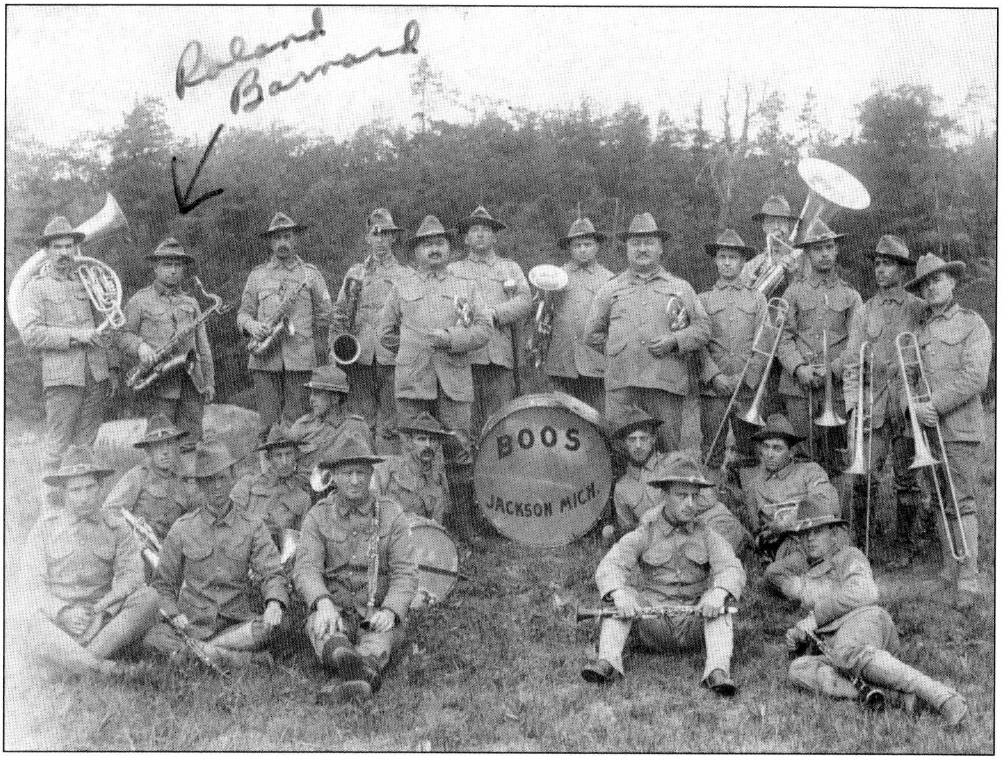

Louis F. Boos started the Boos Band in Jackson. It soon became regarded as one of the best in the state and played at nearly every major function during the late 1800s and early 1900s. The band was named Michigan's best military band during World War I. Boos himself was one of the world's best cornet players. He taught music and lived modestly in Jackson for almost 60 years, then died in his home on Franklin Avenue on January 31, 1935. He was 77. (Both, courtesy of the Jackson Public Library.)

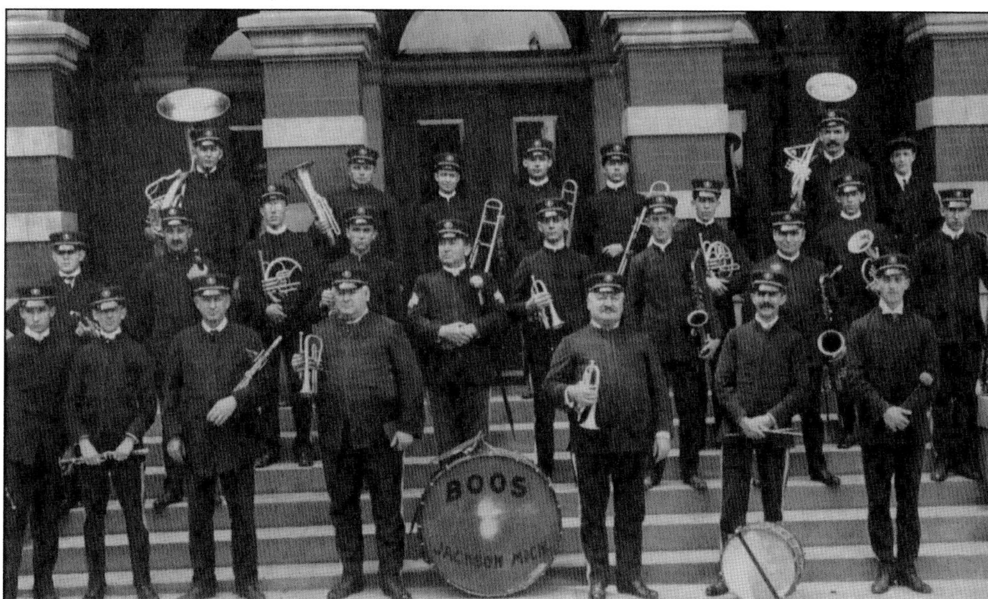

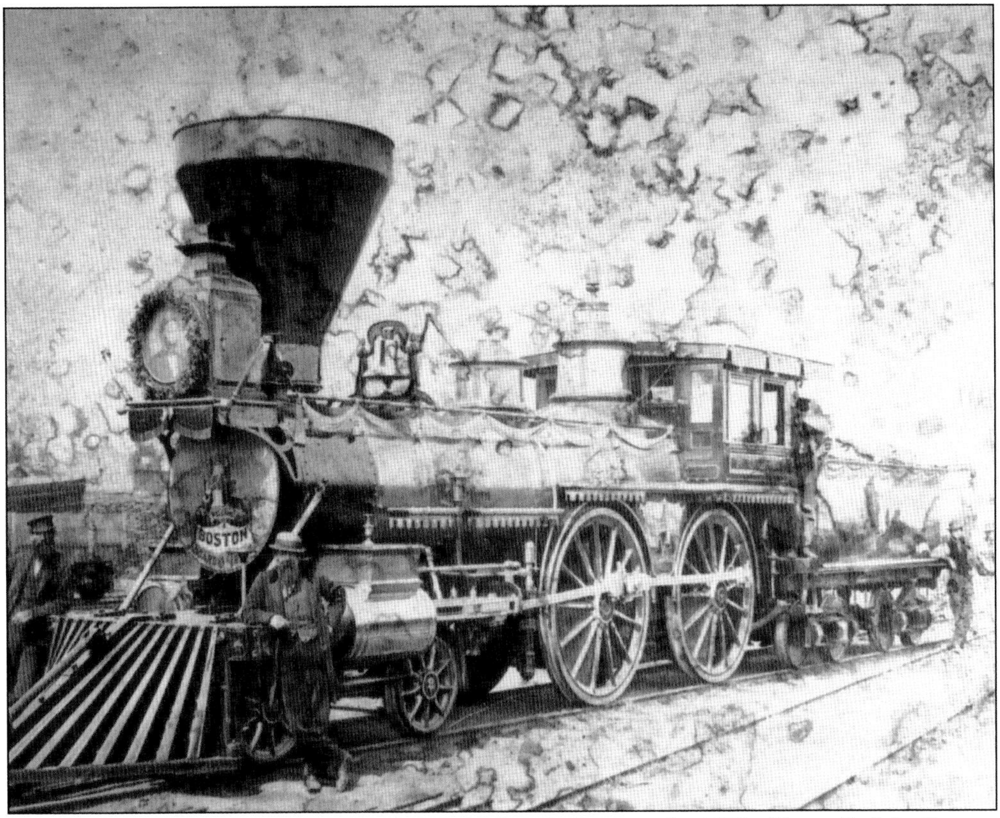

This wood-burning engine named *Ruby* was built in Jackson in the 1870s. She pulled the Boston Board of Trade from Detroit to Chicago, Illinois, becoming the first locomotive on the Michigan Central line to make the 285-mile-run without changing engines. About 10 years later she was renamed *No. 100* and converted to a coal burner. *No. 100*, aka *Ruby*, was scrapped at the turn of the 20th century. (Courtesy of the Capital Area District Library, Lansing.)

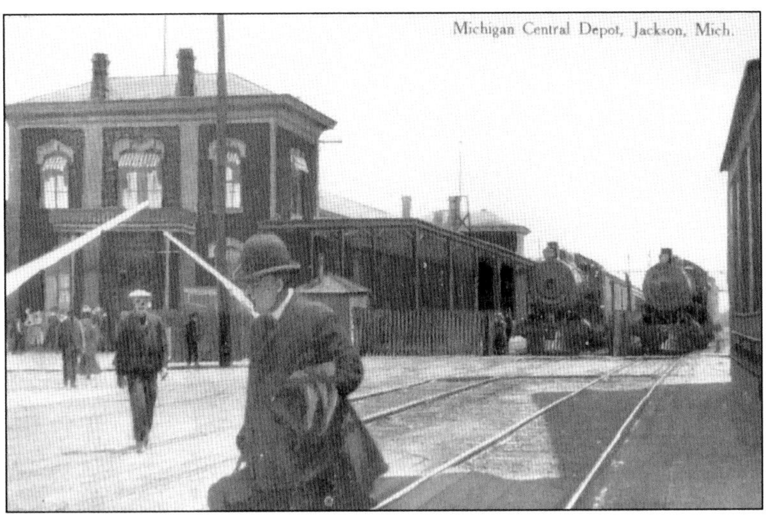

Trains made the transportation of passengers and goods easier and faster than moving them on the river. Jackson's Michigan Central Railroad Depot saw heavy usage until trucking became the method of choice for moving goods. (Courtesy of the Jackson Public Library.)

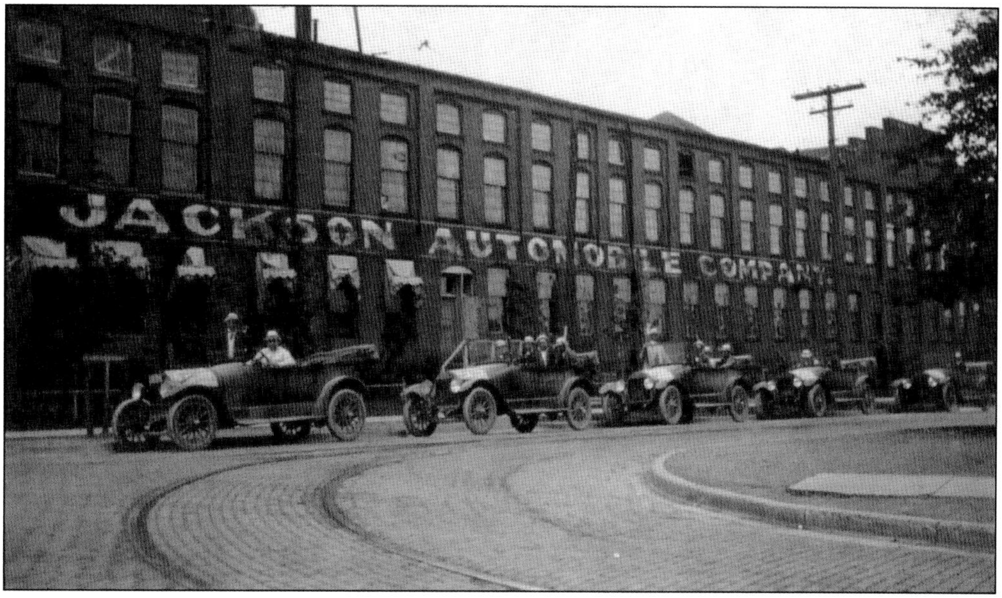

By the turn of the 20th century, the river flowed through a downtown Jackson bustling with commerce and industry, much of which was automobile production. In addition to about 20 other companies, the Jackson Automobile Company produced three-cylinder steam runabouts under the name Jaxon and six-horsepower vehicles called Jacksons. The company's confidence in its products shows in its slogan: "No Hill too Steep and No Sand too Deep." (Both, courtesy of the Ella Sharp Museum, Jackson.)

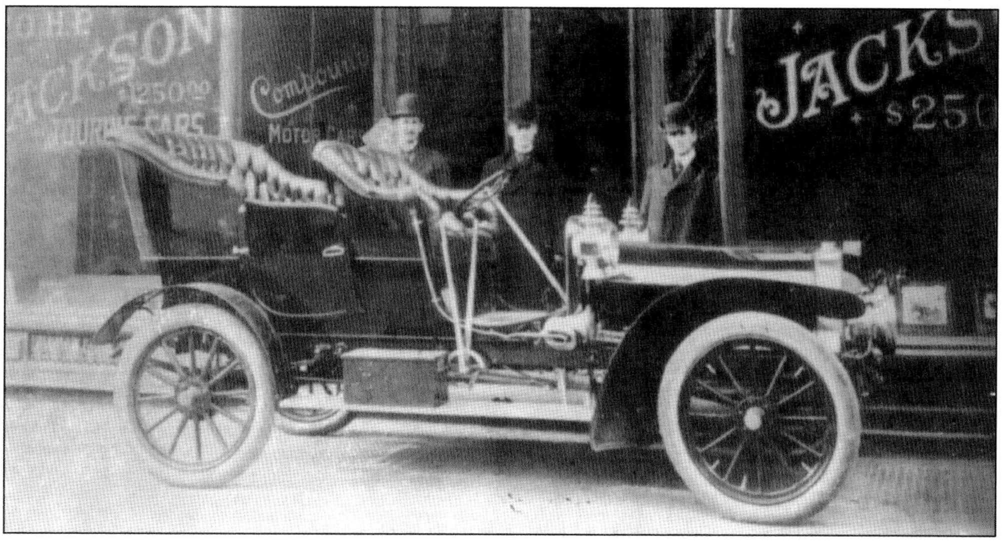

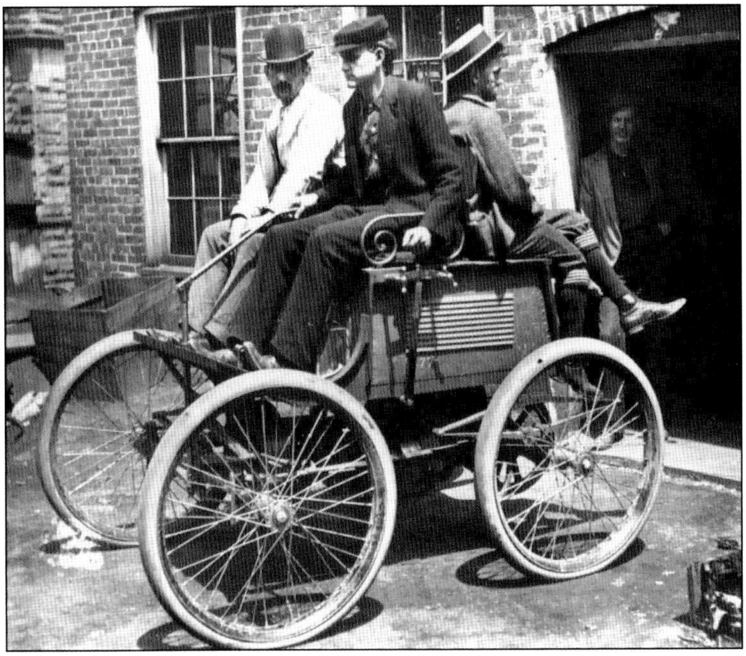

Art Butcher, a local machinist, test-drives an early Butcher and Gage model in 1903. His passengers and the gentleman in the doorway are unidentified. Though primitive, this car has four wheels; the first one built in the city by C.S. Reeves in 1898 consisted of three bicycle wheels mounted on a carriage frame. (Courtesy of the Jackson Public Library.)

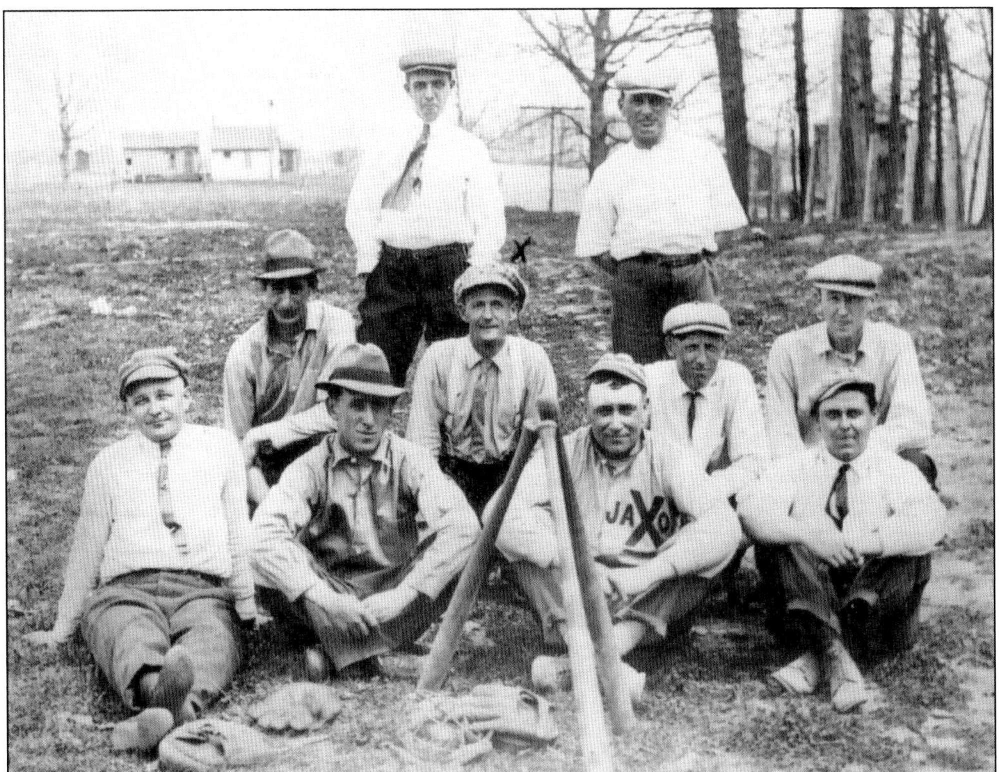

It seems as if employees have always enjoyed representing their companies in athletic competitions. The jersey shows that at least the gentleman behind the bats played for the Jackson Auto Company. (Courtesy of the Jackson Public Library.)

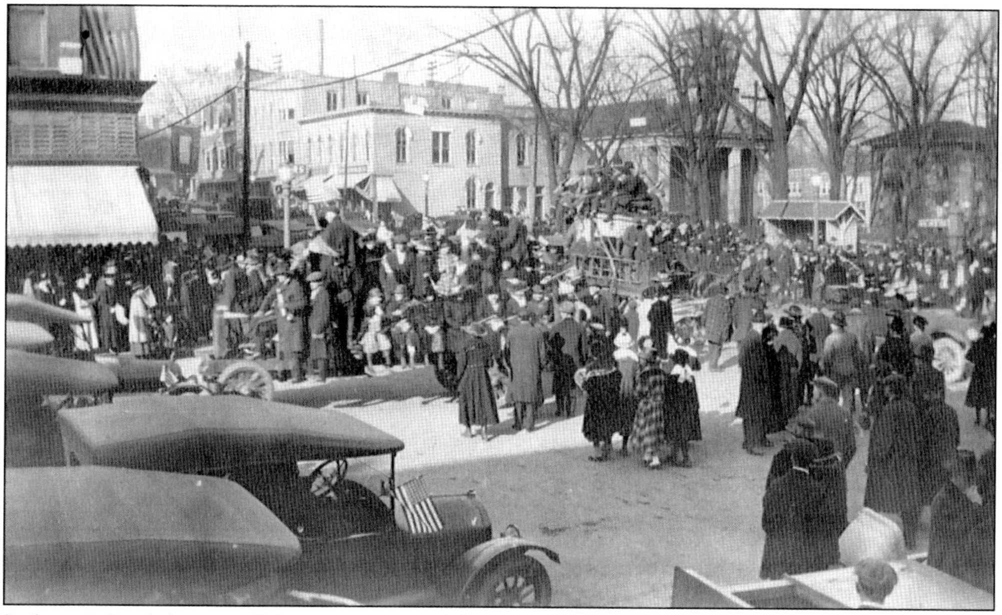

Jackson joined the rest of the country in celebrating Armistice Day on November 11, 1918. Some turned out to wave the American flag, and others decorated their vehicles with flags. The event took place on the corner of Michigan Avenue and Jackson Street by Blackman Park. (Courtesy of the Jackson Public Library.)

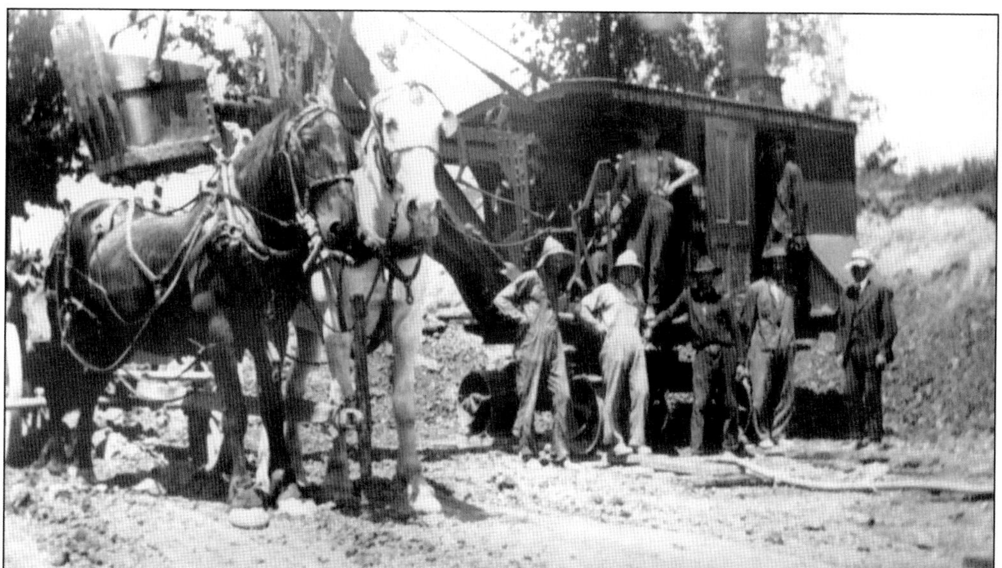

Steam shovels and horses were used to build roads in Jackson to meet the ever-increasing demand of people driving their new automobiles, many of which were produced in the city. (Courtesy of the Jackson Public Library.)

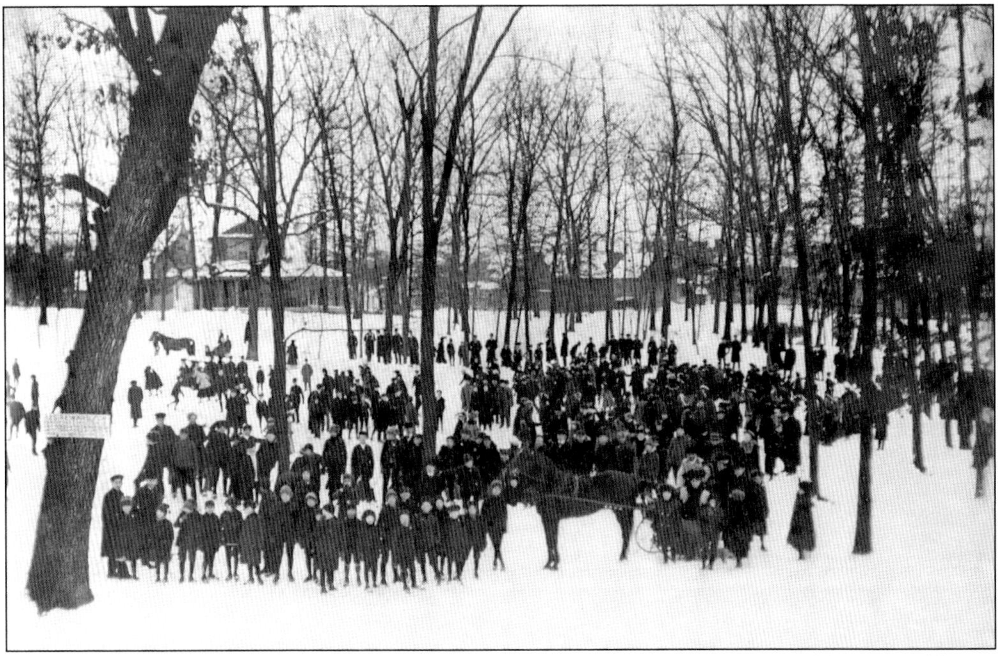

If there was one thing Jackson had plenty of, it was snow. Then, as now, children loved being outside to play in it, and adults accepted the challenges of business as usual. Loomis Park is pictured here, now bordered by East Michigan Avenue and Ganson, Gilbert, and Edgewood Streets. (Courtesy of the Jackson Public Library.)

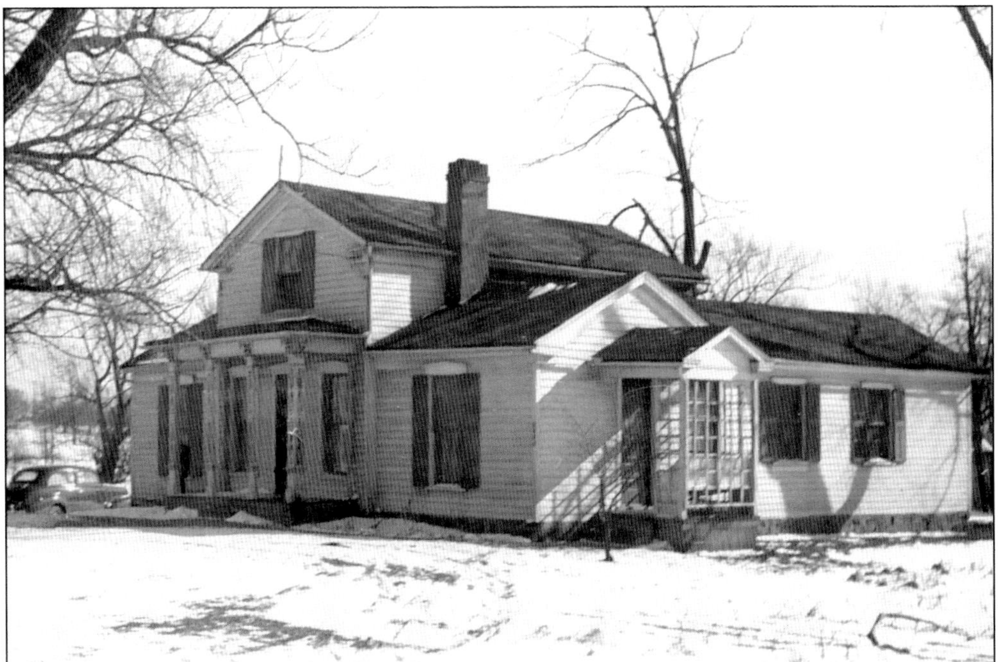

Farmhouses like this one at 2025 Page Avenue were typical in the area. Though the image is undated, the car seen on the left makes it at least in the 1930s. Agriculture is still found in the area, but not in the city limits. (Courtesy of the Jackson Public Library.)

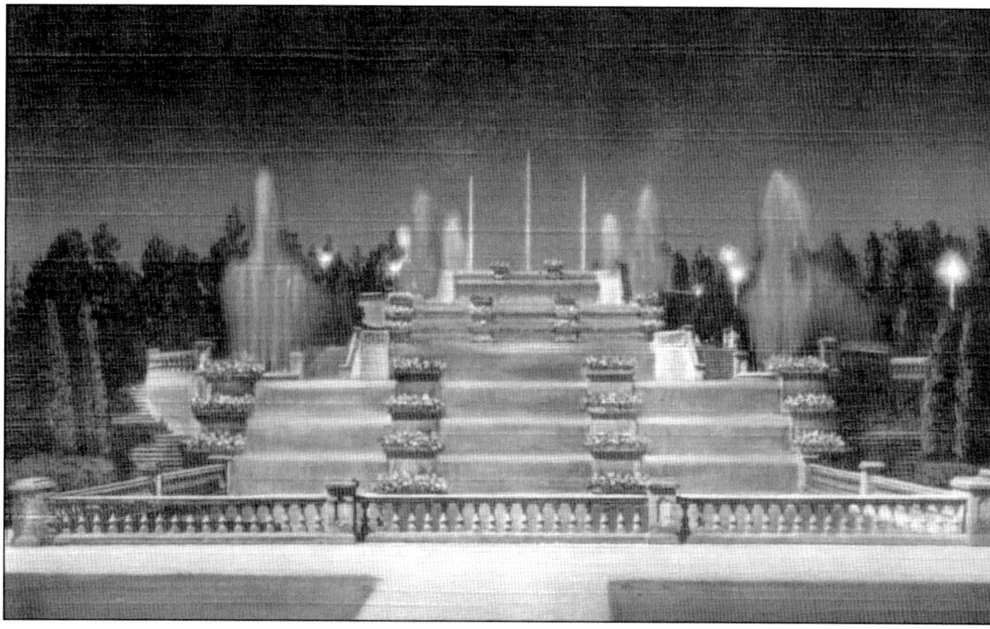

Sparks Avenue County Park is home to Jackson's cascade waterfalls. There are 16 falls in all, and 11 are illuminated. The park covers 465 acres and also features a lagoon, a small museum, picnic areas, and two golf courses. (Above, author's collection; below, courtesy of the Jackson Public Library.)

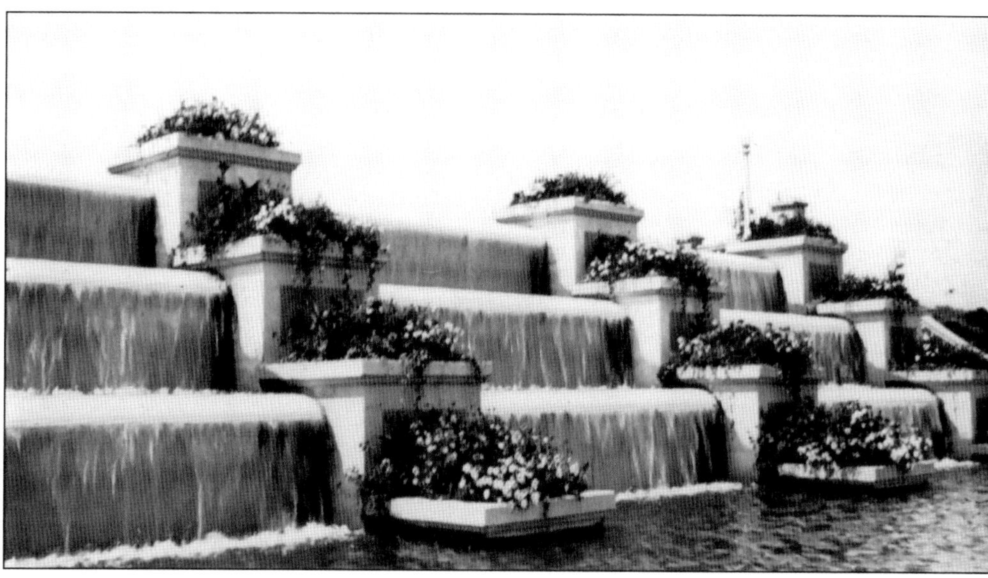

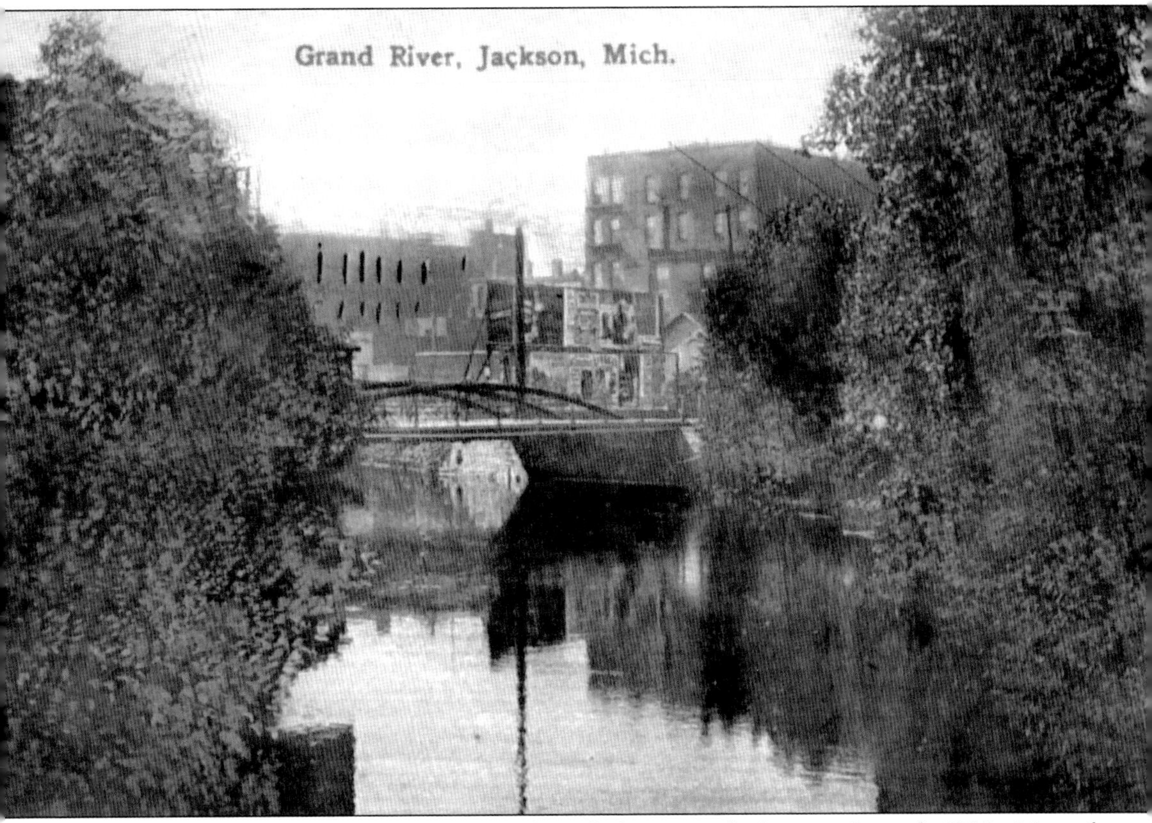

The Grand River is shown here flowing through downtown Jackson in the early 1900s. Most of the city's manufacturing is gone, and the old factories have been razed or divided into spaces for smaller businesses. (Courtesy of the Jackson Public Library.)

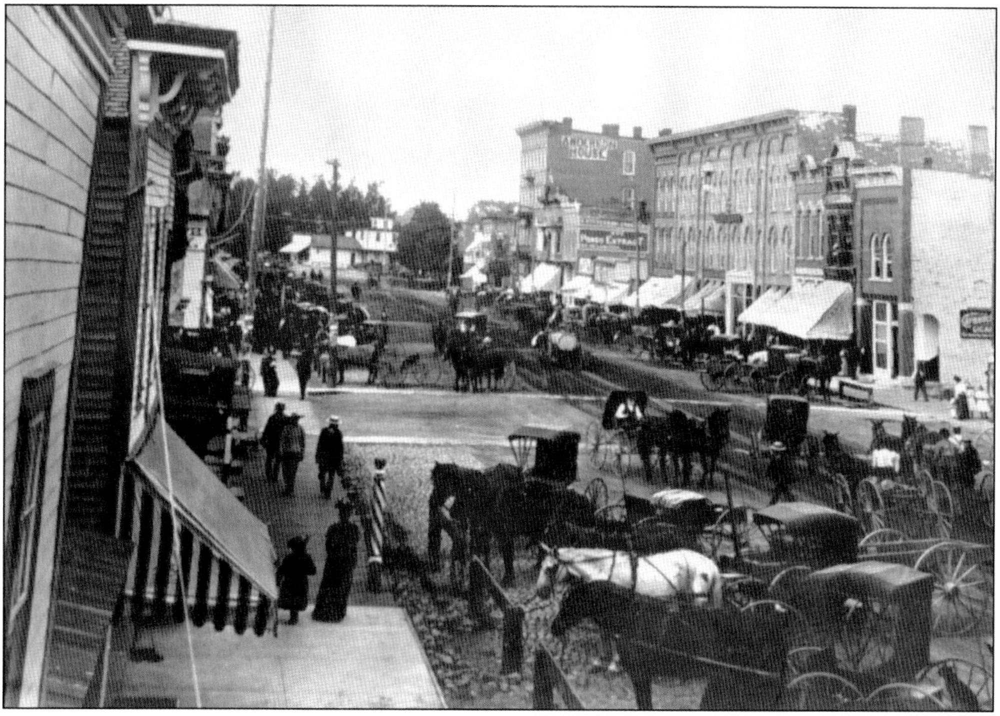

Both Eaton County and the city of Eaton Rapids are named for John H. Eaton, secretary of war in Pres. Andrew Jackson's cabinet. Among the businesses in operation when this image was taken were the Anderson House, Pond's Extract, and Carmichael's Cigar on the right side of the street. Though the barber's name is not known, his pole is visible in the lower left of the foreground. (Courtesy of the Eaton Rapids Area Historical Society.)

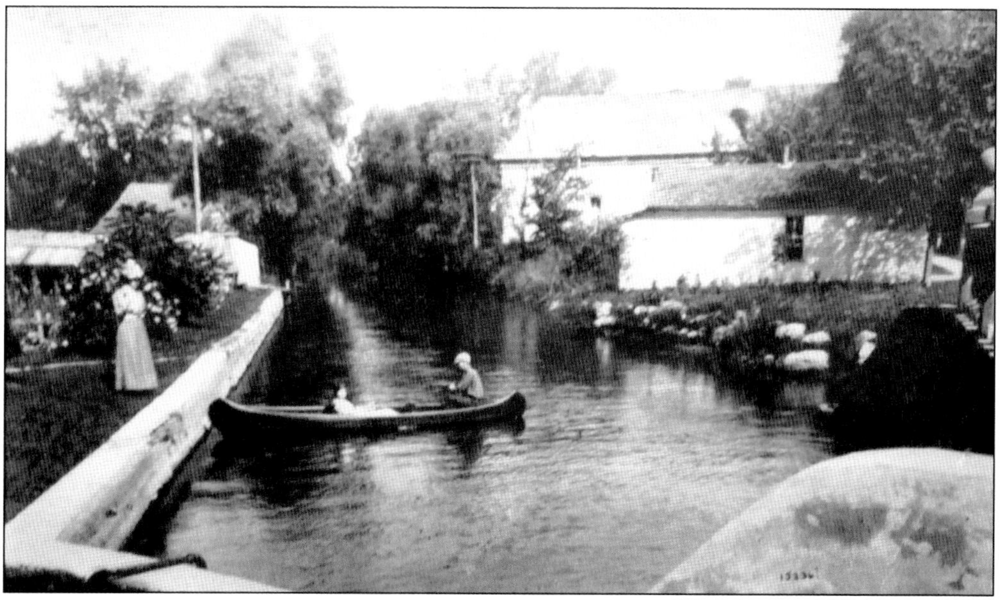

As seen from the Main Street Bridge, a man and child row toward a woman waiting for their return. (Courtesy of the Eaton Rapids Area Historical Society.)

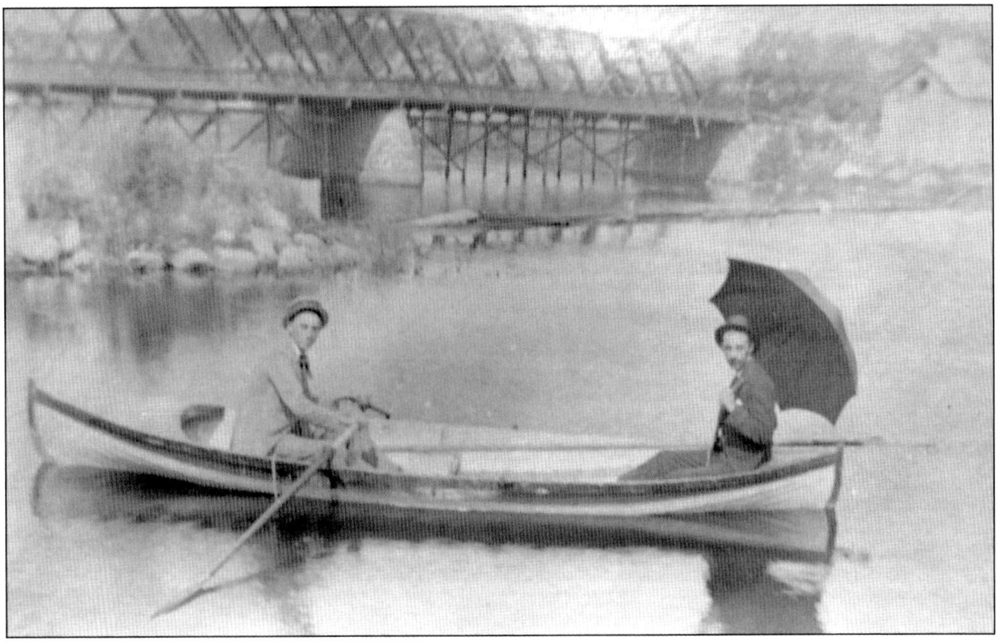

For those living along the river, it was a way of life. Children enjoyed fishing and playing near the State Street dam that provided the area's power. The men crossing the river in the rowboat must have an important destination. Why else would they be out on the water in the rain while wearing suits and ties? (Both, courtesy of the Eaton Rapids Area Historical Society.)

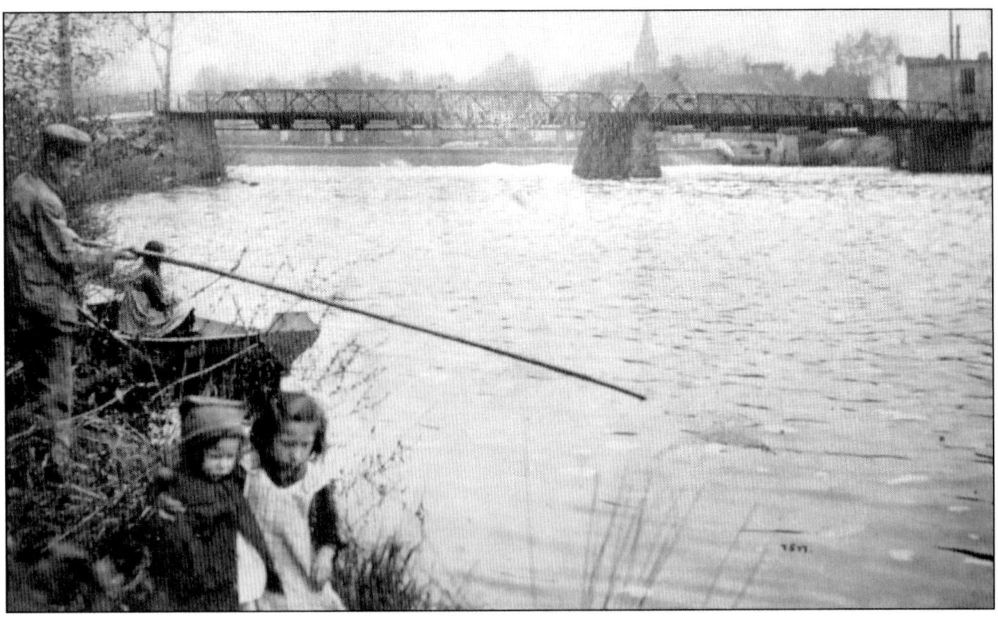

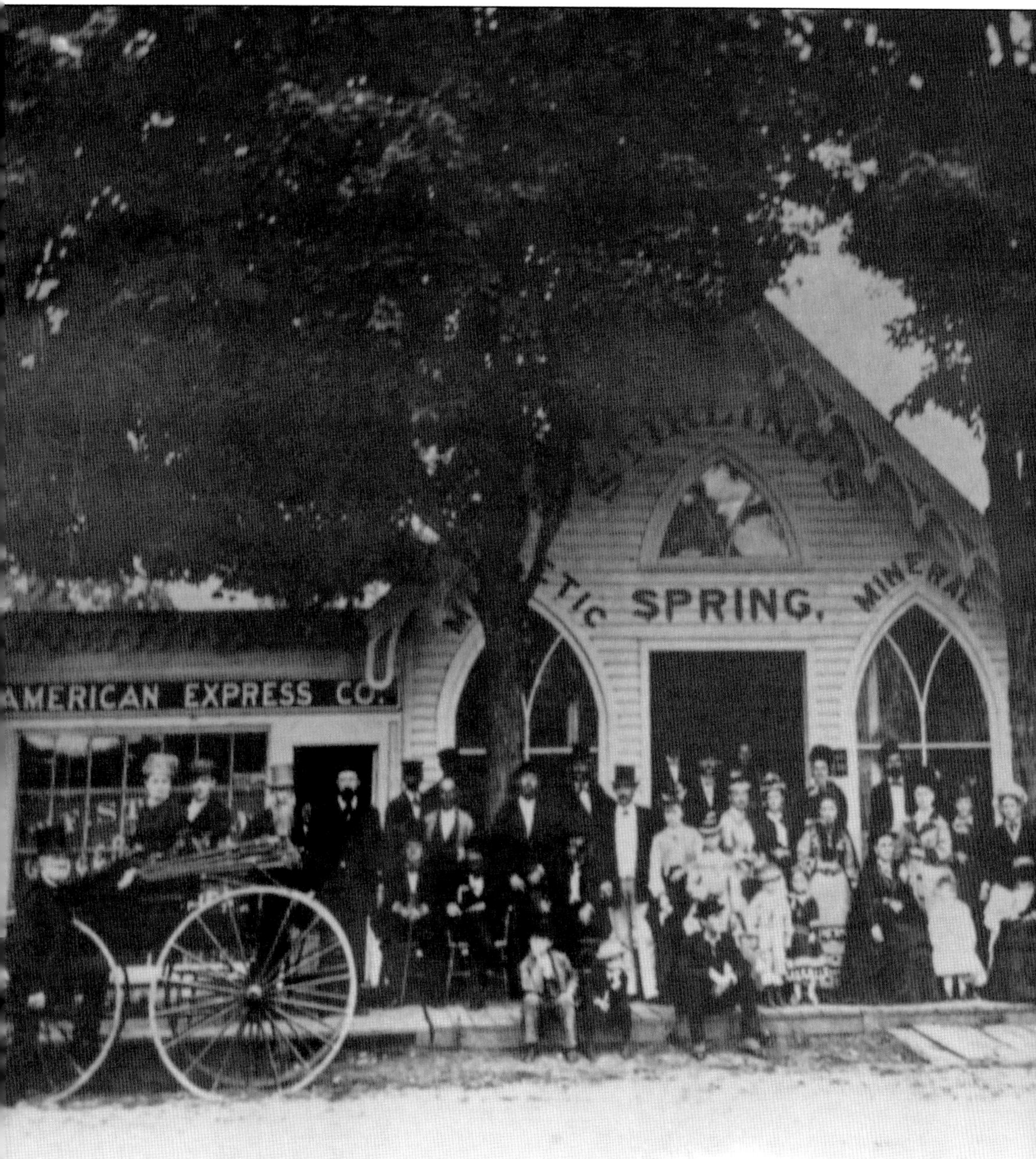

At the height of the popularity of the mineral water springs, several trains a day brought visitors to take the waters. New hotels were built to accommodate the demand, and residents offered their spare rooms to tourists. The Stirling's resort is shown here, and the crowd is most likely made up of guests, along with locals. (Courtesy of the Eaton Rapids Area Historical Society.)

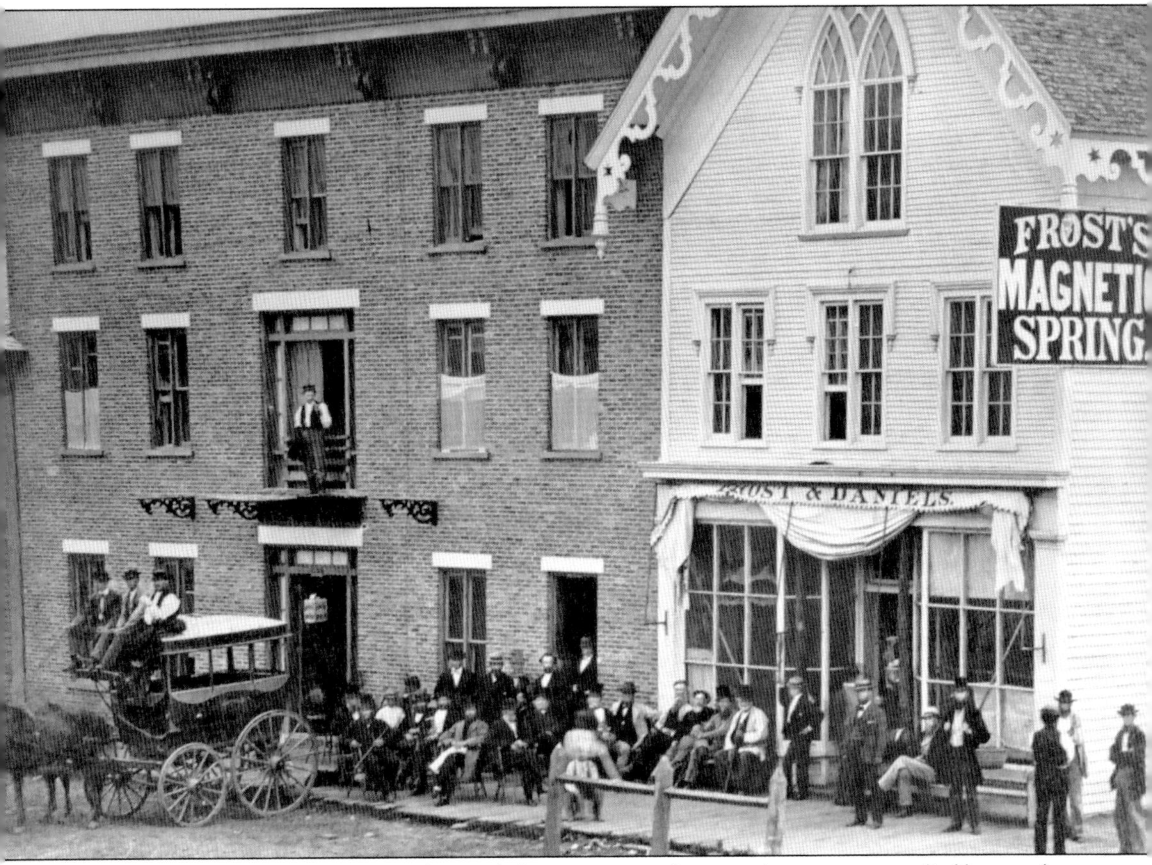

The boom ended when it was learned the springs might provide temporary relief but no long-lasting cures. Resorts like Frost's Magnetic Springs closed, and some of the springs simply dried up. (Courtesy of the Eaton Rapids Area Historical Society.)

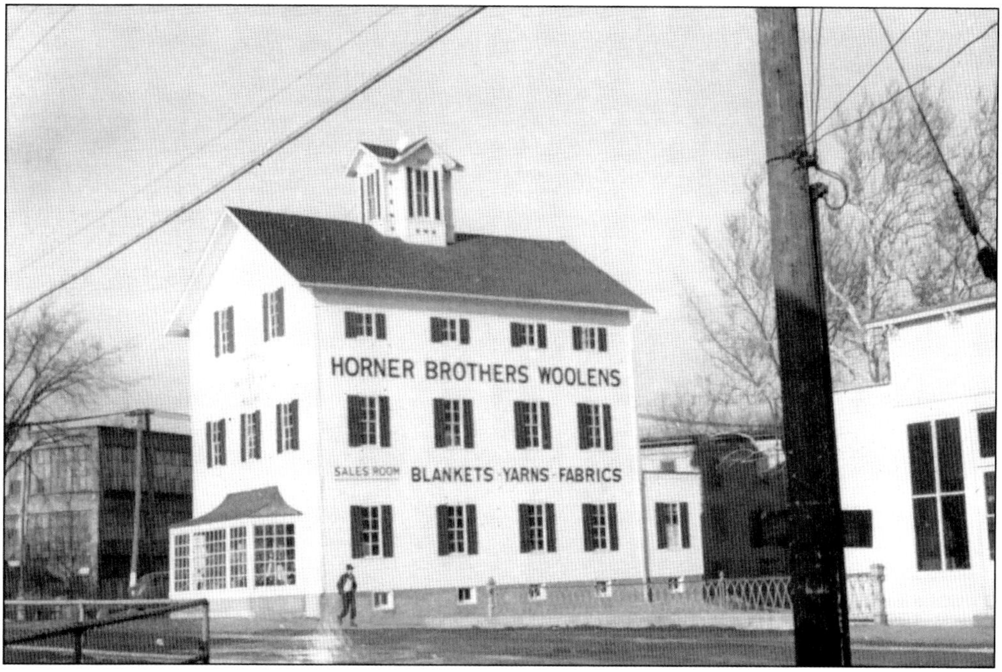

Horner Brothers Woolens came to be when Samuel Horner, a spinner from Yorkshire, England, bought the building from early settlers Pierpont Spicer and C.C. Darling. It quickly became an Eaton Rapids fixture. Today, the building is known as Horner Commerce Park and houses several businesses. (Above, courtesy of the Bentley Historical Library, University of Michigan; below, courtesy of the Eaton Rapids Area Historical Society.)

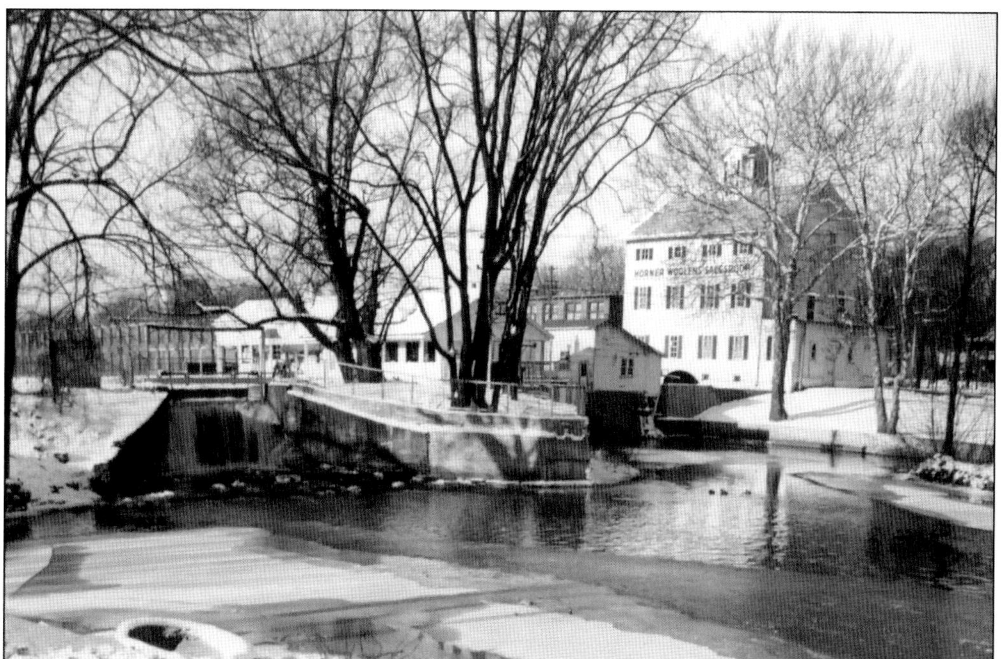

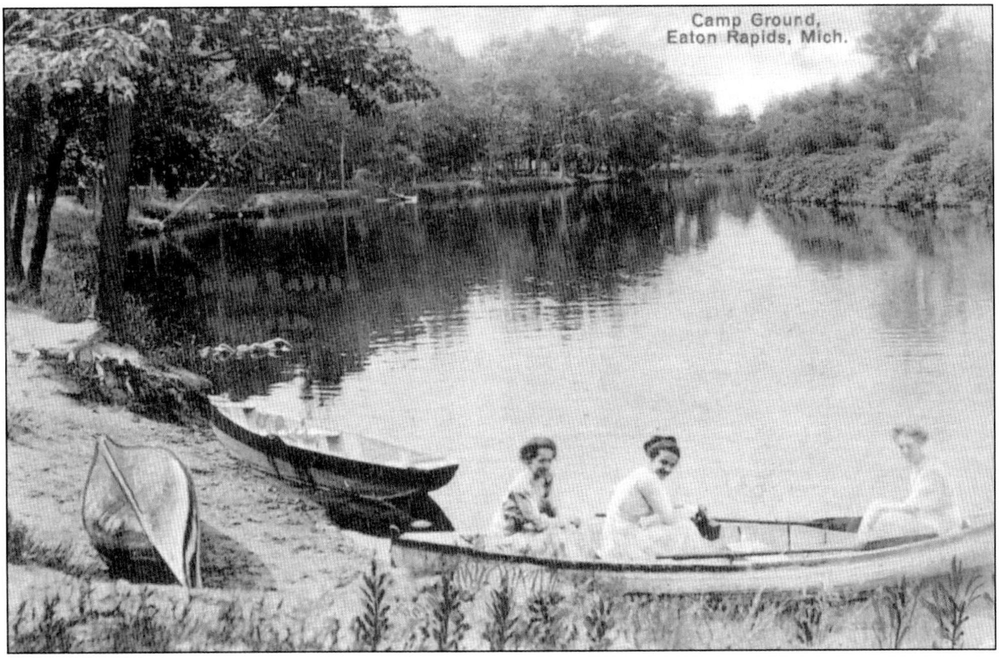

A young lady named Lillian wrote to her friend Kittie that she was attending the Eaton Rapids Camp Meeting, and the boat pictured on the card was the one she had rowed. Camp meetings were popular during the early decades of the 20th century, and the river provided a perfect destination. The camp meeting Lillian attended welcomed visitors with "Holiness unto the Lord" emblazoned on the arch over the entrance. (Above, author's collection; below, courtesy of the Eaton Rapids Area Historical Society.)

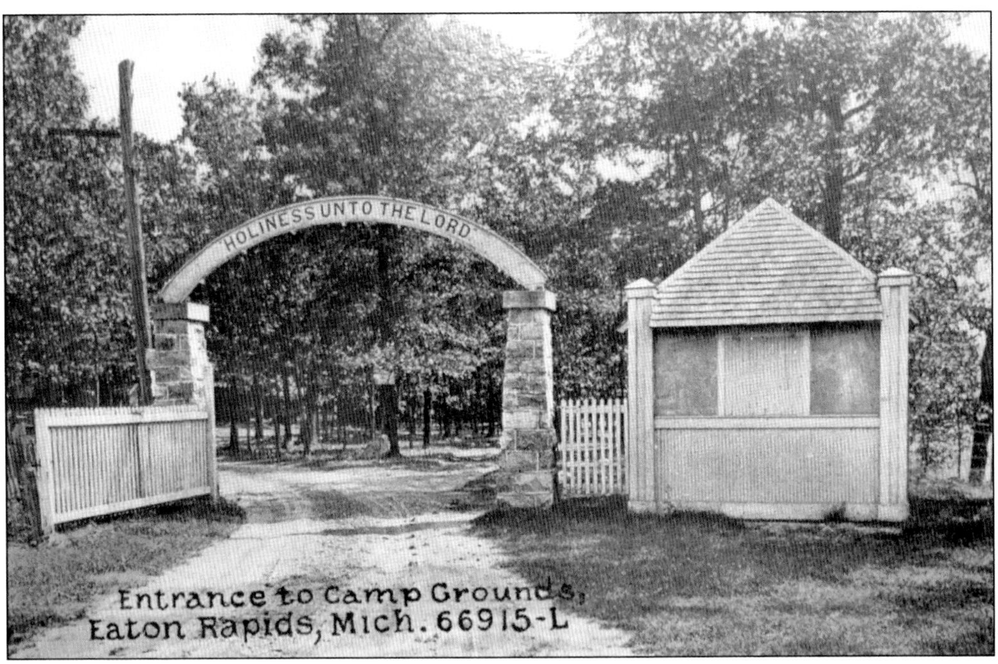

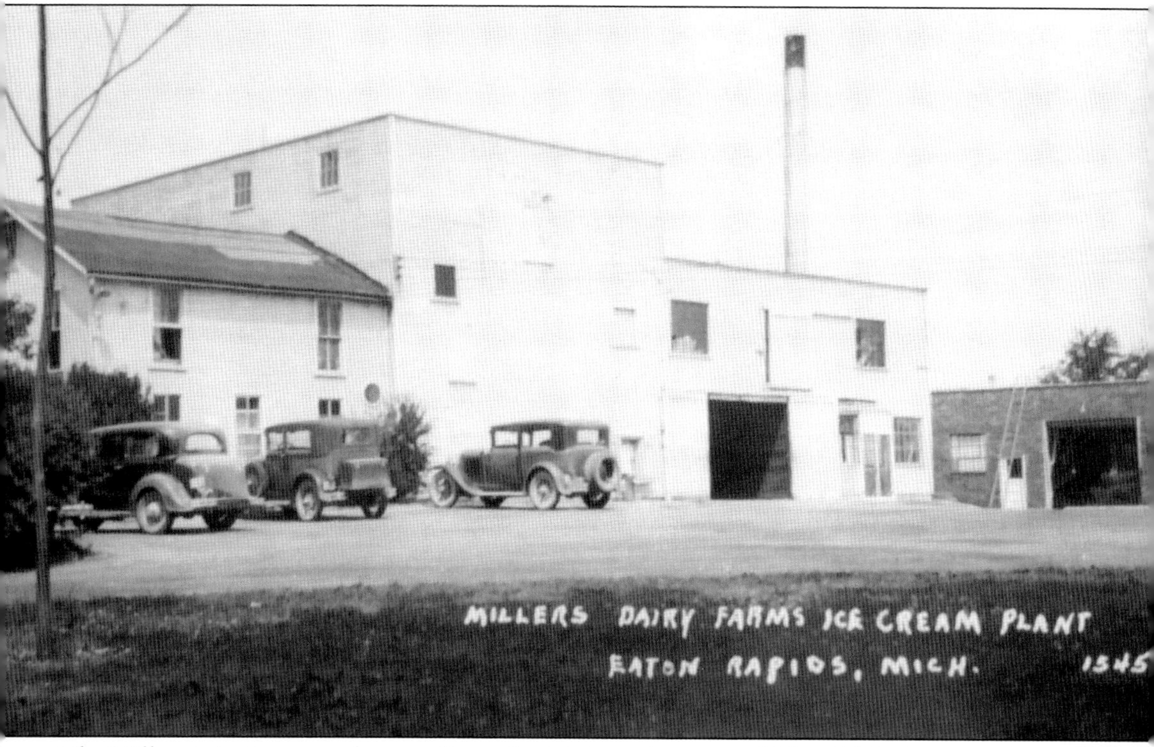

The Miller Dairy Farm was long an Eaton Rapids icon. Dennis and Mary Miller began making ice cream here in 1896. Considered one of the longest barns in the state, this is actually two barns combined into one, and the silo is the original. Now owned by the Eaton Rapids Area Historical Society, it is a favorite school field trip attraction, and tours end with a treat from the ice-cream shop. (Courtesy of the Eaton Rapids Area Historical Society.)

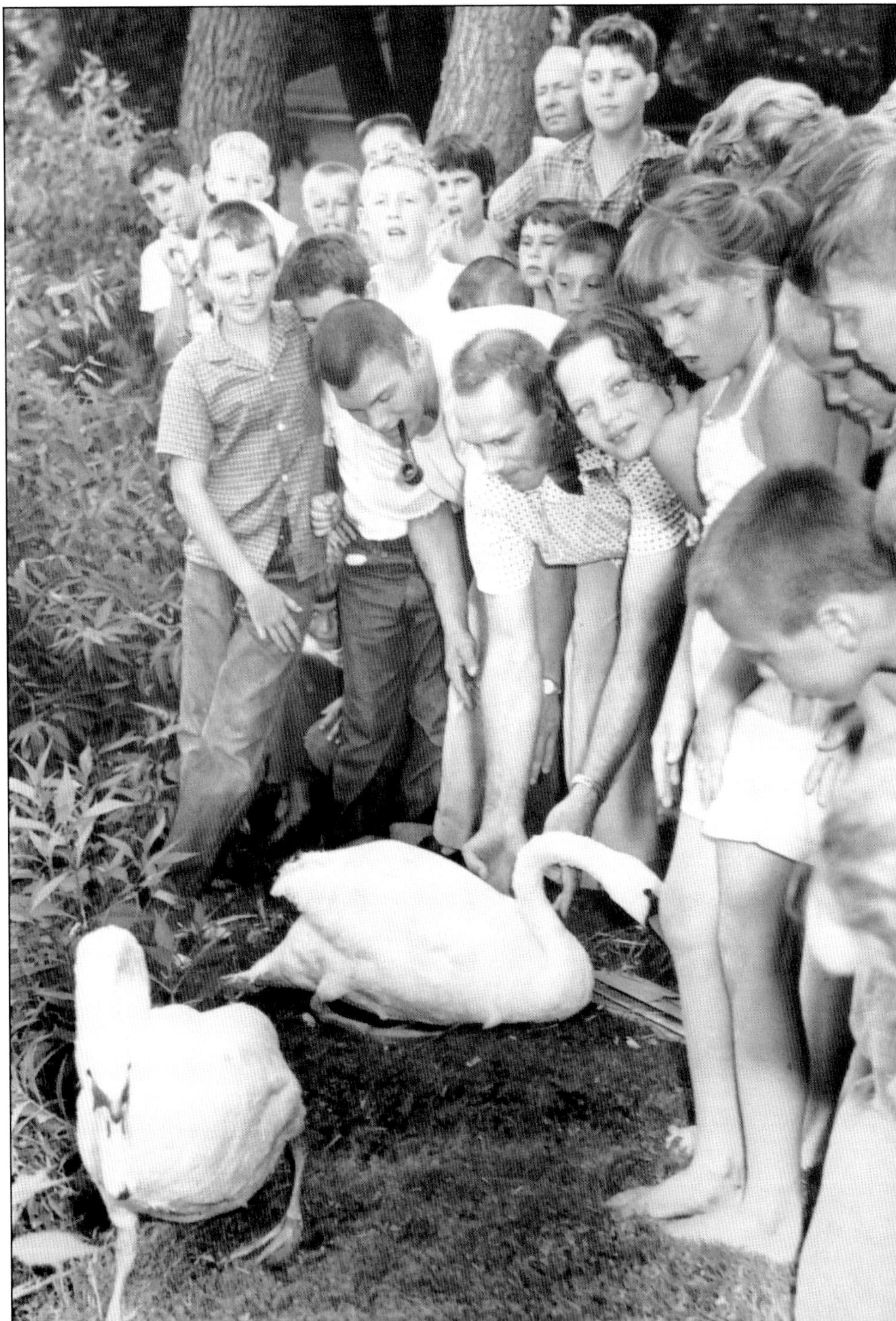

People are not the only ones who enjoy the Riverfront Park; swans gather here too, even if it sometimes means posing for pesky photographers. Though swans can be ornery, these two seem to be taking the attention in stride. (Courtesy of the Eaton Rapids Area Historical Society.)

Two

Lansing to Grand Rapids

When the Grand River reaches Michigan's capital city, it is joined by the Red Cedar River. The Grand River flows through downtown Lansing, while Michigan State University is on its tributary, the Red Cedar River. Here, too, the river was a trading post site. George Campeau, whose brother Louis first settled Grand Rapids, set up operations in 1826. Commerce and industry followed, including the Oldsmobile production plant, started by Ransom E. Olds. Michigan State University, now a Big Ten heavyweight, had humble beginnings here as Michigan Agricultural College and was known for cows long before the "Sparty" mascot came on the scene.

Just beyond Lansing, the river flows west to Grand Ledge and one of the most scenic spots on its course. Cliffs reach as high as 35 feet on the banks there and challenge climbers. Portland comes next, at the confluence of the Grand and the Looking Glass Rivers. Portland calls itself the "City of Two Rivers" and is justifiably proud of its eight-mile river walk, which is part of a larger 15-mile trail system looping through the area.

Then on to Saranac, which was once called Boston, but the name was changed to reflect its American Indian roots. This part of the river is now sparsely populated, but it is rich in history. Saranac's former depot is now a museum and holds treasures of the past, particularly railroad history. Next on the river's path, Lyons and Muir have a combined museum and historical society. In all three, the river looks much as it did a century ago and is still a magnet for fishing and boating. Ionia comes next and is the largest city on this part of the river. It is best known today as the site of the annual Ionia Free Fair.

Lowell and Ada are in Kent County and considered part of Greater Grand Rapids. Lowell still has the iconic showboat, and Ada is where Rix Robinson first settled in Michigan. Robinson worked for John Jacob Astor and took over the Ada trading post. The Flat River joins the Grand River at Lowell; the Thornapple River, at Ada.

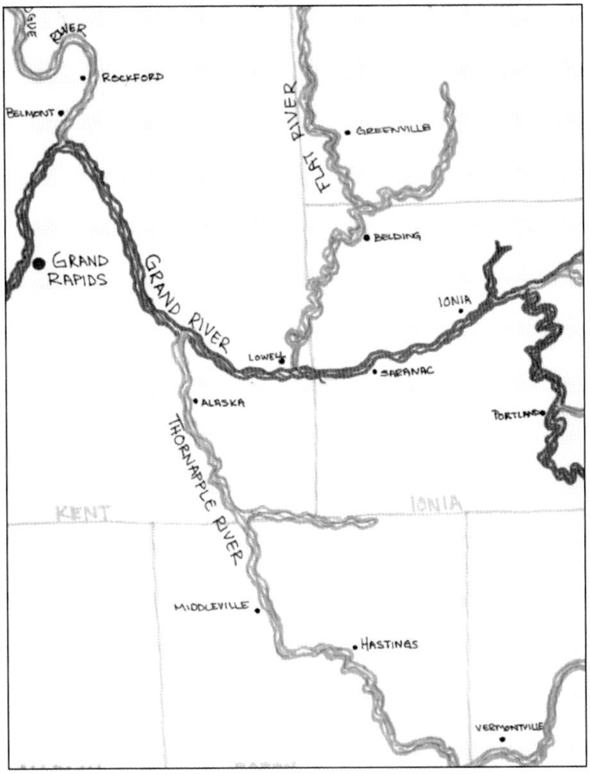

At Lansing, the river flows north into Clinton and Ionia Counties, heads east near the city of Ionia into Kent County, and turns north again to Michigan's second-largest city, Grand Rapids. (Map by Jillian Berry.)

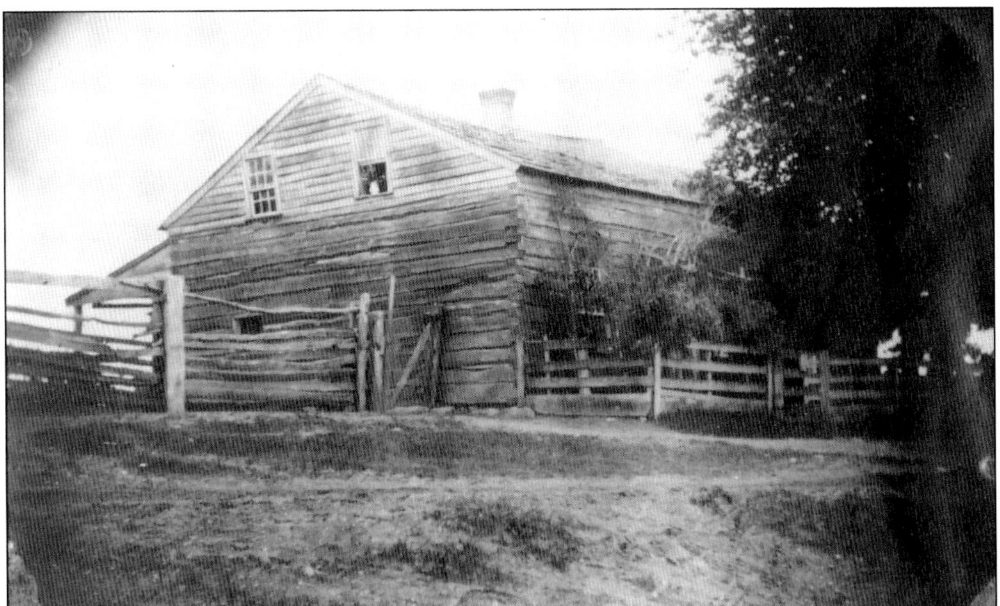

George Campeau, brother of Louis Campeau, the first settler in Grand Rapids, opened a trading post in Maple village in 1826, the remains of which are shown here. Campeau's building was the first erected in Clinton County, and he became the first landowner there when he received a land grant signed by Pres. Andrew Jackson in 1834. (Courtesy of the Bentley Historical Library, University of Michigan.)

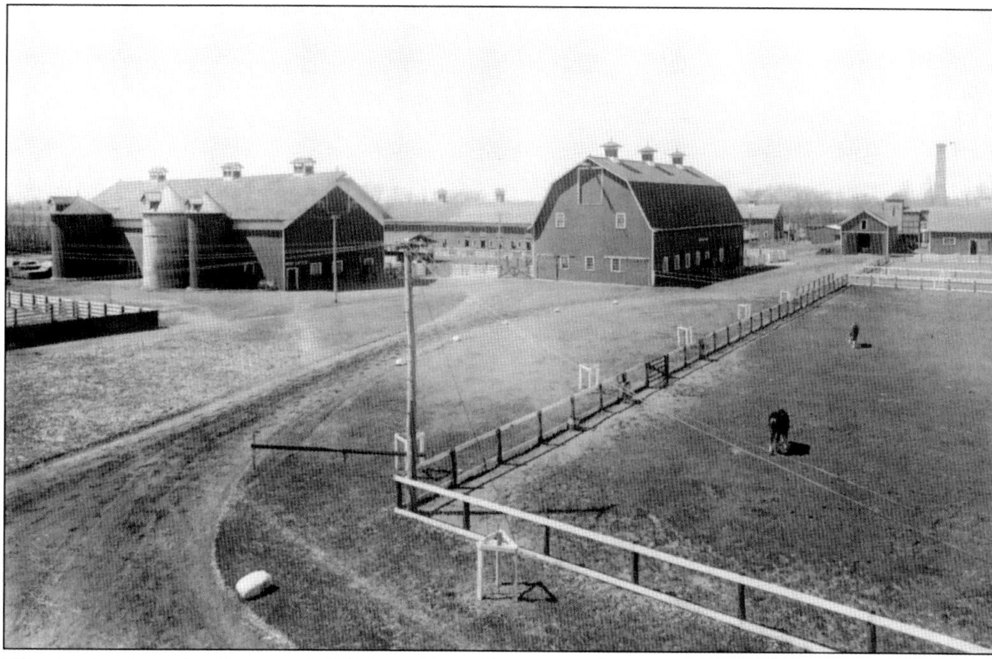

The institution that became Michigan State University first opened its doors in 1855 and was named Michigan Agricultural College. There were 63 male students taught by five faculty members, and livestock outnumbered people. Pictured here are the college barns. (Courtesy of the Capital Area District Library, Lansing.)

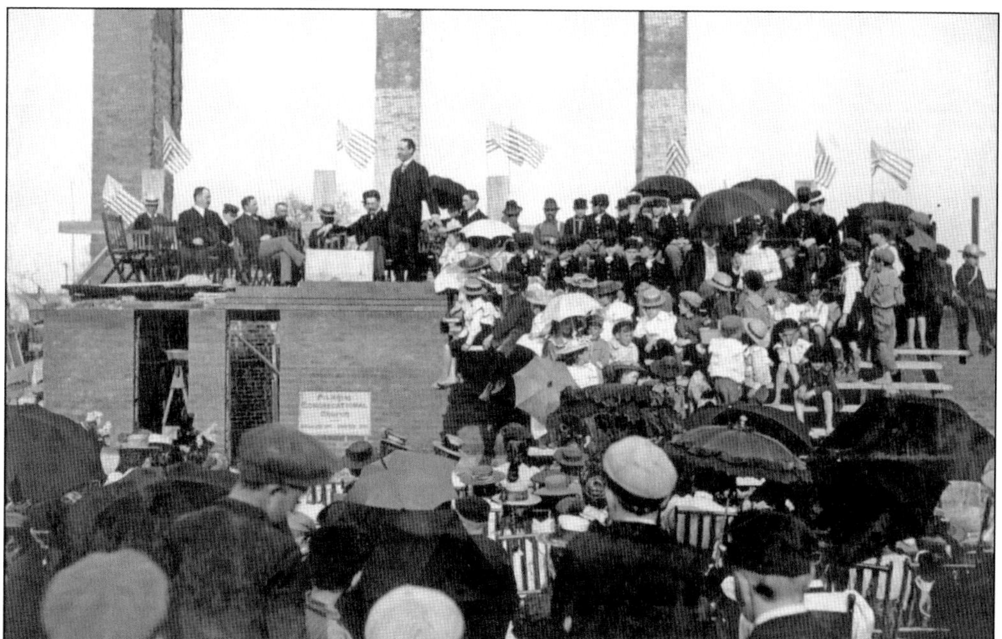

The Pilgrim Congregational Church held a cornerstone-laying ceremony in 1893. The church began with Sunday School classes in the Larch Street School. In 1959, Pilgrim Congregational voted to join the United Church of Christ and is now known as Pilgrim Congregational United Church of Christ. (Courtesy of the Capital Area District Library, Lansing.)

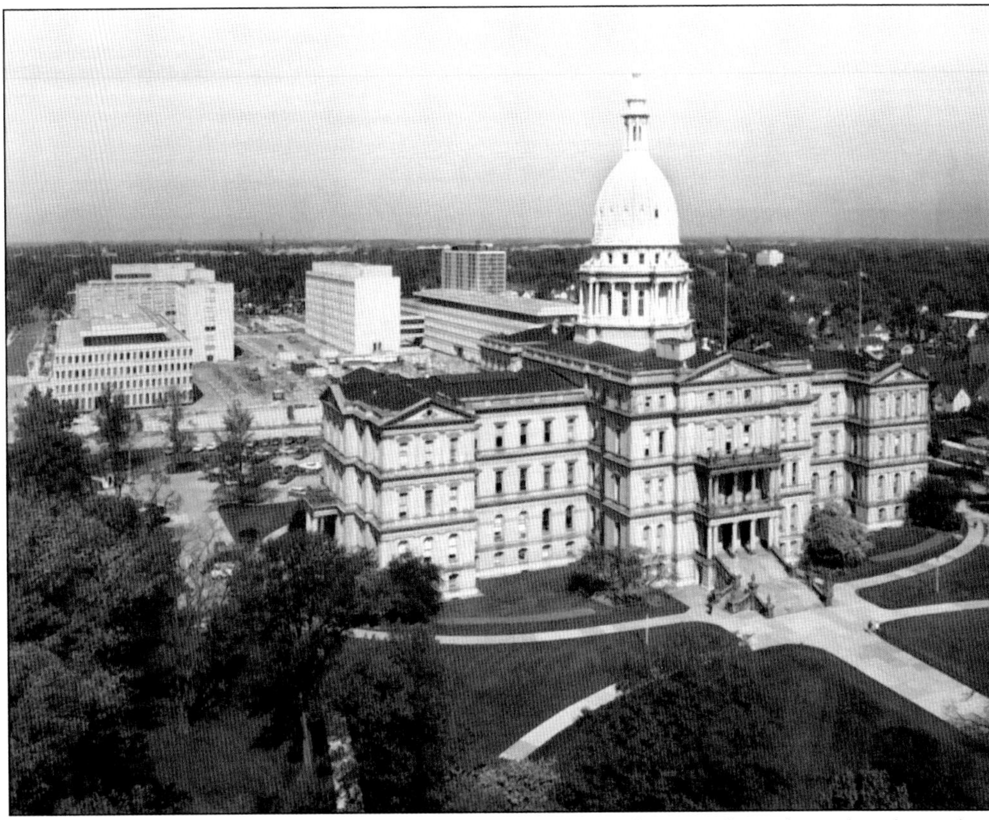

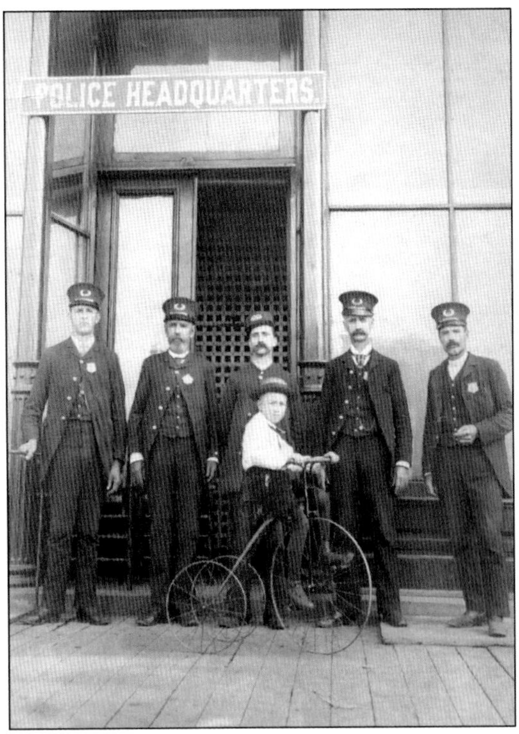

This is the view from the railroad switch at Saginaw Avenue near Center Street, with the state capitol, built in 1869, in the background. This area is now Riverfront Park. The Grand River runs through downtown Lansing. Michigan State University is located on its tributary, the Red Cedar River. (Courtesy of the Capital Area District Library, Lansing.)

Lansing's first police department poses outside its 204 East Michigan Avenue headquarters in 1890. From left to right are George Kohler, John N. Bush, Ed Bates (chief), Ben Harrington, and John Collins. The boy on the tricycle is Harrington's son Claude. (Courtesy of the Capital Area District Library, Lansing.)

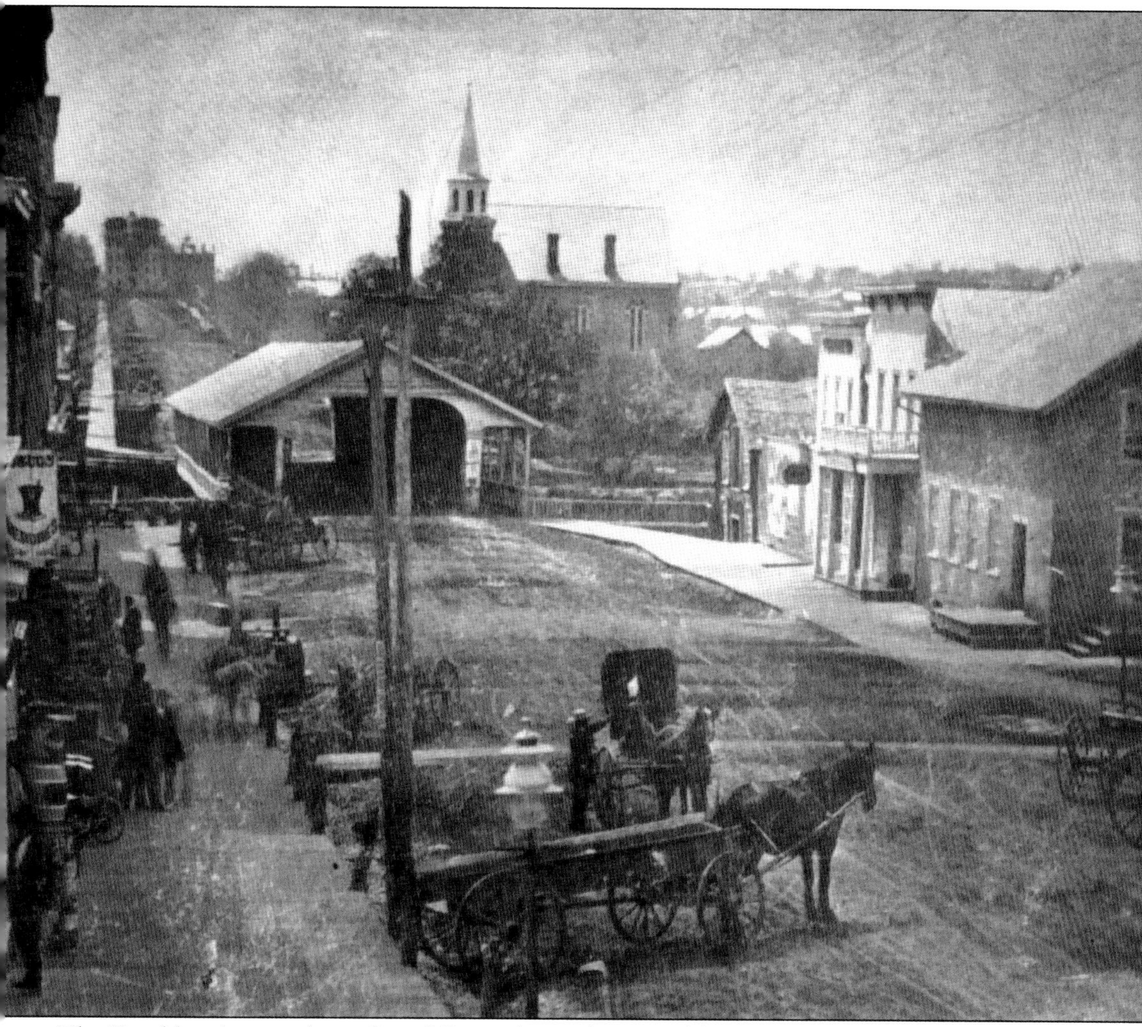

The Franklin Avenue (now Grand River Avenue) covered bridge was built in 1848, making it easier to reach the state capitol shown behind it. (Courtesy of the Capital Area District Library, Lansing.)

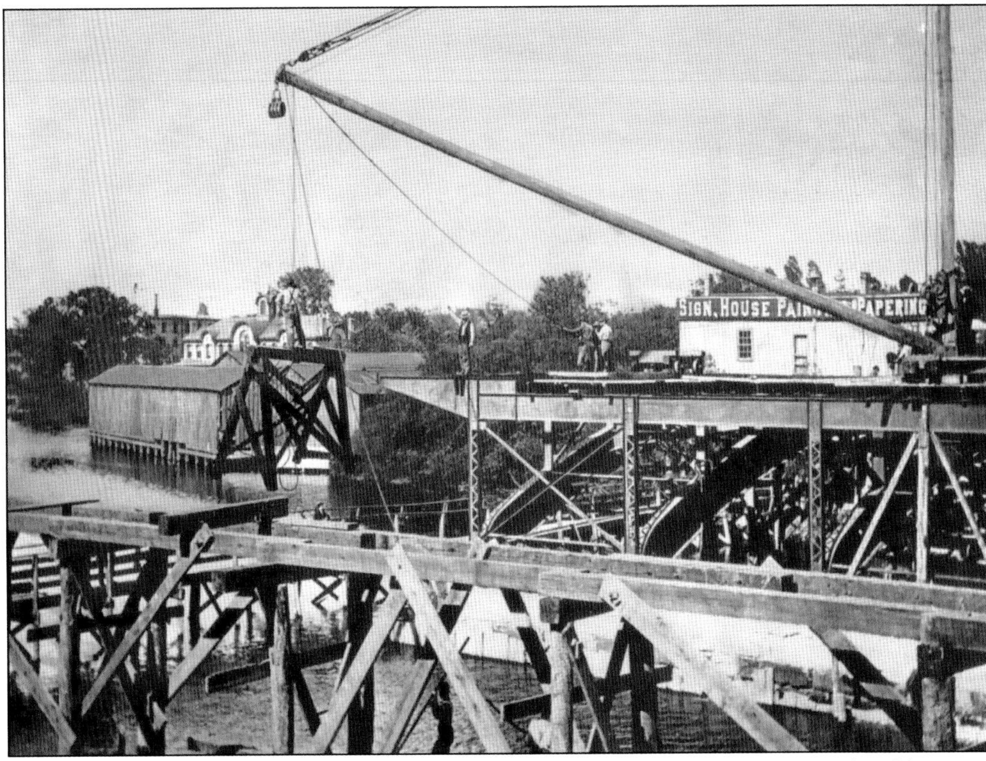

Work started in 1893 on this concrete and steel bridge on Michigan Avenue. Note the old covered bridge showing in the background. That structure was later replaced by the iron span shown in the image below. (Both, courtesy of the Capital Area District Library, Lansing.)

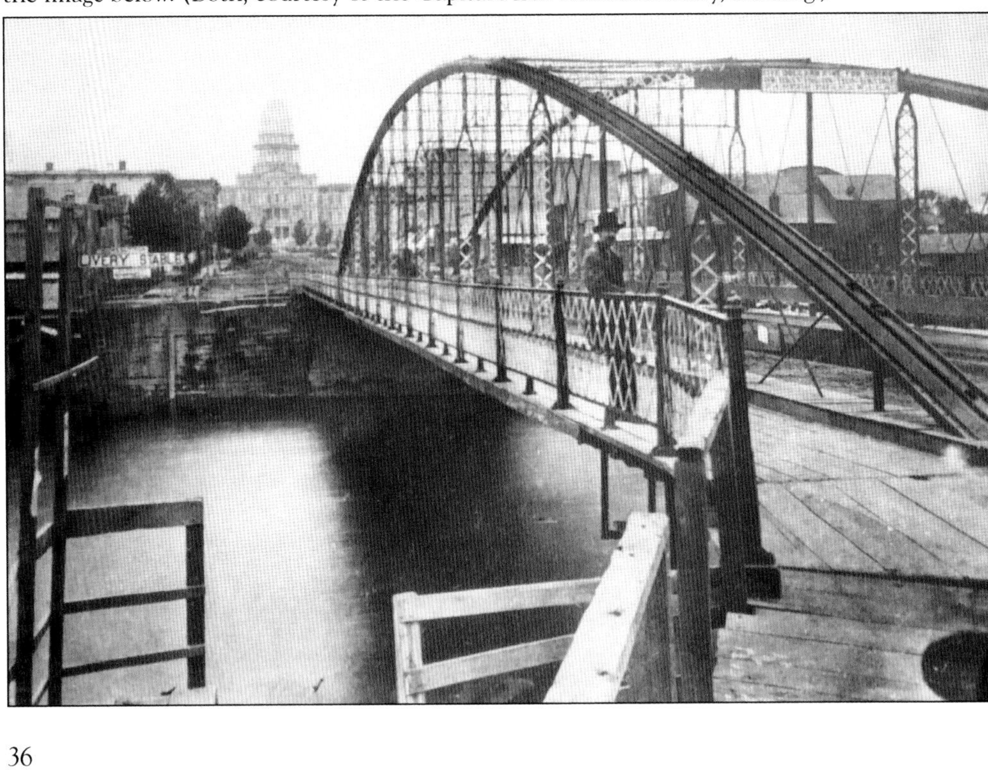

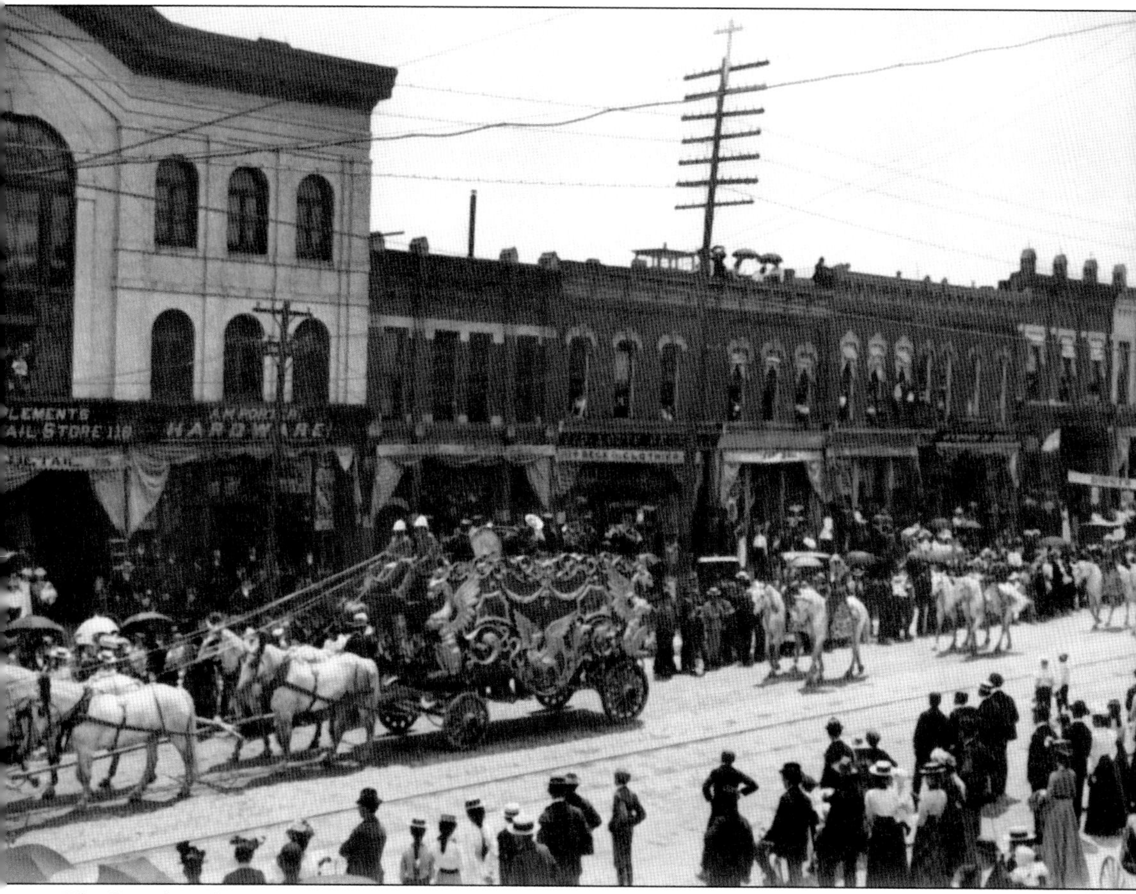

The Ringling Bros. circus came to Lansing on June, 14, 1900, and enjoyed rave reviews. The *Lansing Journal* reported that it came with "the finest array of horses, the handsomest wagons, and by far the most elaborate parade ever seen in the city." Here, the parade is shown on Washington Avenue. (Courtesy of the Capital District Area Library, Lansing.)

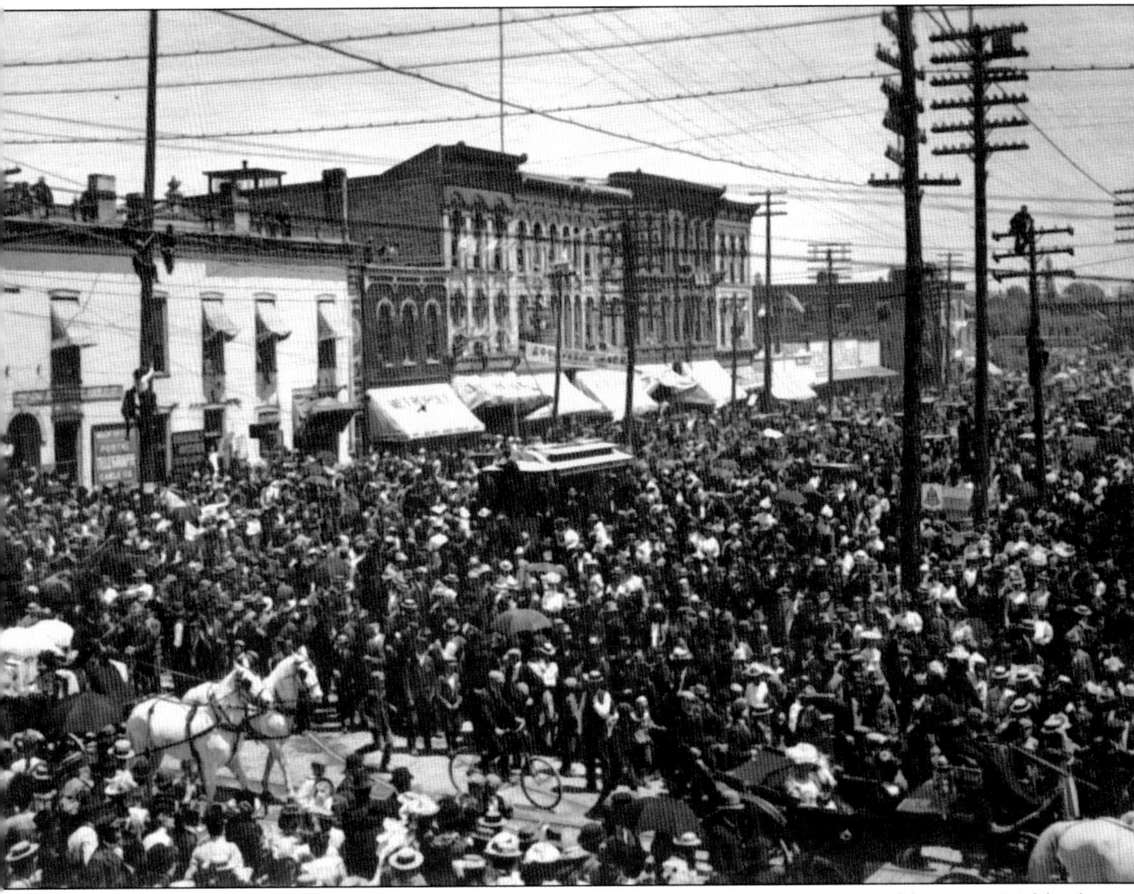

In 1900, Lansing hosted another major event, Admiral Dewey Day. Pictured here are Mildred Dewey, J.F. Hammill, and Ida Longyear in the carriage. Most of the city turned out to greet one of the heroes of the Spanish-American War. In those pre-television days, people had to leave their living rooms to see a celebrity. (Courtesy of the Capital District Area Library, Lansing.)

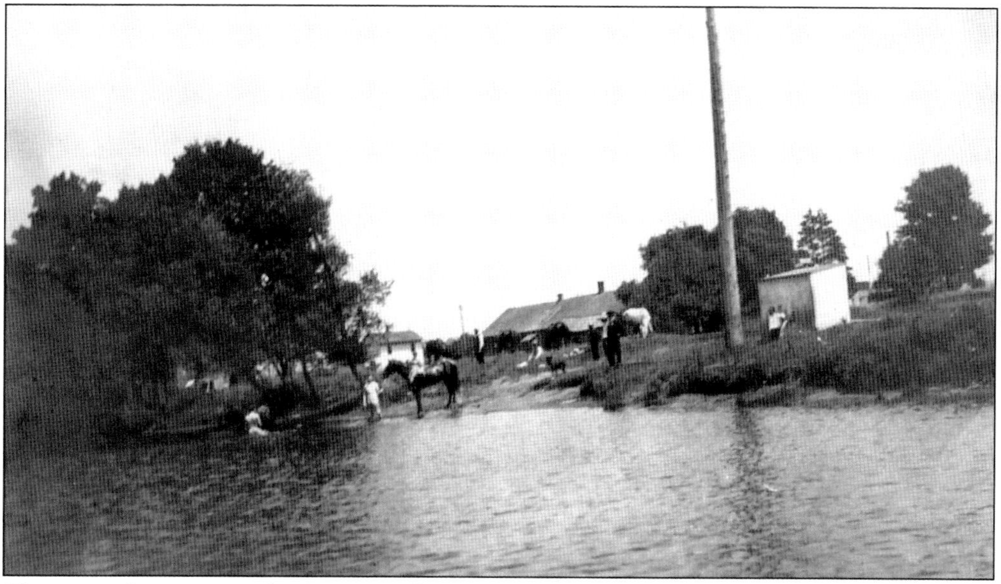

The mineral water craze hit Lansing when springs were discovered there as well as other sites along the river. In Lansing, too, people lost interest when it was revealed there was no lasting therapeutic value. This old well at the far right was photographed in 1901. (Courtesy of the Capital Area District Library, Lansing.)

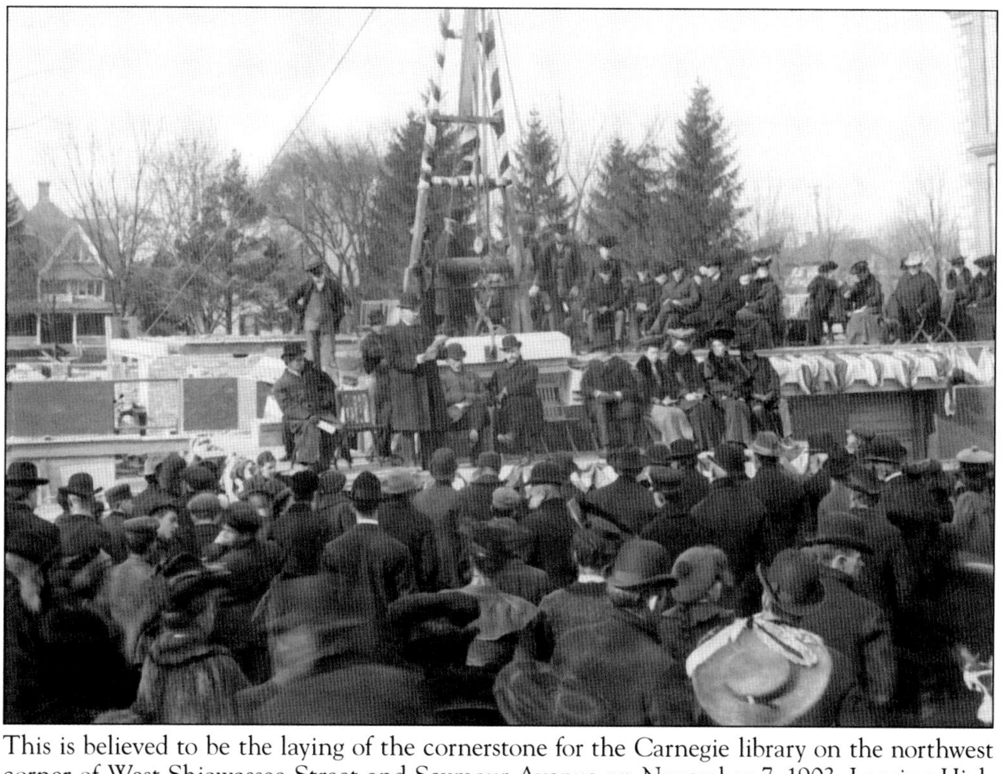

This is believed to be the laying of the cornerstone for the Carnegie library on the northwest corner of West Shiawassee Street and Seymour Avenue on November 7, 1903. Lansing High School is at the far right, and the Jenison family lived in the house in back. (Courtesy of the Capital Area District Library, Lansing.)

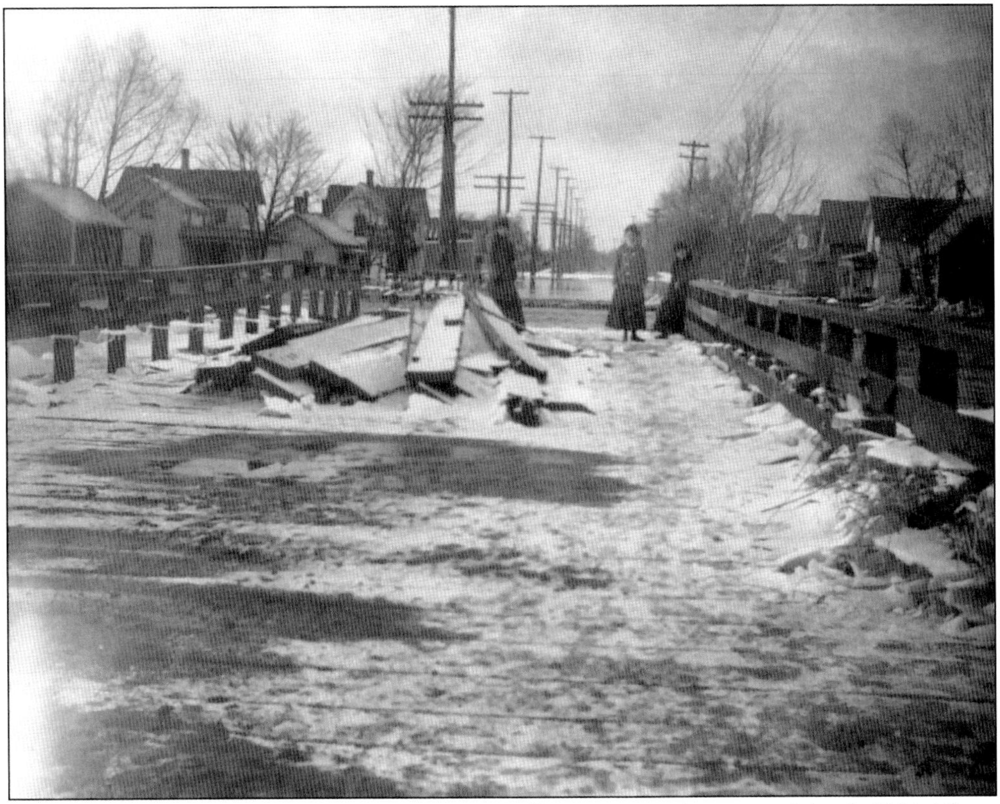

Severe flooding all along the river took a huge toll in property damage in March 1904. Three Lansing women stand on a flooded bridge in a hard-hit residential area. The river wreaked havoc for most of its length, and scenes like this were repeated in other cities and towns. (Courtesy of the Capital Area District Library, Lansing.)

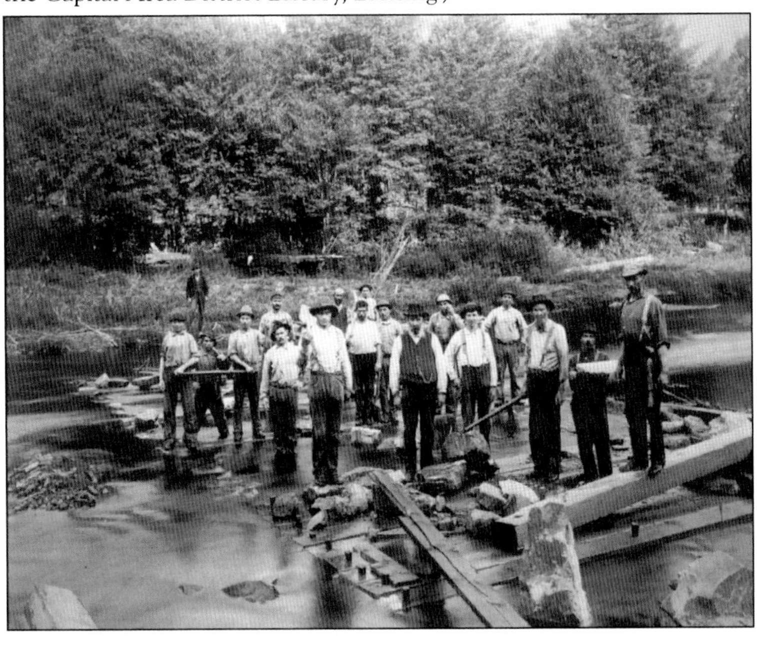

Lumbermen are examining the damage done to a bridge so they can determine how much will have to be done to repair the structure. The image is undated, so it is unknown whether this followed a flood or normal wear and tear. (Courtesy of the Capital Area District Library, Lansing.)

In 1886, a little over a decade before he founded the Olds Motor Vehicle Company, Ransom E. Olds built this, his first steam car. It became the first self-propelled vehicle sold in Michigan when a British Company bought it and shipped it to Bombay, India, in 1893. (Courtesy of the Capital Area District Library, Lansing.)

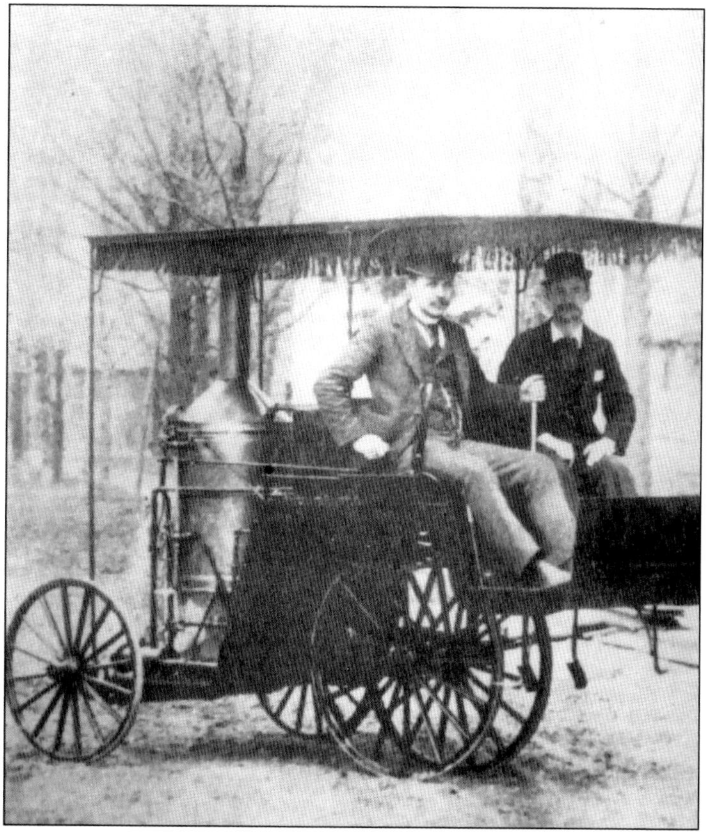

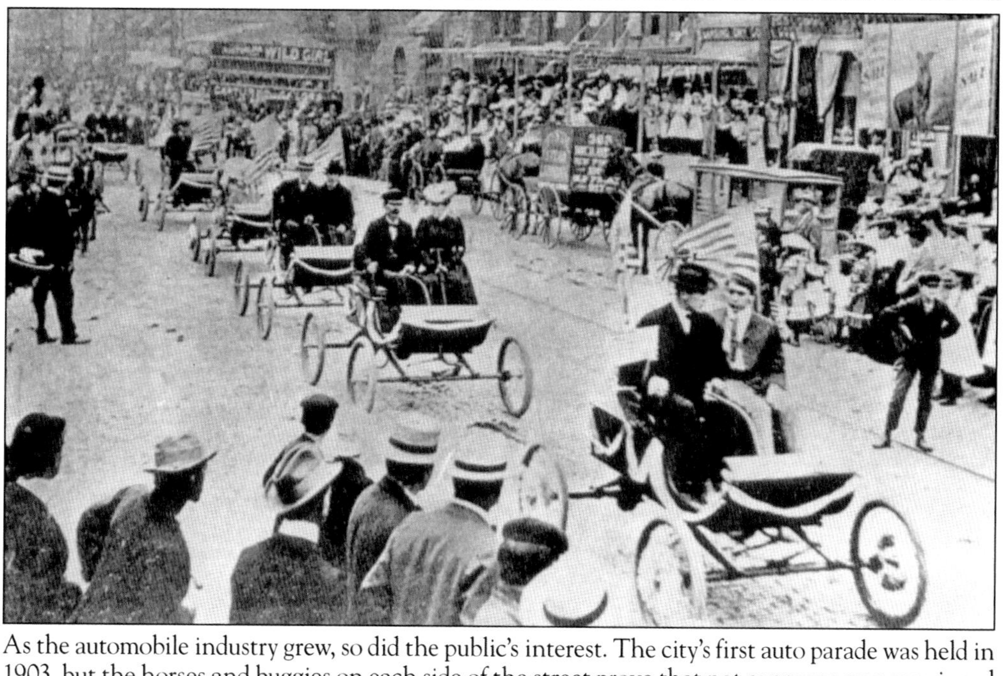

As the automobile industry grew, so did the public's interest. The city's first auto parade was held in 1903, but the horses and buggies on each side of the street prove that not everyone was convinced the fad would last. (Courtesy of the Capital Area District Library, Lansing.)

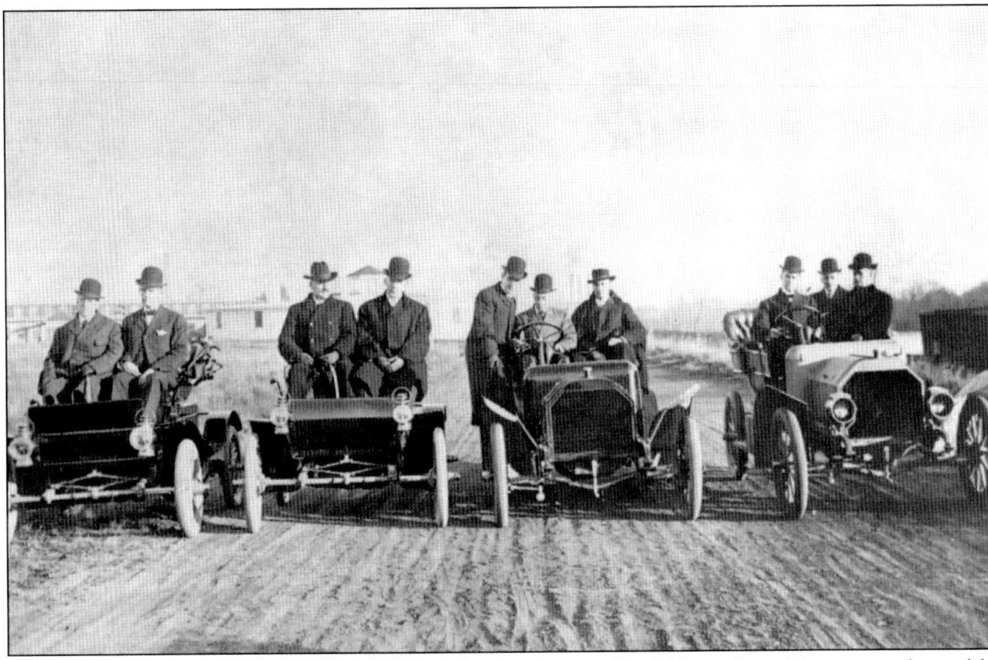

Ransom Olds was convinced his Curved Dash autos were affordable and could compete favorable against the era's favorite mode of transportation, the horse. He argued that once a car was purchased it did not have to be fed, and gasoline was cheap and readily available. The cars being test driven here in 1906 went on to become the first that were mass produced. (Courtesy of the Bentley Historical Library, University of Michigan.)

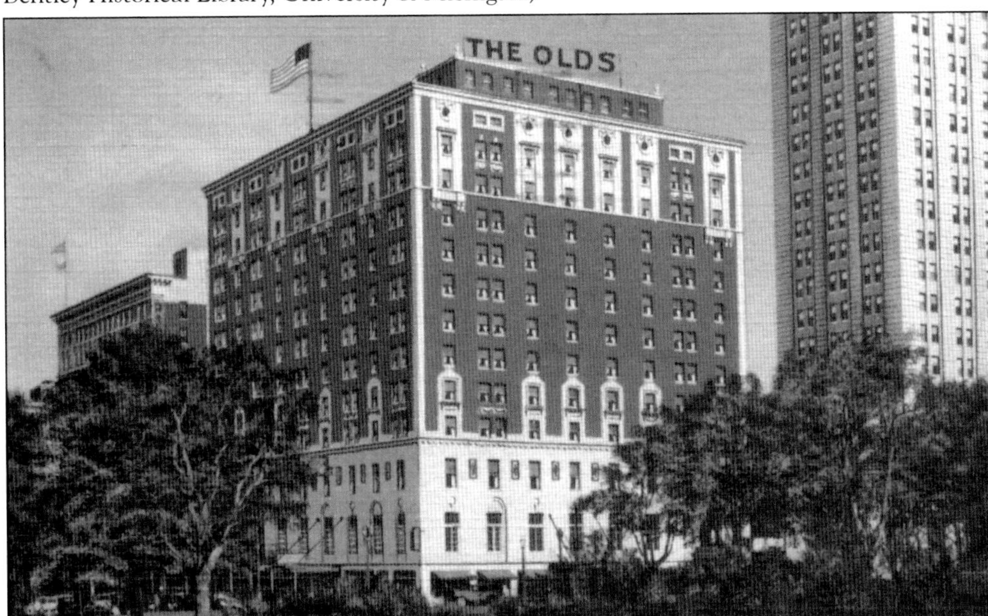

A postcard mailed on September 19, 1934, showing the Olds Hotel in downtown Lansing demonstrates the impact R.E. Olds had on the city. The message on the back addresses the economic challenges of the time with cautious optimism: "George is back at Oldsmobile working every day and sometimes six or seven hours. Other factories are picking up some too." (Author's collection.)

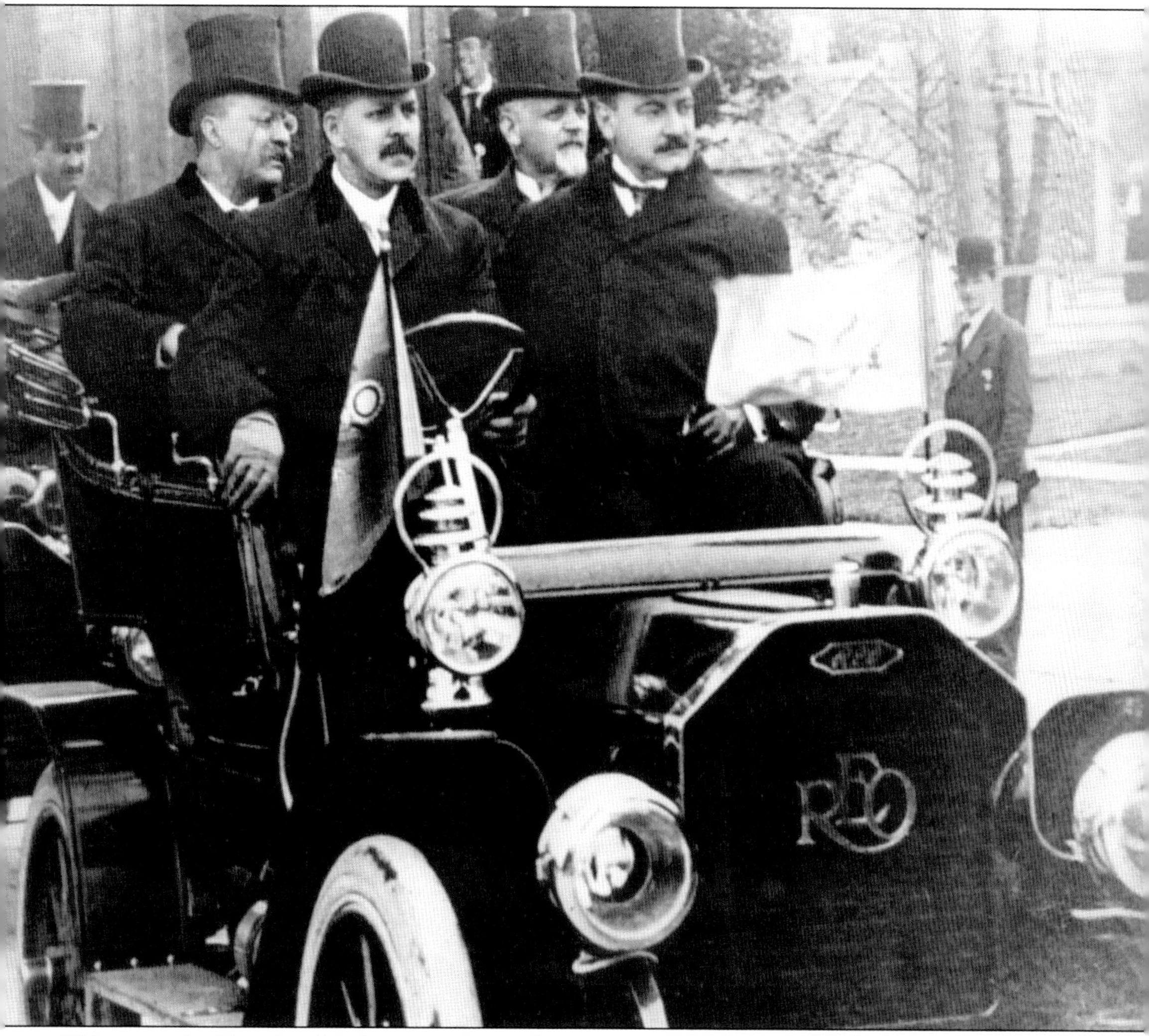

Olds recognized Lansing, Michigan, as the perfect spot to open an automobile factory. He founded the Olds Motor Vehicle Company in 1897; in 1915, his REO Motor Car Company line included a light truck named the REO Speed Wagon. This 1907 image shows Olds driving Pres. Theodore Roosevelt (backseat, left) to Michigan Agricultural College, where the president made a speech. In the back with Roosevelt is college president Jonathon Snyder. The passenger in the front seat is Roosevelt's secretary, William Loeb. (Courtesy of Michigan State University.)

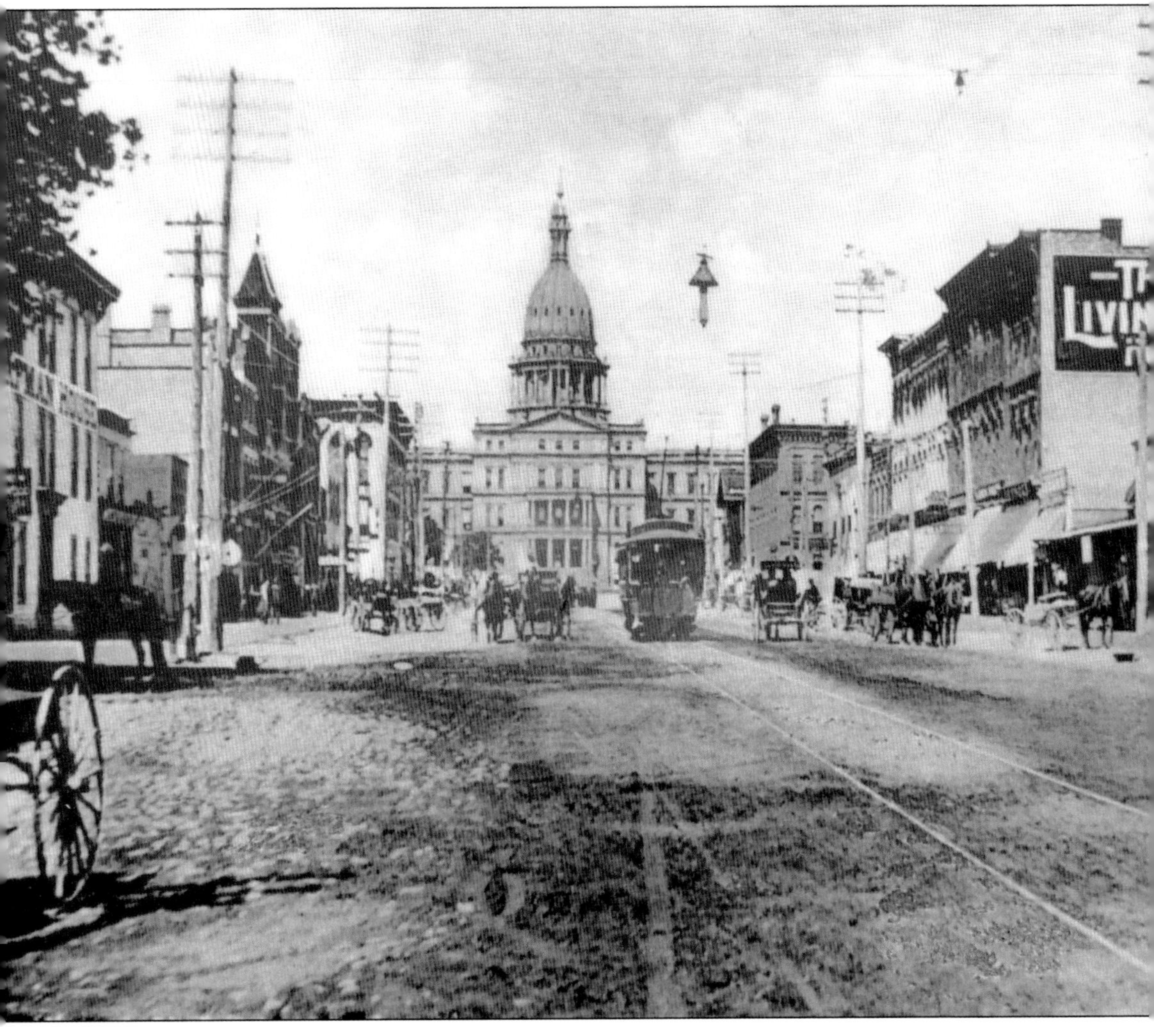

Michigan's first capital was Detroit, but the seat of government was relocated to Lansing in 1847, with the first building a simple wood-frame structure. The Italianate building shown here was dedicated in 1879 and, though it has undergone renovations, is still in use today. The image was taken in 1869. (Courtesy of the Bentley Historical Library, University of Michigan.)

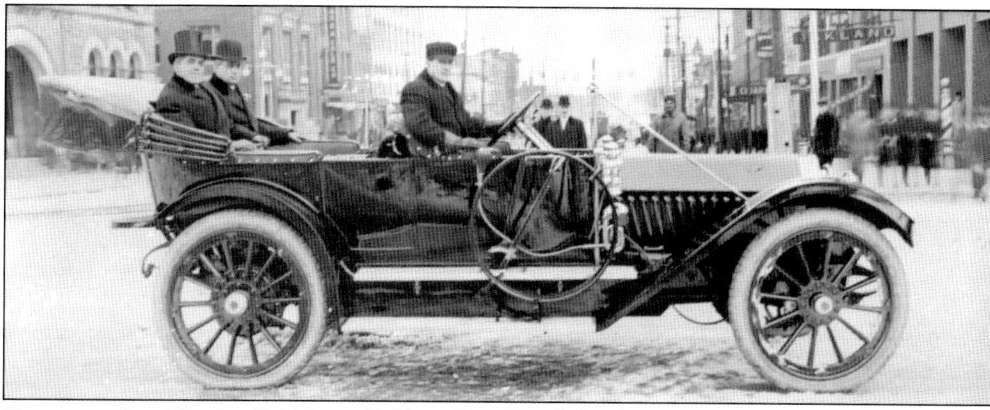

Governor-elect Charles S. Osborn (left) and Lt. Gov. John Ross arrive at the capitol in fine style on the day of their inauguration, January 2, 1911. Osborn was Michigan's 27th governor. (Courtesy of the Bentley Historical Library, University of Michigan.)

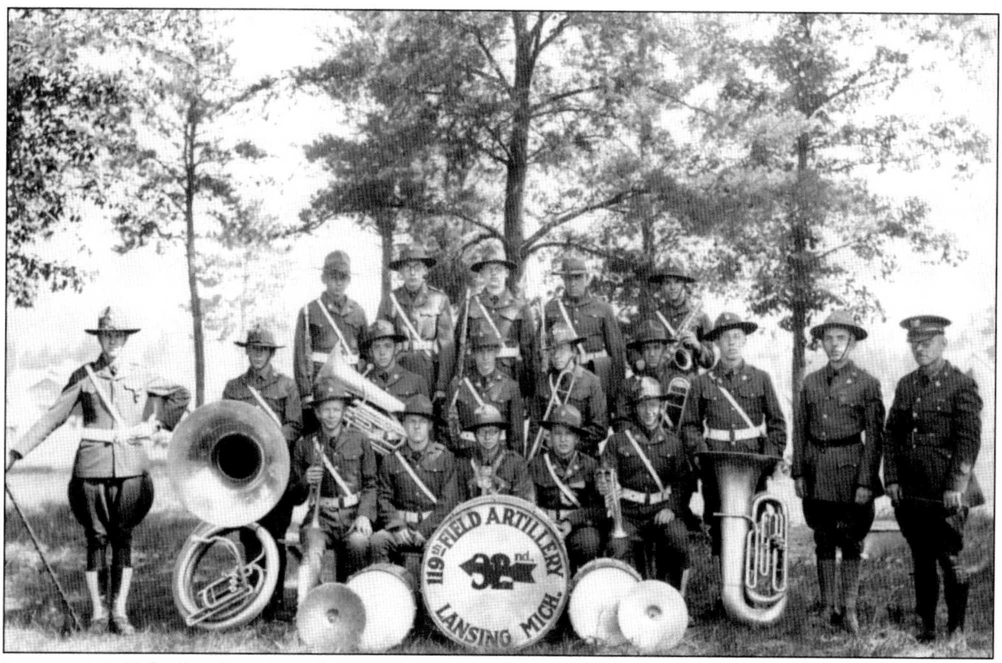

Lansing's 119th Artillery Band poses at Camp Grayling in Northern Michigan in 1929. Today, that military installation is the largest National Guard training facility in the United States. (Courtesy of the Capital Area District Library, Lansing.)

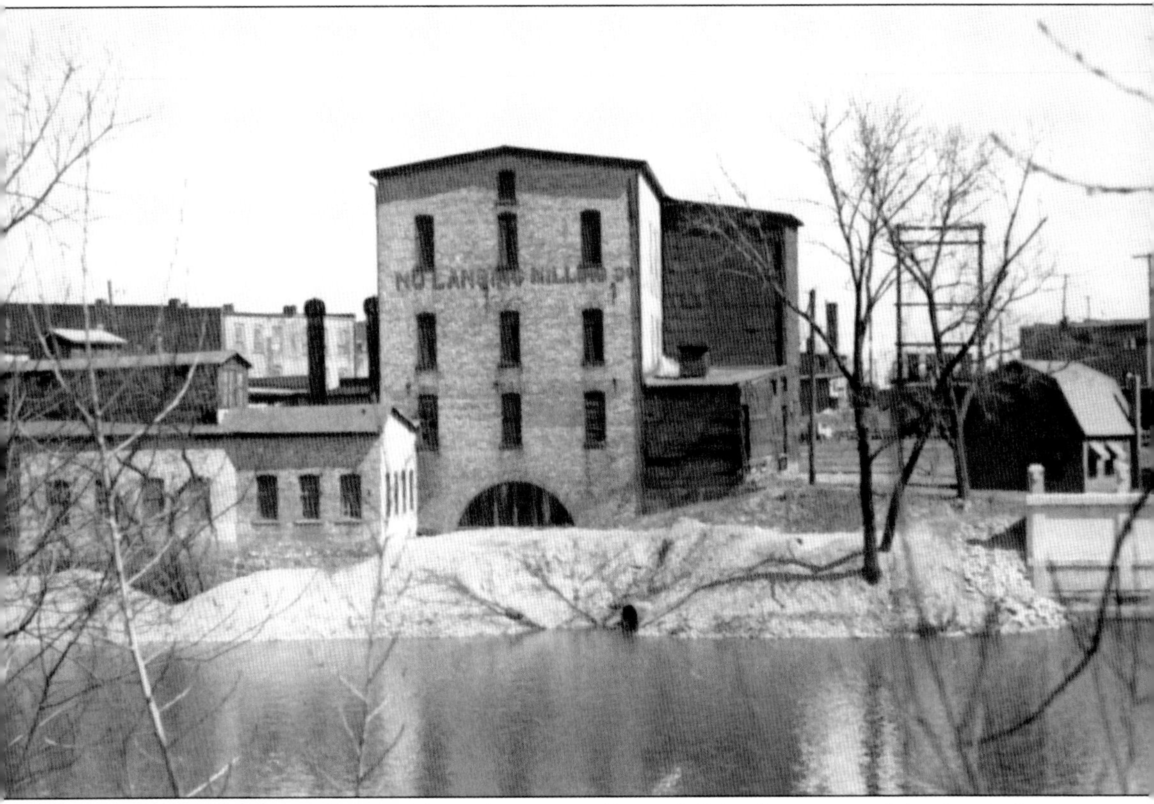

As in most of the settlements along the river, milling of all kinds was one of the first industries, and many of them milled flour. The North Lansing Milling Company was still producing flour in 1937 when this photograph was taken on March 23. (Courtesy of the Bentley Historical Library, University of Michigan.)

Three 1914 students in the women's residence hall at Michigan Agricultural College prepare for the next day's classes. Women were first admitted to the college in 1870. (Author's collection.)

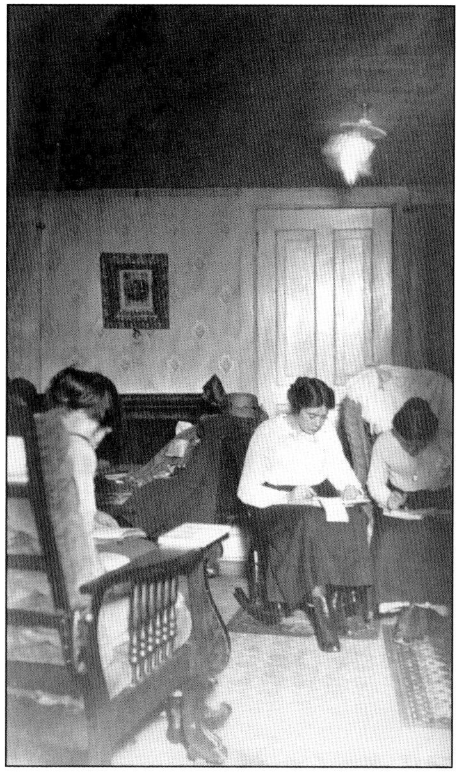

Michigan State students change classes on the campus in 1954. It was a big year for the school, whose football team won the first of four Rose Bowl titles for the Spartans. The other three were in 1956, 1988, and 2014. (Courtesy of the Capital Area District Library, Lansing.)

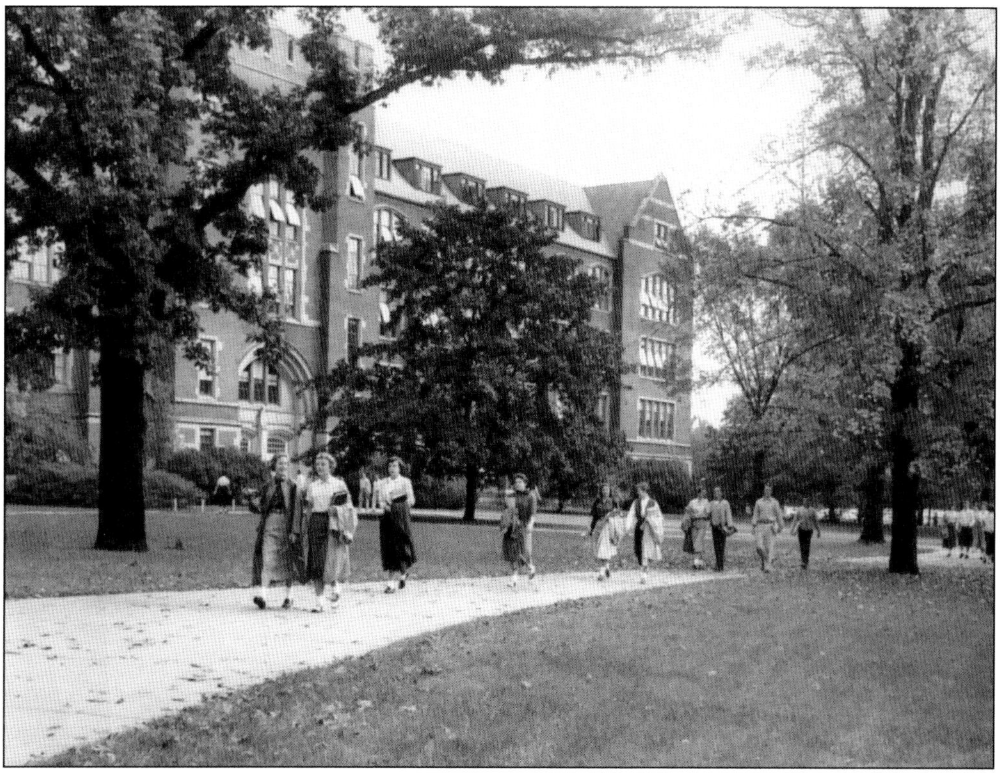

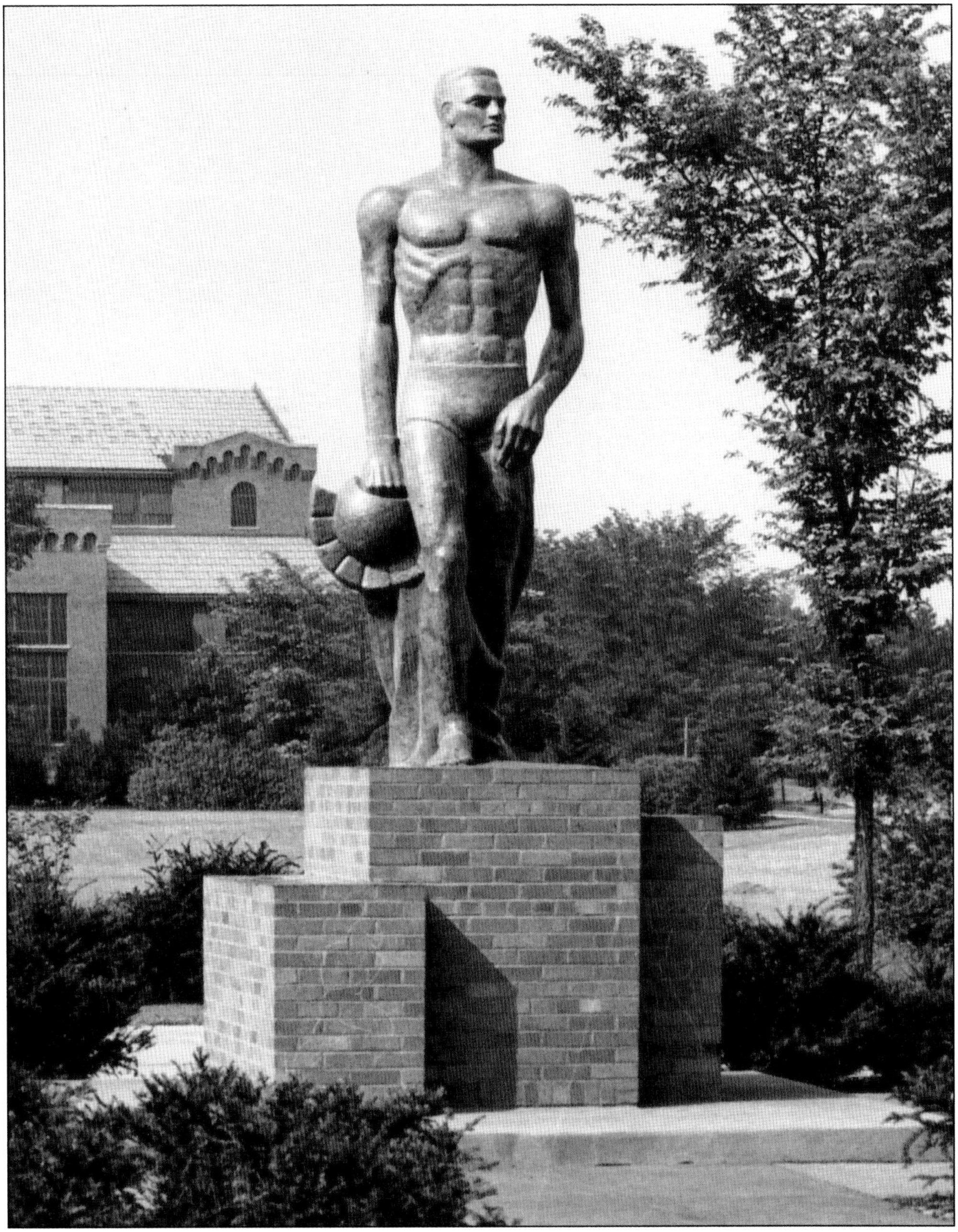

In 1943, an MSU art director, Leonad D. Jungwirth, designed *The Spartan*, a nine-foot-seven-inch statue to represent the school's mascot. Sparty, as he is known, was built of terra-cotta due to World War II rationing, and the statue eventually deteriorated and had to be moved inside. Today, a bronze replica stands at the original site. (Courtesy of the Capital Area District Library, Lansing.)

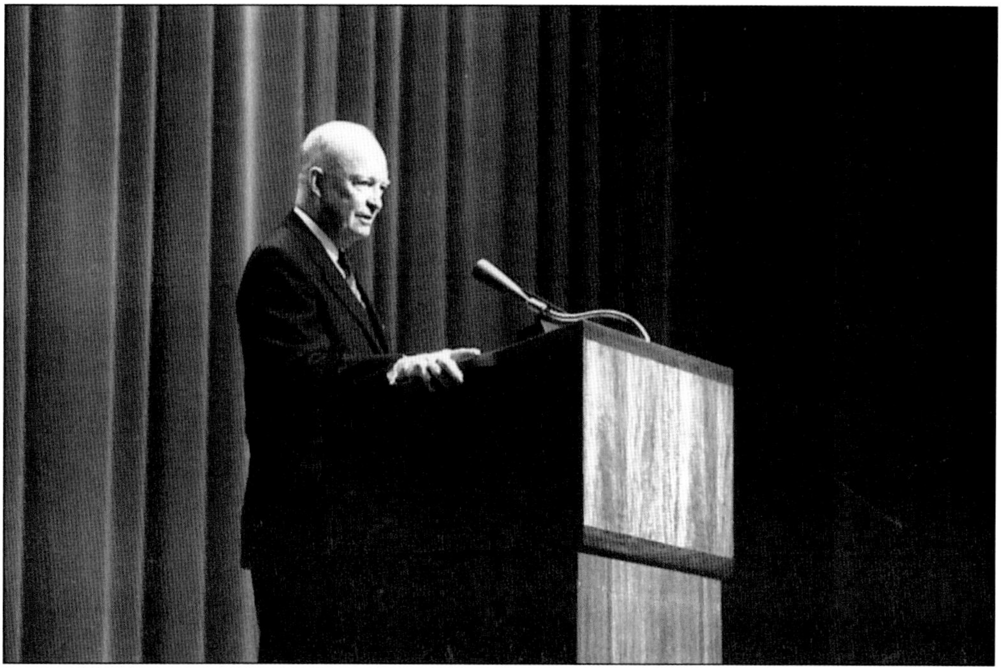

Pres. Dwight D. Eisenhower came to the campus in 1960 and is shown delivering a speech. In the image below, he greets students, faculty, and others who have lined up to see him. Increased security after the assassination of his successor, John F. Kennedy, in 1963 would make this kind of presidential access impossible. (Both, courtesy of Michigan State University.)

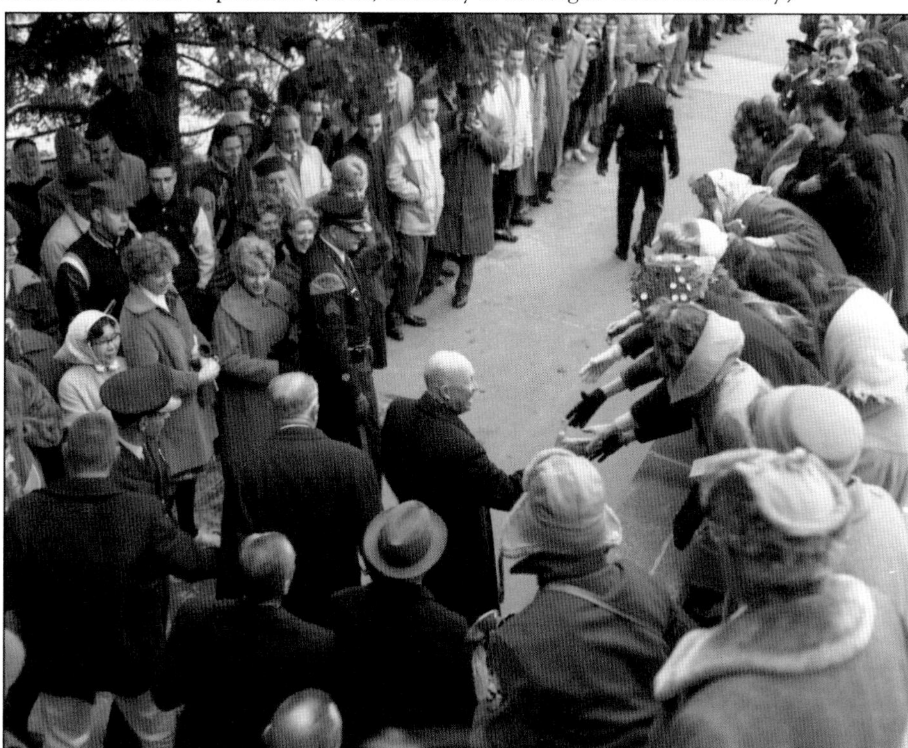

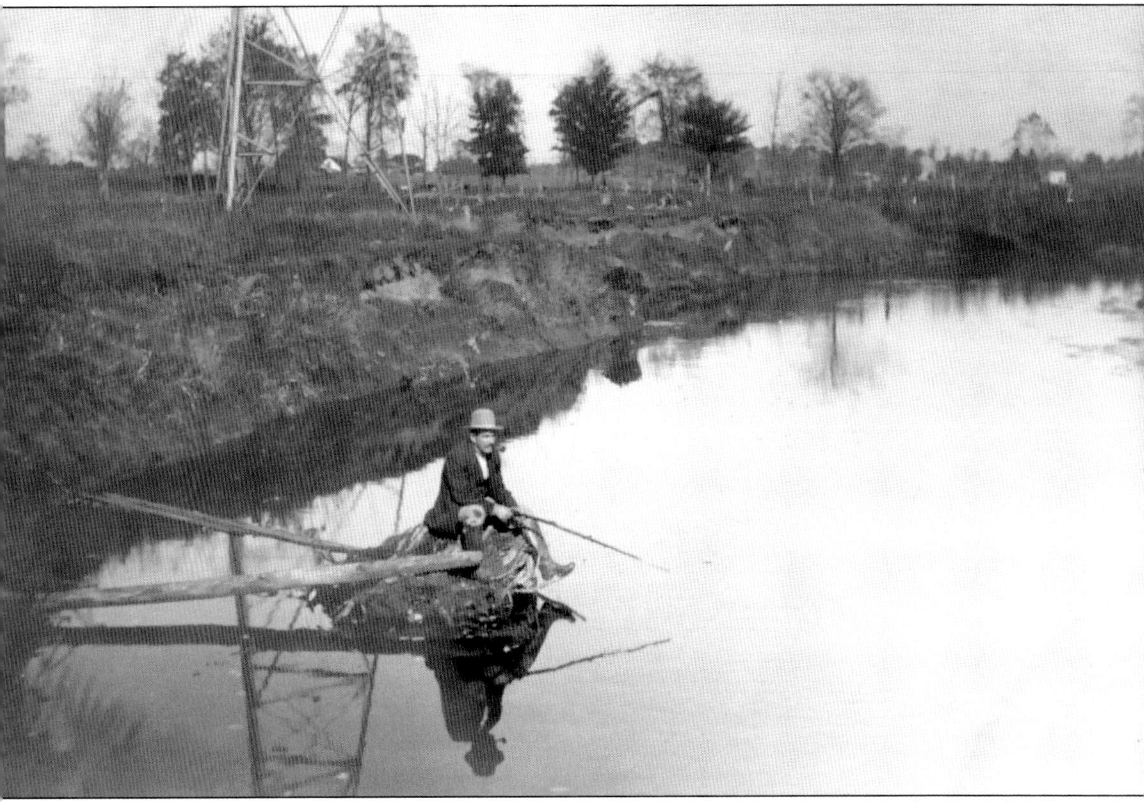

This postcard showing a fisherman on the Grand River near Lansing is postmarked 1918 and written to someone in Diamondale, Michigan. The writer asks if the recipient knows the photograph, as it was taken by his neighbor. (Courtesy of the Capital Area District Library, Lansing.)

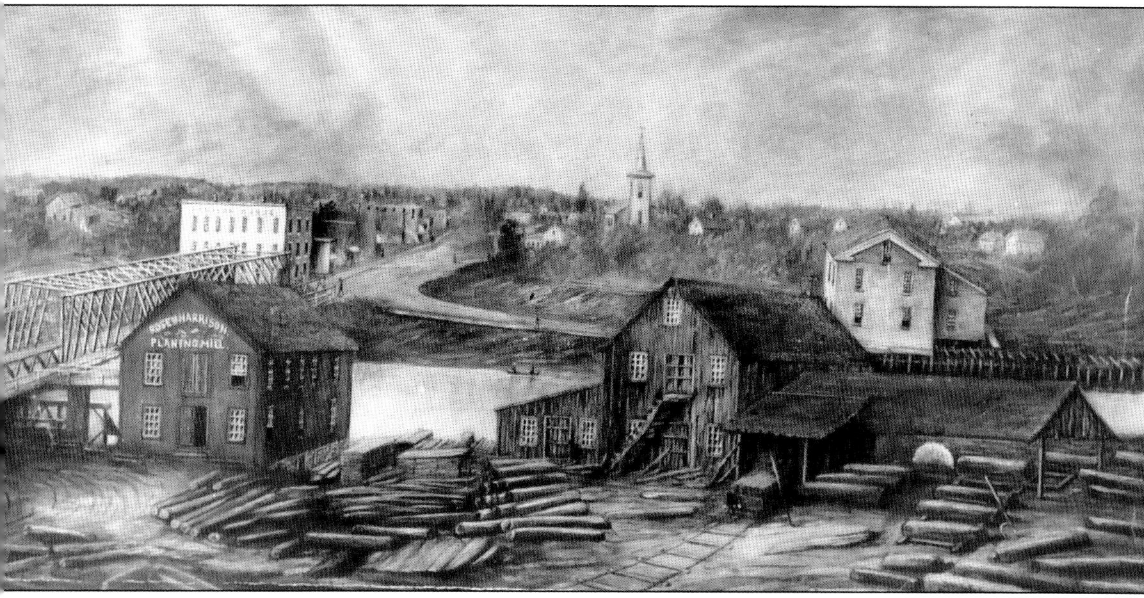

This is what Grand Ledge looked like in 1874, in a view looking north away from the river and toward the village. The old cliff house on the right burned a short time later. (Courtesy of the Grand Ledge Area Historical Society.)

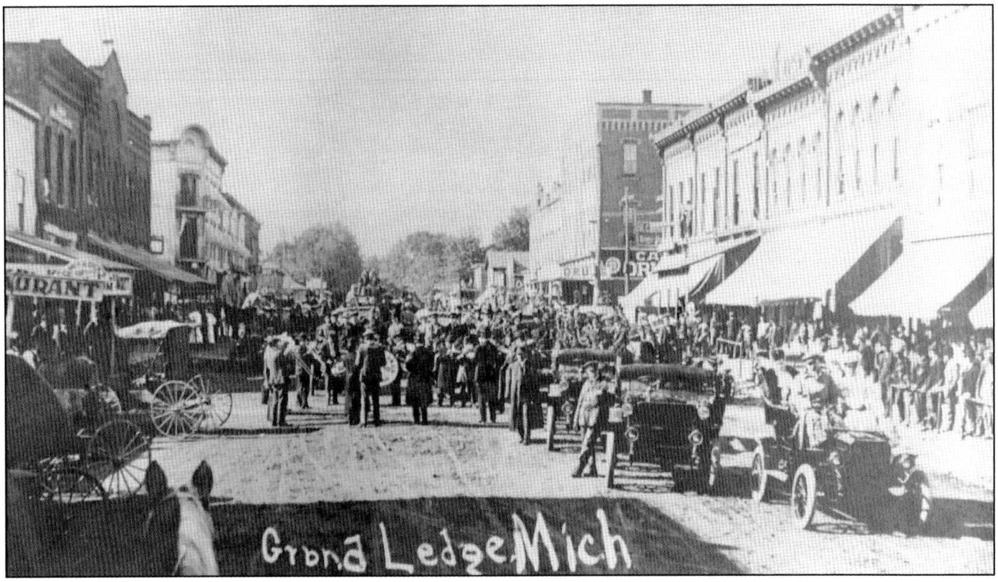

A parade on the 200 and 300 blocks of South Bridge Street in 1905 celebrated the first cars in Grand Ledge. Ransom E. Olds is driving the first car, and the next two may have been driven by D.D. Shane and Thomas Astley. Olds enjoyed arranging parades in area towns to create interest in his vehicles. He brought other automobile owners and was often accompanied by a band, as the drum in the center of this image illustrates. (Courtesy of the Grand Ledge Area Historical Society.)

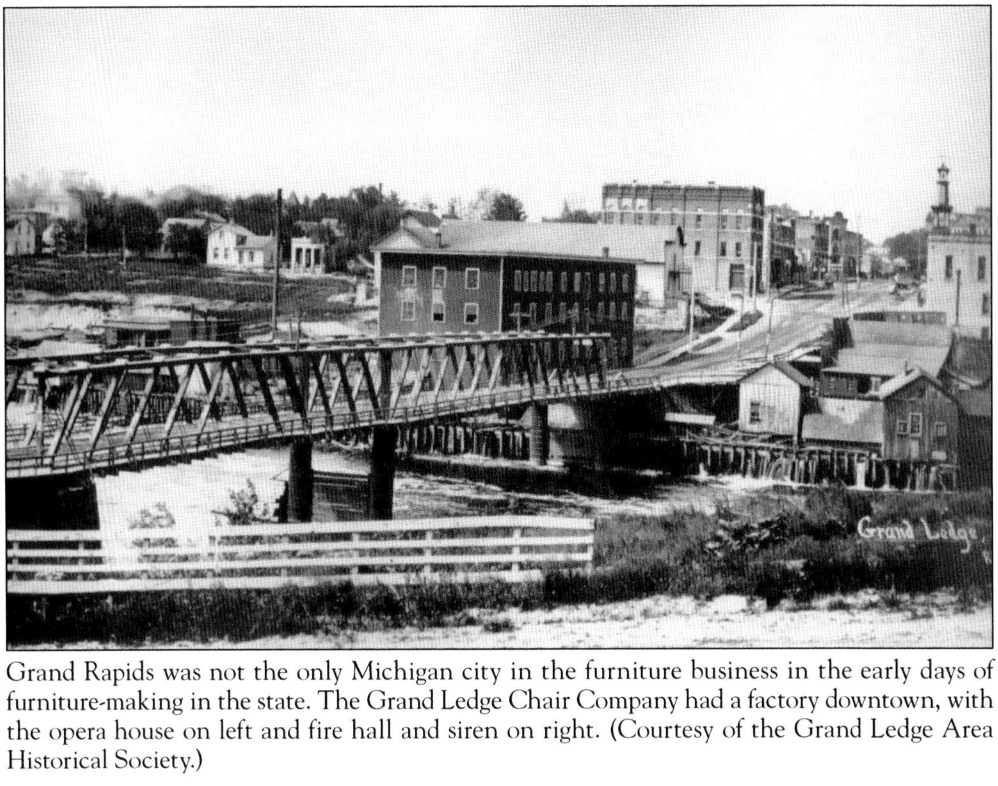

Grand Rapids was not the only Michigan city in the furniture business in the early days of furniture-making in the state. The Grand Ledge Chair Company had a factory downtown, with the opera house on left and fire hall and siren on right. (Courtesy of the Grand Ledge Area Historical Society.)

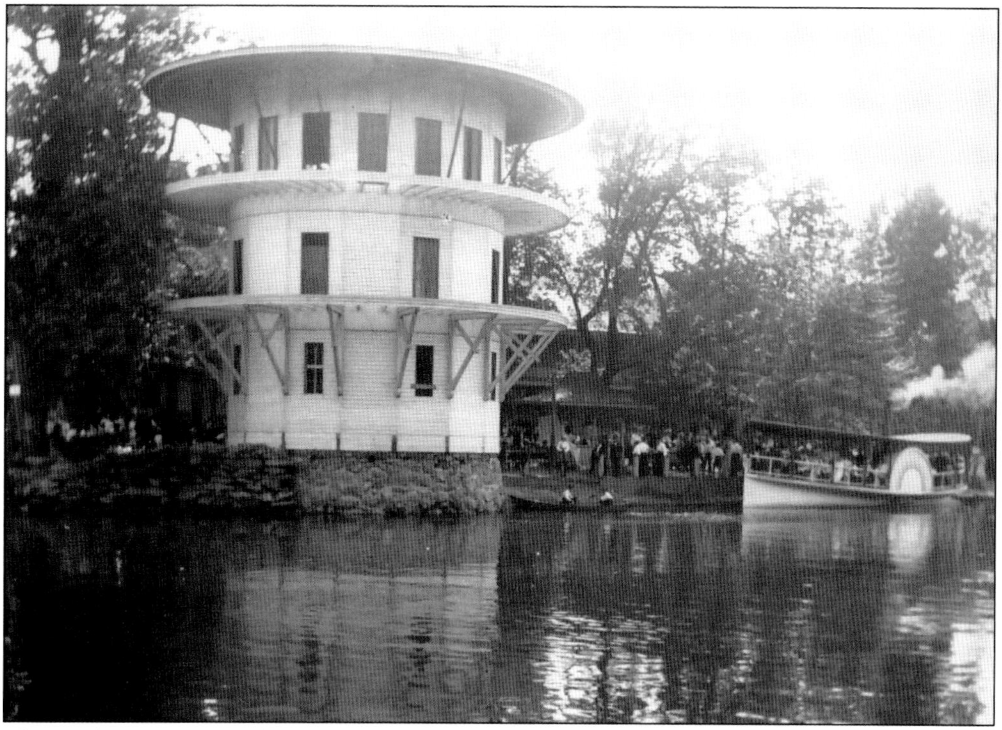

The Mudge Resort, on the second of the three islands, was one of several such facilities in the area in the 1890s. The image below shows the resort during its heyday when weddings, parties, and other events were frequent occurrences. Though the resort is gone, the island is still a draw. (Both, courtesy of the Grand Ledge Area Historical Society.)

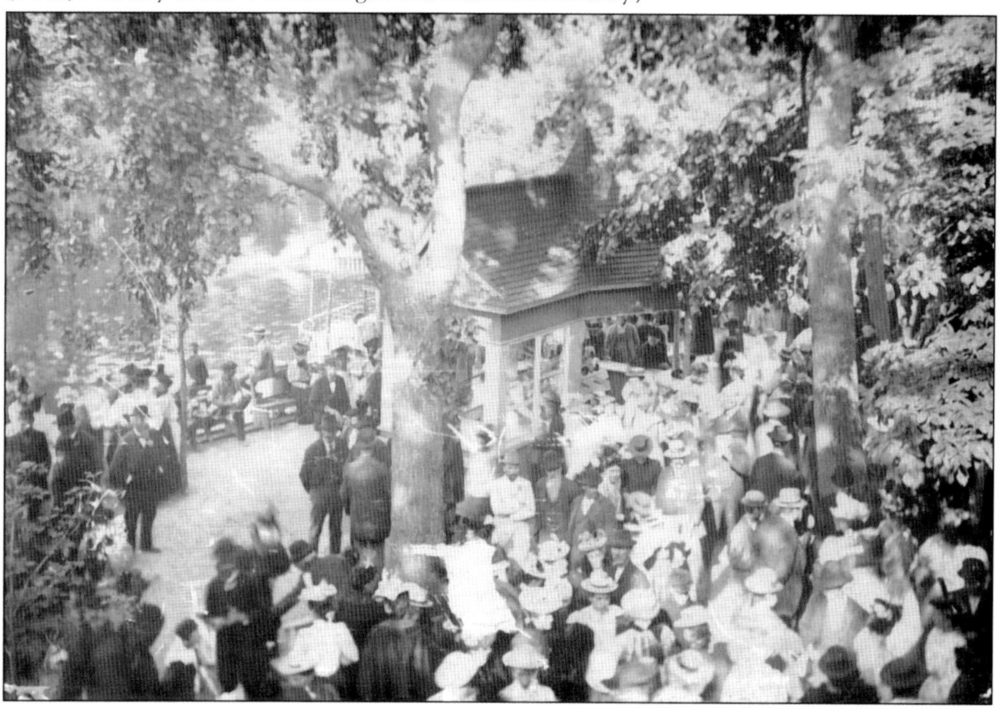

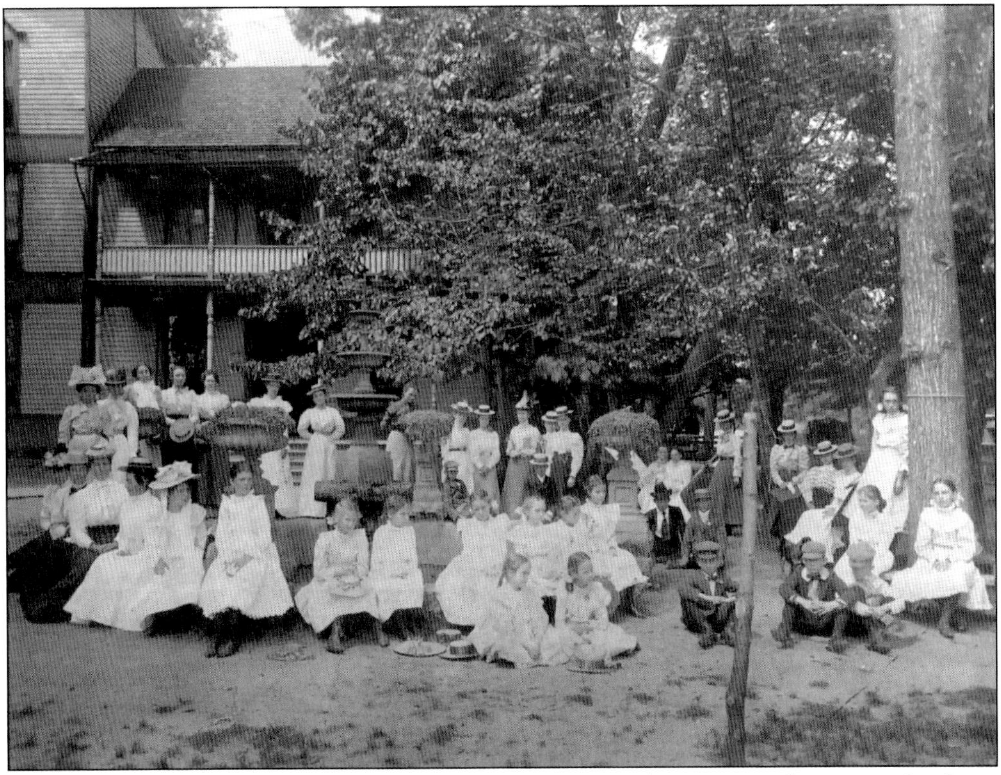

The resorts on the islands also hosted smaller gatherings. Local musician and music teacher Irene Reed chose a resort on the second island as the venue for her music class recital. (Courtesy of the Grand Ledge Area Historical Society.)

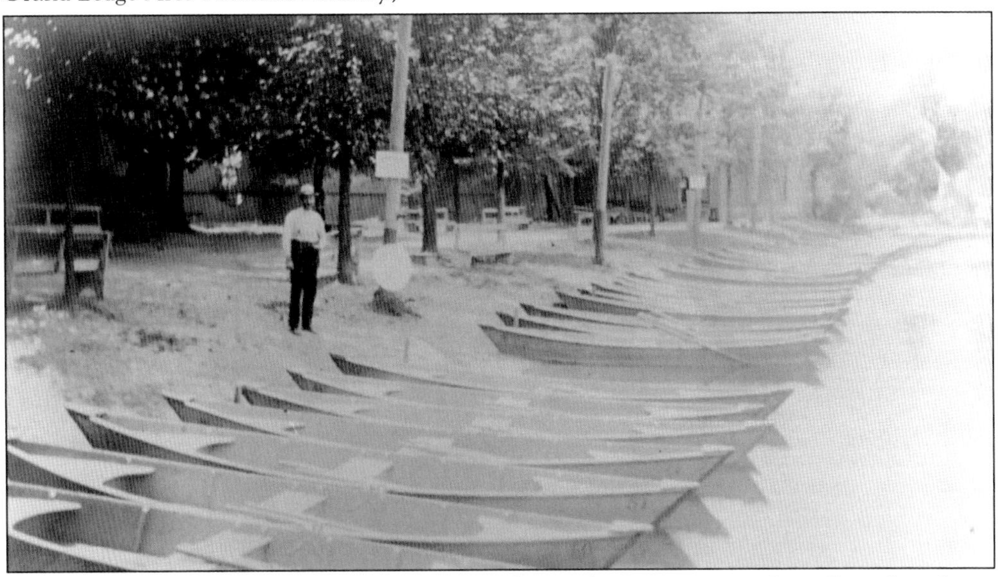

Even after the resorts closed, the islands continued to see heavy recreational use. Rental rowboats were a necessity, and the situation seems to be under control. Rental fees for the 75 or so boats on the island ran from 10¢ to 25¢ an hour, depending on the time of day. (Courtesy of the Grand Ledge Area Historical Society.)

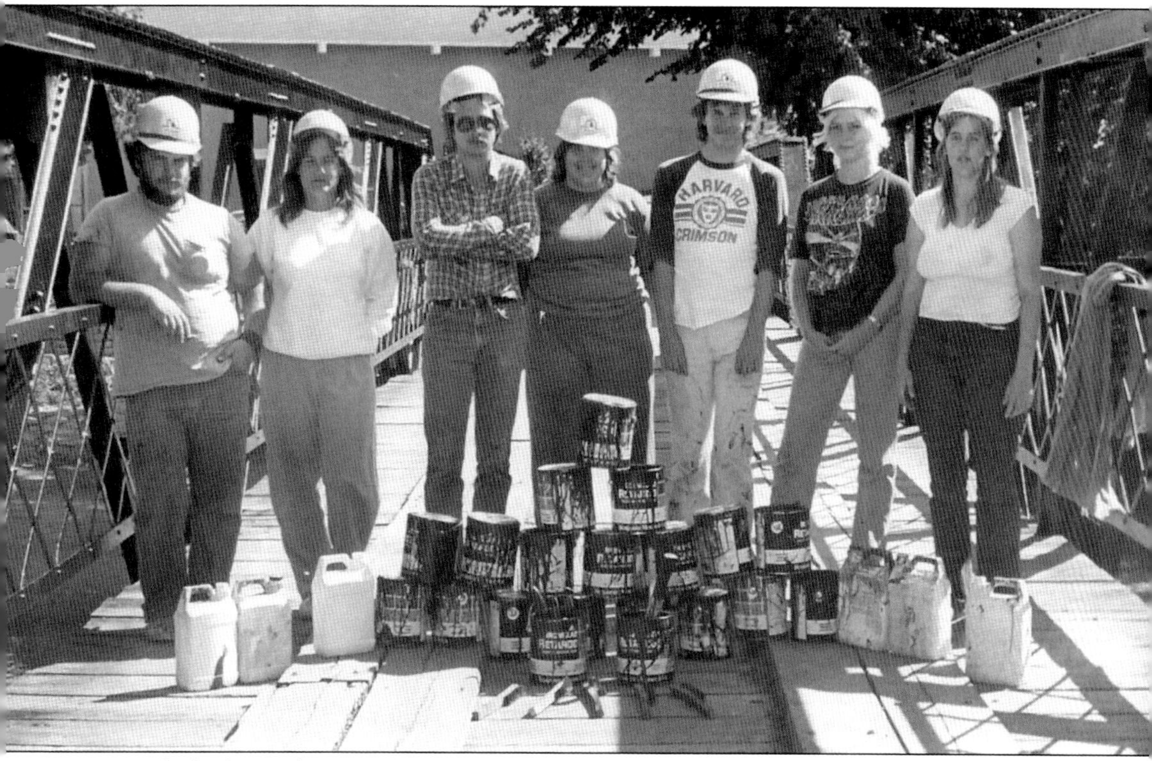

In 1983, the bridge to the second island needed to be painted. On September 22, the Grand Ledge Youth Corps rose to the challenge. Pictured, from left to right, are Vance White, Karen Browning, Dave Rocheleau, Pam Carl, John Doxsie, Cindy Feldpausch, and Rose Dorman.

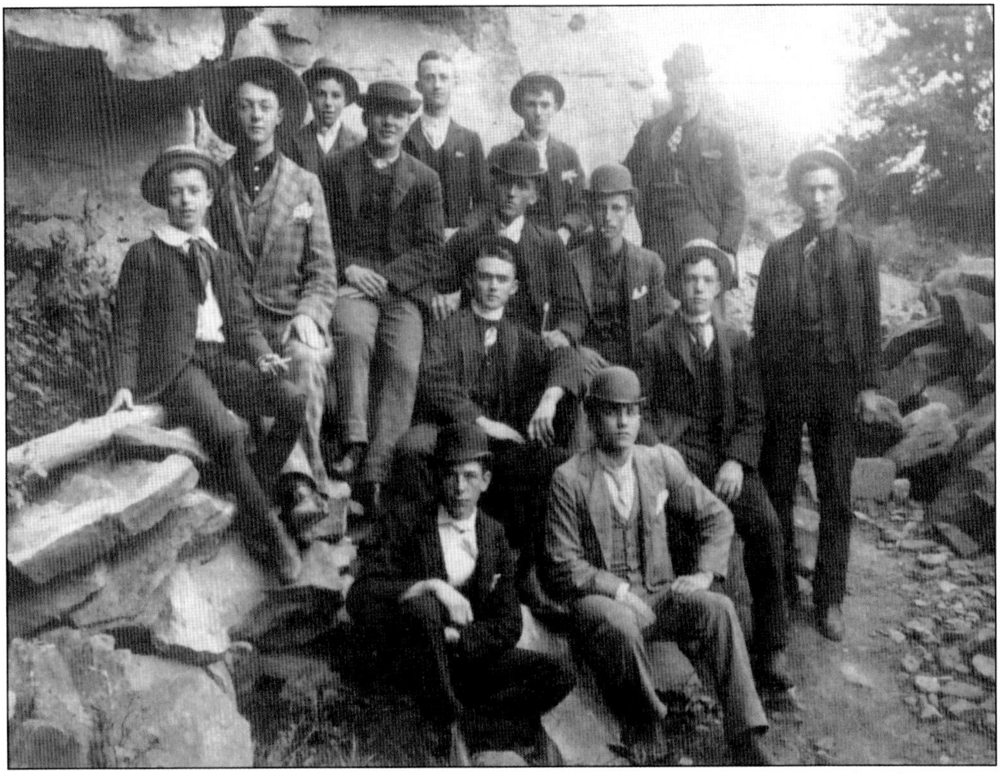

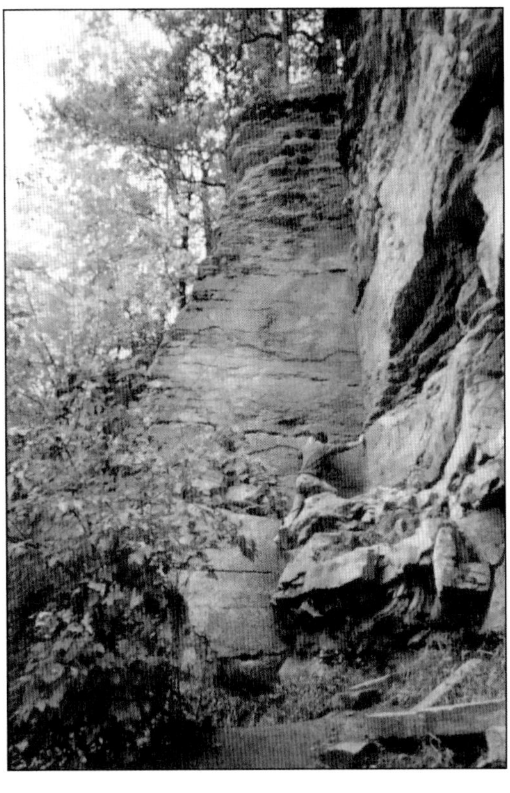

The best reason to visit Grand Ledge is the ledges. Unlike any other spot along the river, 35-foot cliffs of exposed rock have always tempted climbers. Some climb to find the perfect photo opportunity. Others use the local anomaly to learn or practice climbing skills before tackling more challenging sites. (Both, courtesy of the Grand Ledge Area Historical Society.)

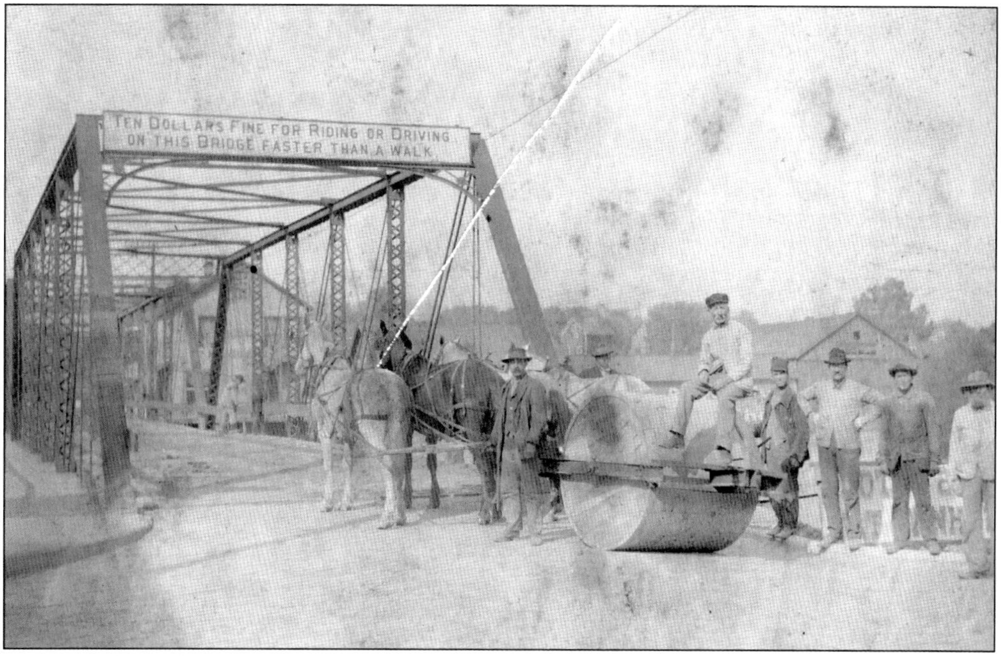

This is perhaps the oldest image in the Portland Area Historical Society's collection. Note the warning sign on the downtown bridge: "Ten dollars fine for riding or driving on this bridge faster than a walk." That was a lot of money back then, so the men had to make sure their horses refrained from prancing. (Courtesy of the Portland Area Historical Society.)

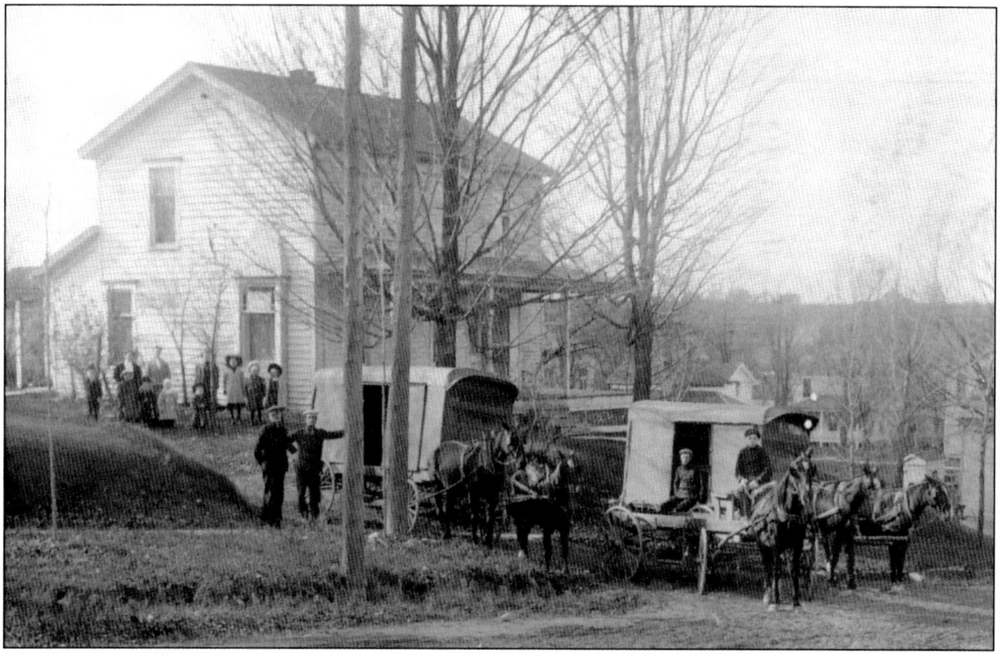

This is a typical farm near Portland, with a house large enough to shelter a growing family. The horses and buggies are probably the farm delivery conveyances. On the family's precious few days off, they stood ready to take the family out for a social event or even a pleasure ride. (Courtesy of the Portland Area Historical Society.)

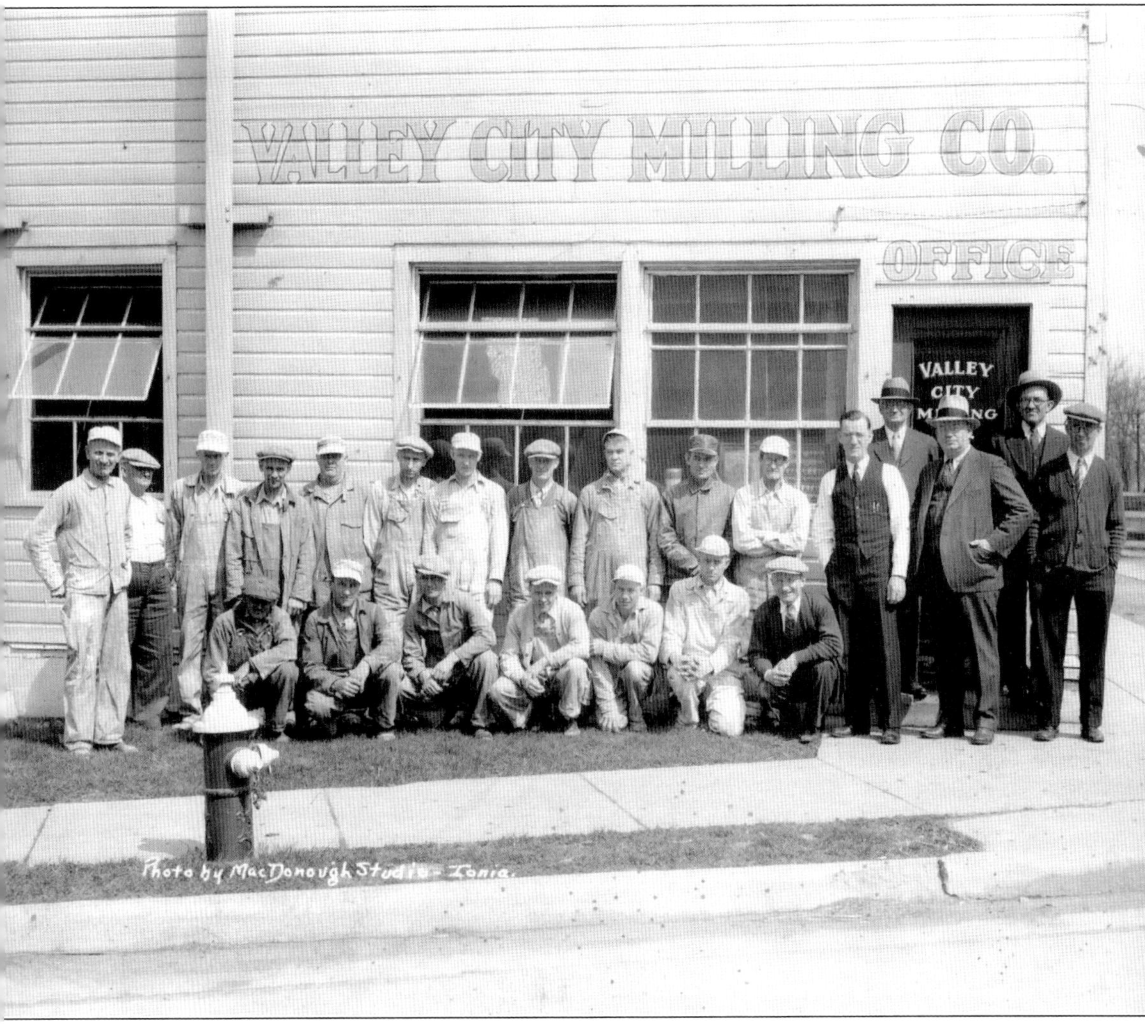

Employees of the Valley City Milling Company pose for a group photograph. Attached to the image are names of those shown. They are, from left to right, (first row) Mervin Sellech, George Bauer, Charles Rock, Alden Young, Arnold Gross, Julius Smith, and Bob Saline; (second row) Peter Roberts, Emory Swank, George Guilford, Frank Snow, unidentified, Ray Cross, Herb Baldwin, John Schaffer, Arlo Smith, Henry Densmore, John Grass, Bill Tranick, unidentified, Frank Martin, Oscar Rice, and Robert Holz. Unfortunately, the list contains two fewer names than the number of people pictured and identification is not 100 percent certain. (Courtesy of the Portland Area Historical Society.)

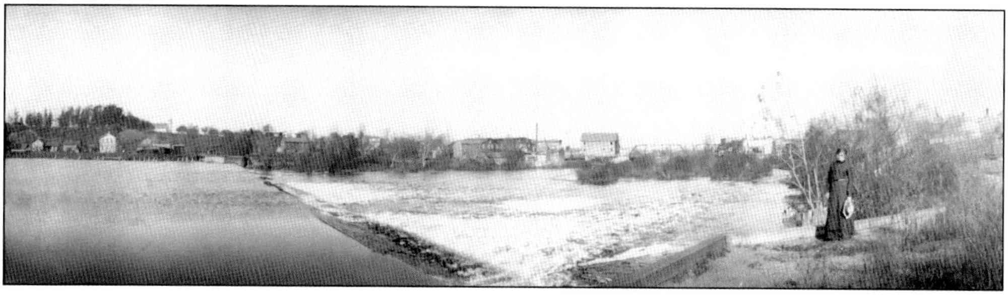

The woman in the above view of the river is looking west from where the library stands today, while the photograph below shows the downtown area. (Both, courtesy of the Portland Area Historical Society.)

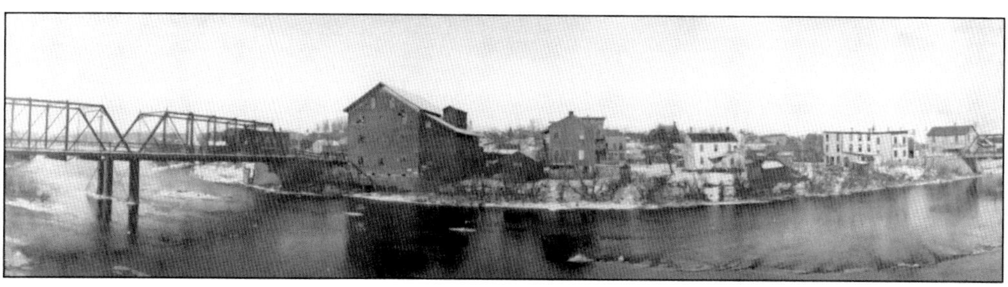

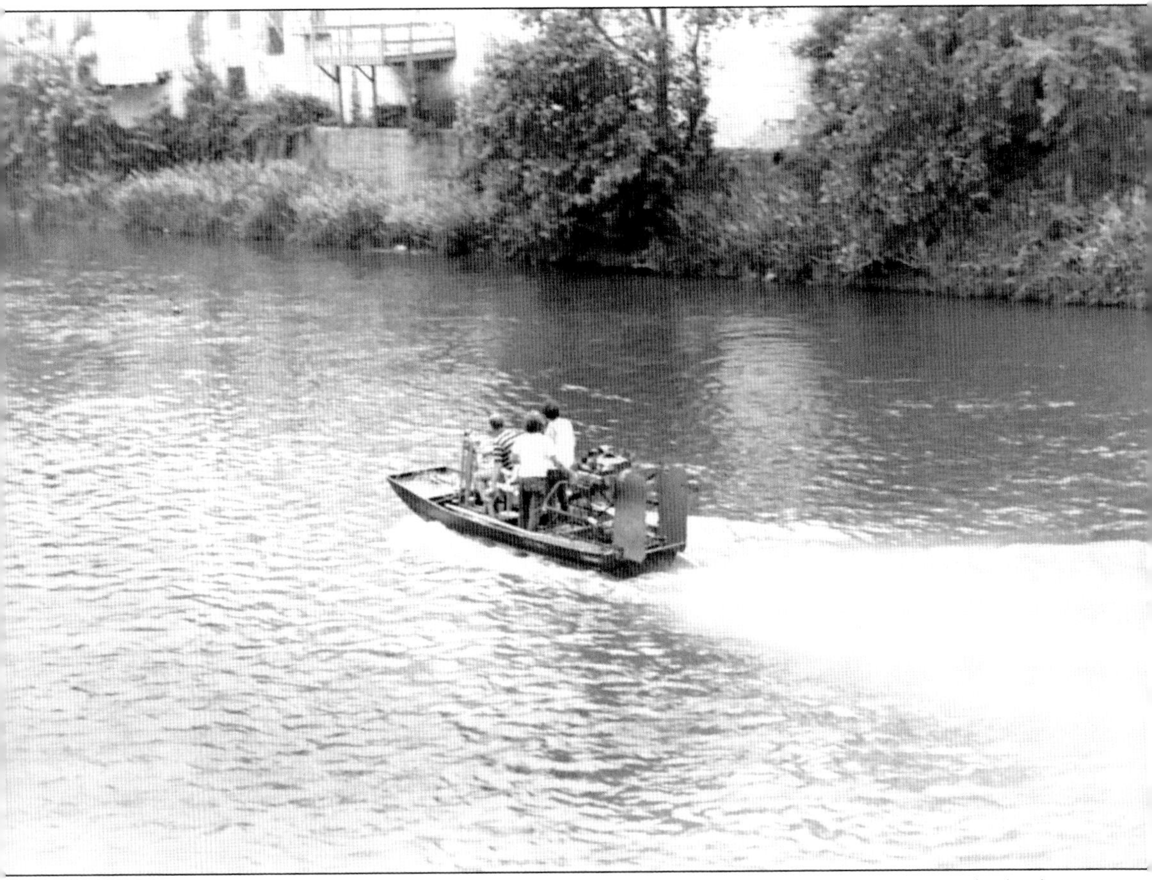

In the mid-20th century, Portland was a good place to put a boat on the river. And whether a person is fishing or pleasure boating, it still is. The scenery along the way remains unchanged. (Courtesy of the Portland Area Historical Society.)

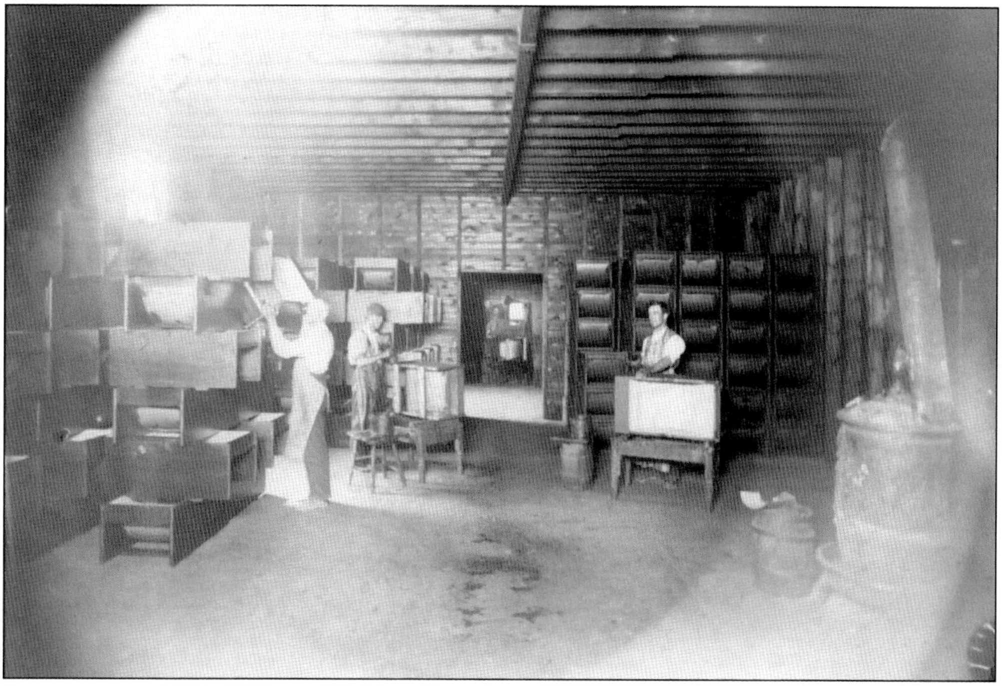

Beginning in 1890, William W. Terriff produced Terriff's Perfect Washers in his Portland Manufacturing Company starting. The early versions were little more than square tubs, but compared to washboards, they must have seemed luxurious indeed. (Both, courtesy of the Portland Area Historical Society.)

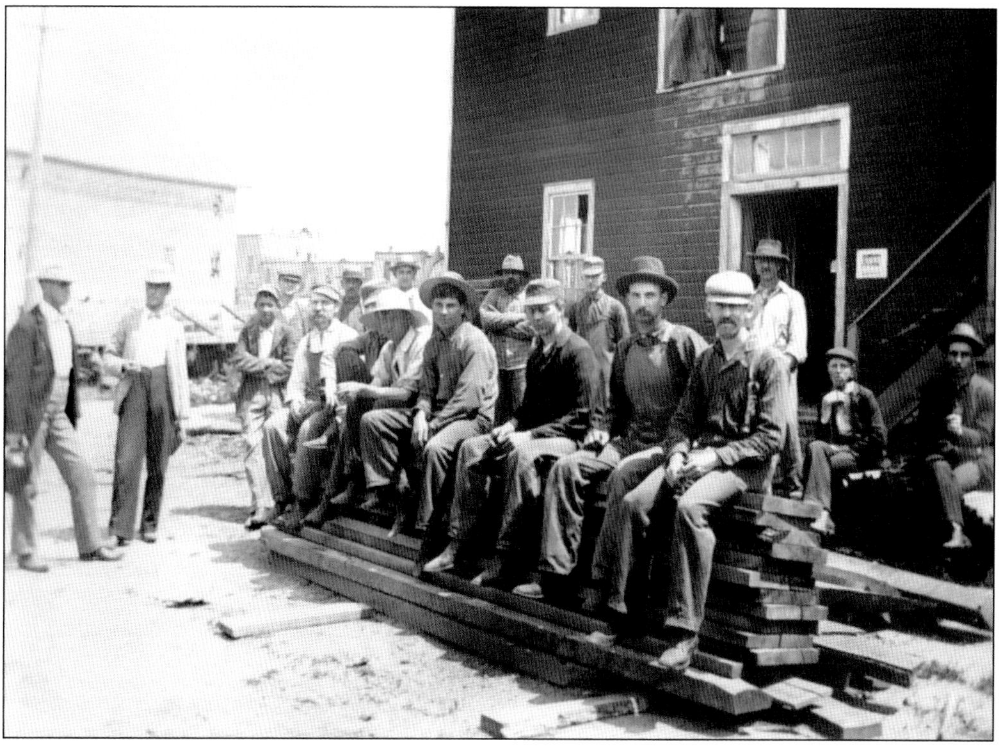

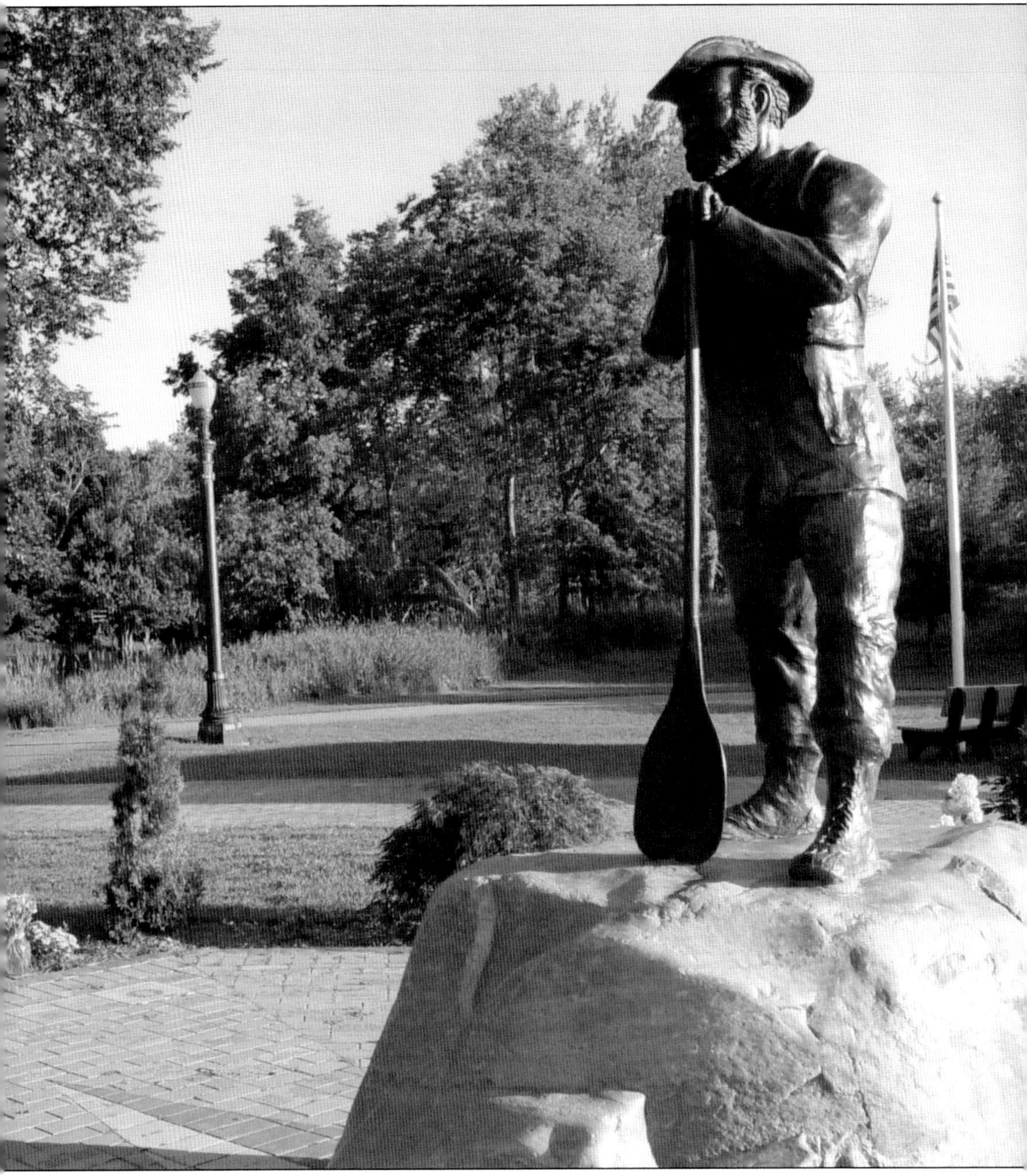

Verlen Kruger began canoeing at age 42 and turned it into an endurance sport. He canoed more than 100,000 miles, including a 28,000-mile trip through and around North America and from the Arctic Ocean to Cape Horn, South America. When he died at age 82, the people of Portland, his hometown, raised money to erect this statue facing the river to honor his memory. (Photograph by Shelby Ayers.)

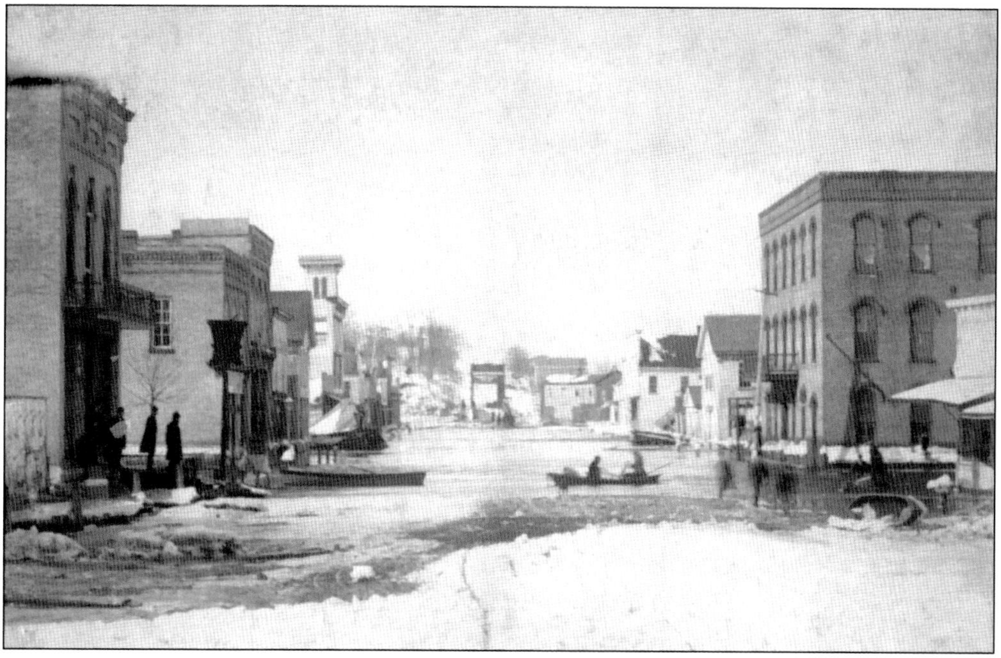

Living on the river meant the risk of floods. In February 1887, the village of Lyons was hit hard when a large buildup of ice cut off the flow of water on the river. Even dynamite failed to stop the blockage, and 83 businesses and residences were flooded. The post office had to open a temporary office in the Methodist church. (Both, courtesy of the Lyons/Muir Historical Society Museum.)

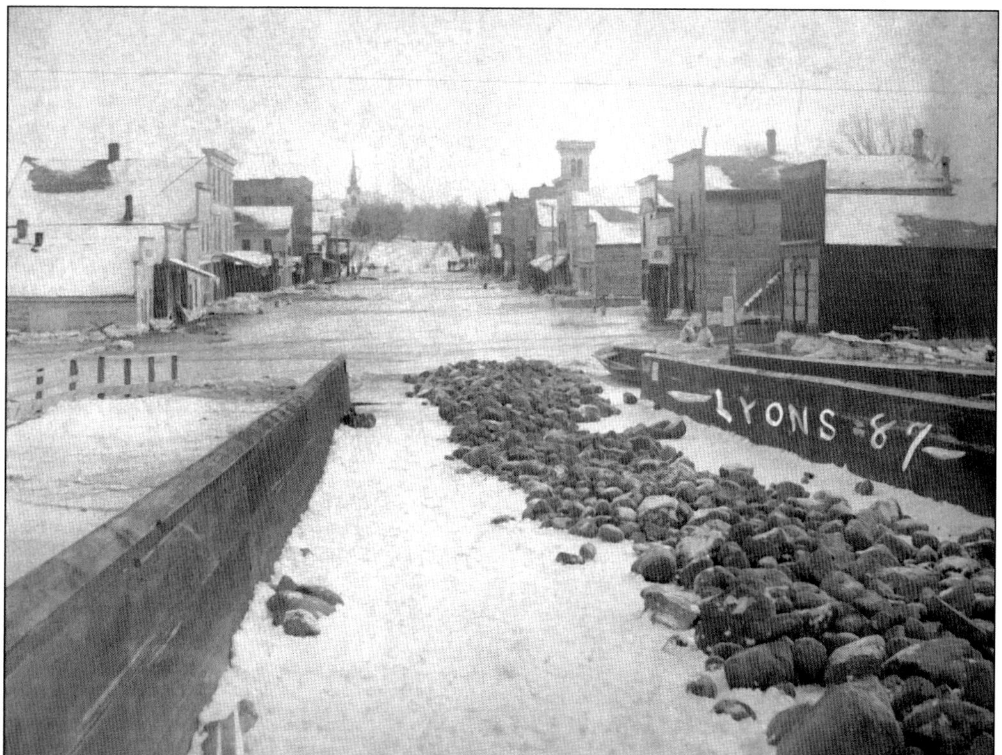

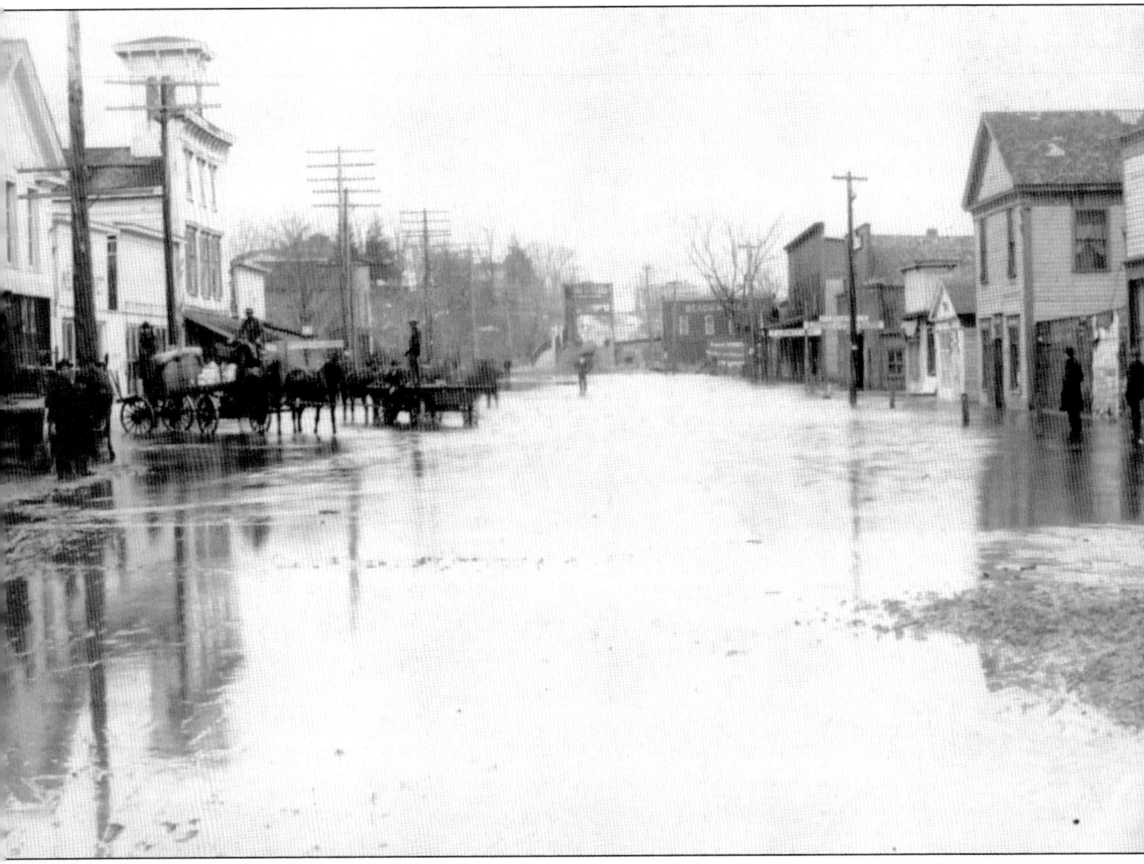

Flooding could not be avoided, and the rising waters often spilled over into the downtown area without doing significant damage. The flood of 1887, however, was an exception. Muir's main street shows another view of the devastation caused. (Courtesy of the Lyons/Muir Historical Society.)

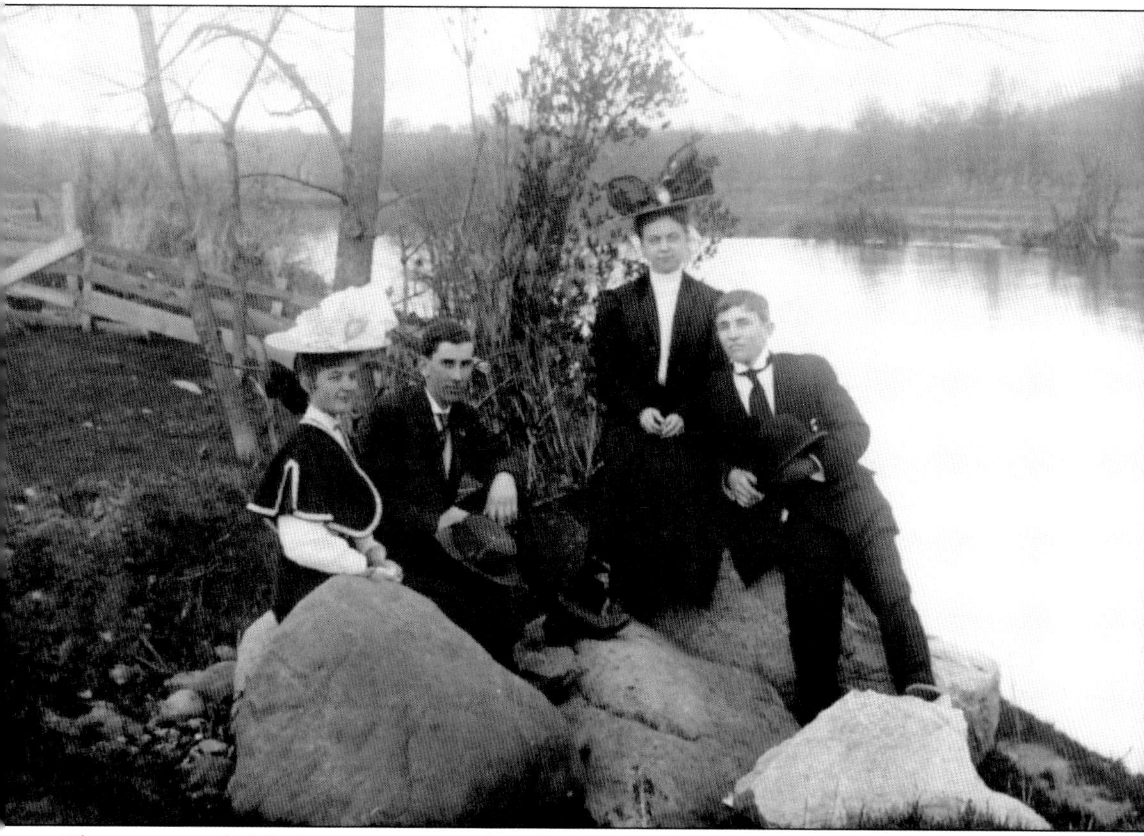

The river provided the best spot in town for taking photographs, as demonstrated by these young people. Pictured, from left to right, are Jennie Kelly, unidentified, Gladys Bradh, and Oliver Kelly. (Courtesy of the Lyons/Muir Historical Society.)

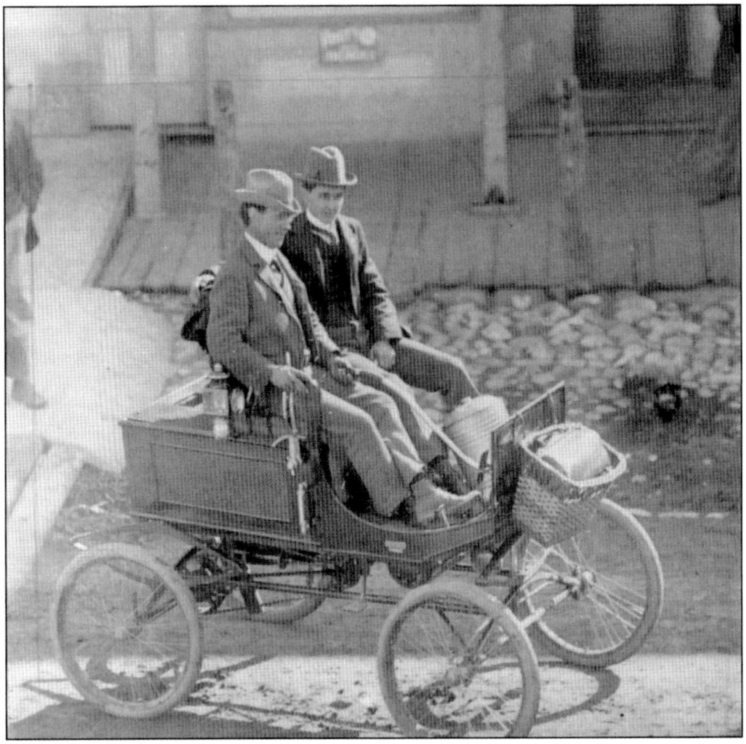

Brothers Jay and Jerry Hayes drove their new automobile home from Detroit. It took them three days to make the 102-mile trip. Theirs was the second car owned by Muir residents. (Courtesy of the Lyons/Muir Historical Society.)

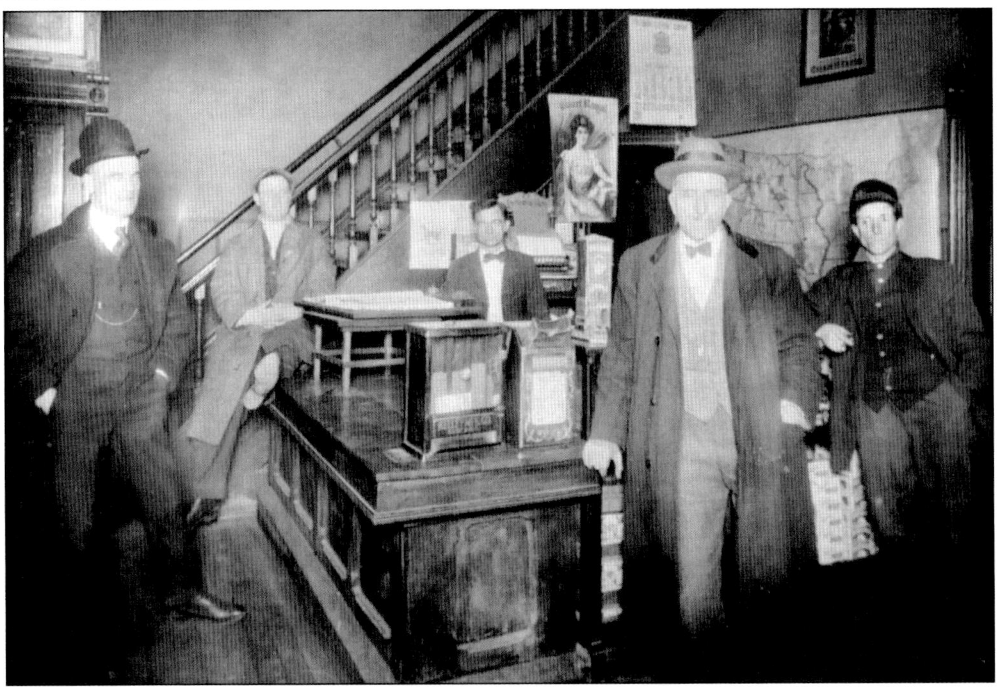

Muir residents around the turn of the 20th century pose in what appears to be a hotel lobby. They are, from left to right, William Dilley, Bert Hechathorne, unidentified gentleman behind counter, Frank Rohler, and Silas Huested. Huested was the first mail carrier in Muir. (Courtesy of the Lyons/Muir Historical Society.)

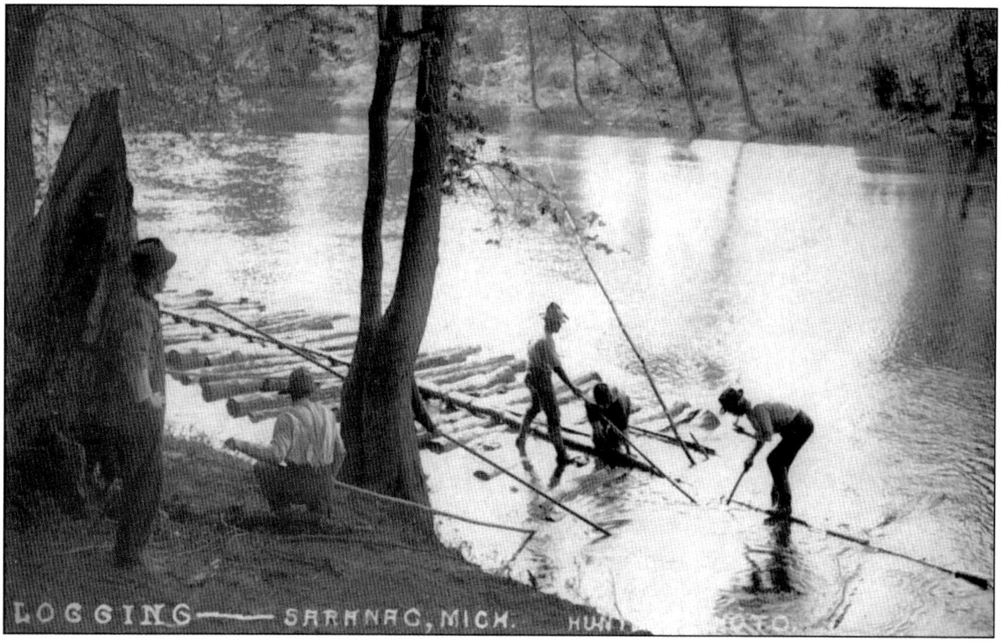

Clams were abundant in the Grand River here in Saranac, and they were harvested for food and buttons. Though there was great demand, the clammers received only pennies per bushel. This was not a problem for these loggers, who are only gigging for a steamed clam dinner. (Courtesy of the Boston-Saranac Historical Museum.)

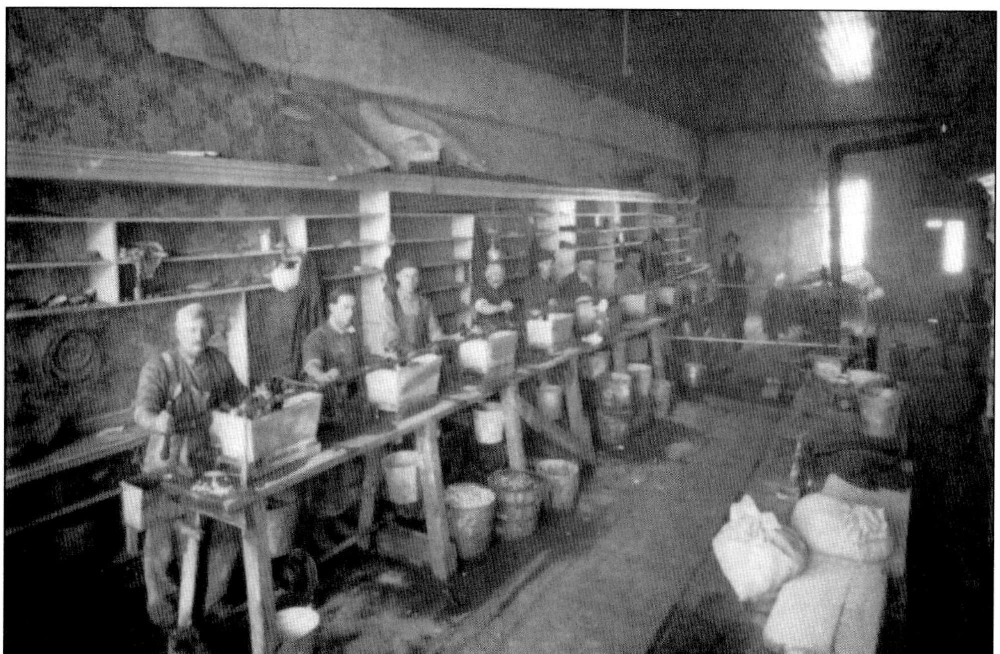

The clamming industry on the river provided food, the occasional pearl, and the shells that yielded mother-of-pearl, the top choice for buttons at the time. This is one of the button factories that profited from the clammers. (Courtesy of the Lyons/Muir Historical Society.)

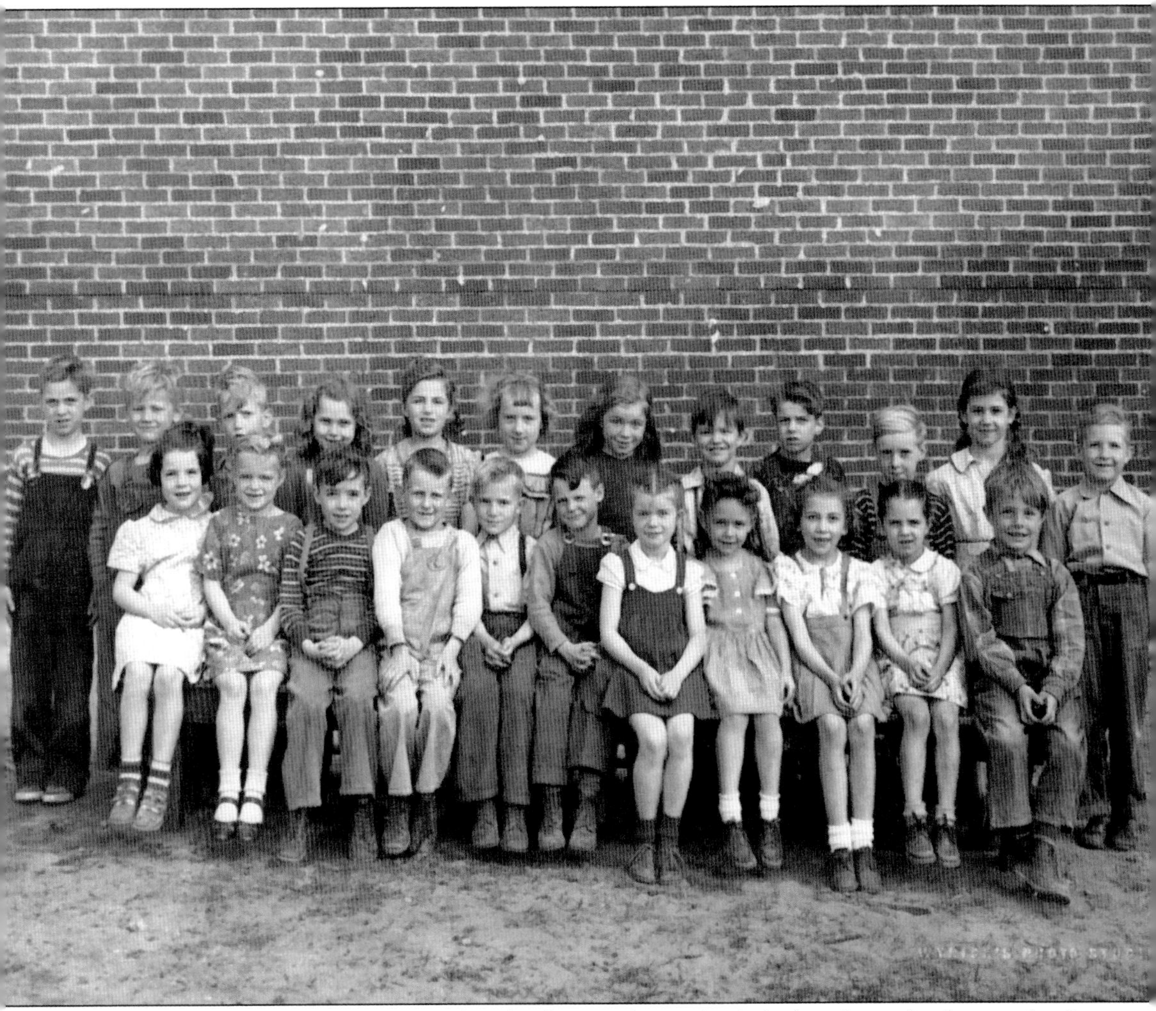

They are all in their places with bright shining faces. A 1940s fourth grade class smiles for the camera and becomes a part of the Muir school's history. (Courtesy of the Lyons/Muir Historical Society.)

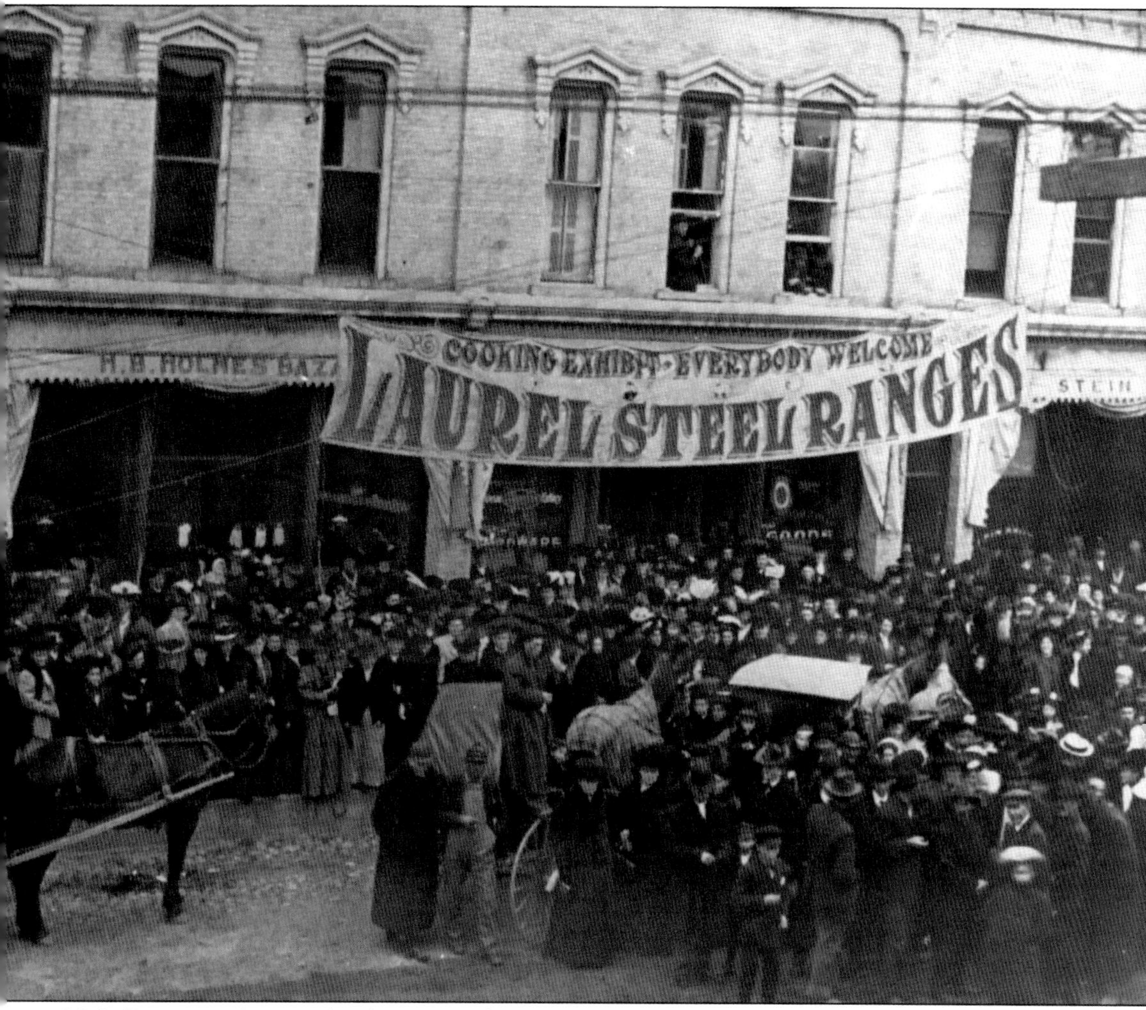

M.A. Benson, a Saranac hardware merchant, knew how to create a buzz for his kitchen stoves. He enlisted a few fine cooks to demonstrate the features of the Laurel range line. People came from all over the area to taste Clarissa Wallington's tea biscuits. (Courtesy of the Boston-Saranac Museum.)

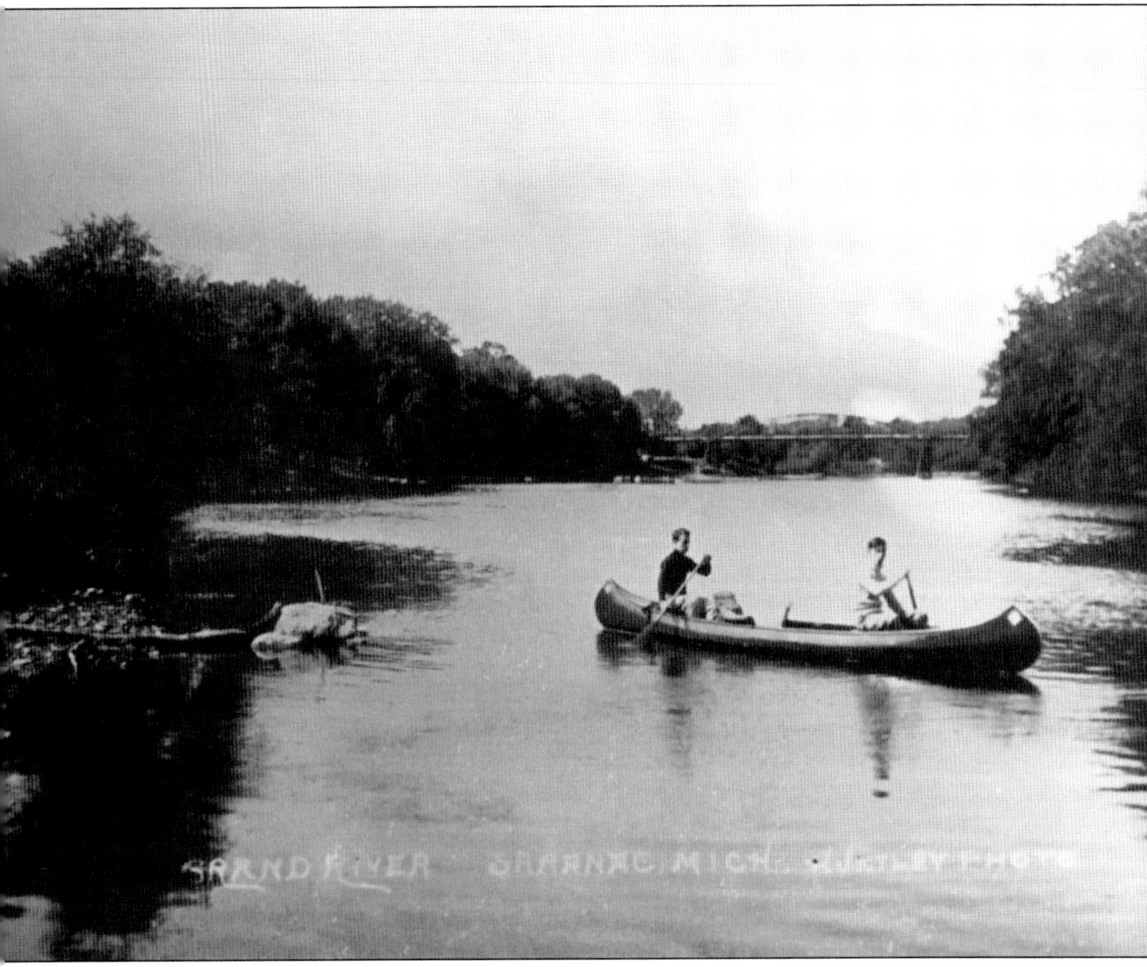

With its twists and turns through scenic towns like Saranac, the river always provided a pleasant diversion for anyone who had time to row, row, row his boat gently down the stream. It still does. (Courtesy of the Boston-Saranac Historical Society.)

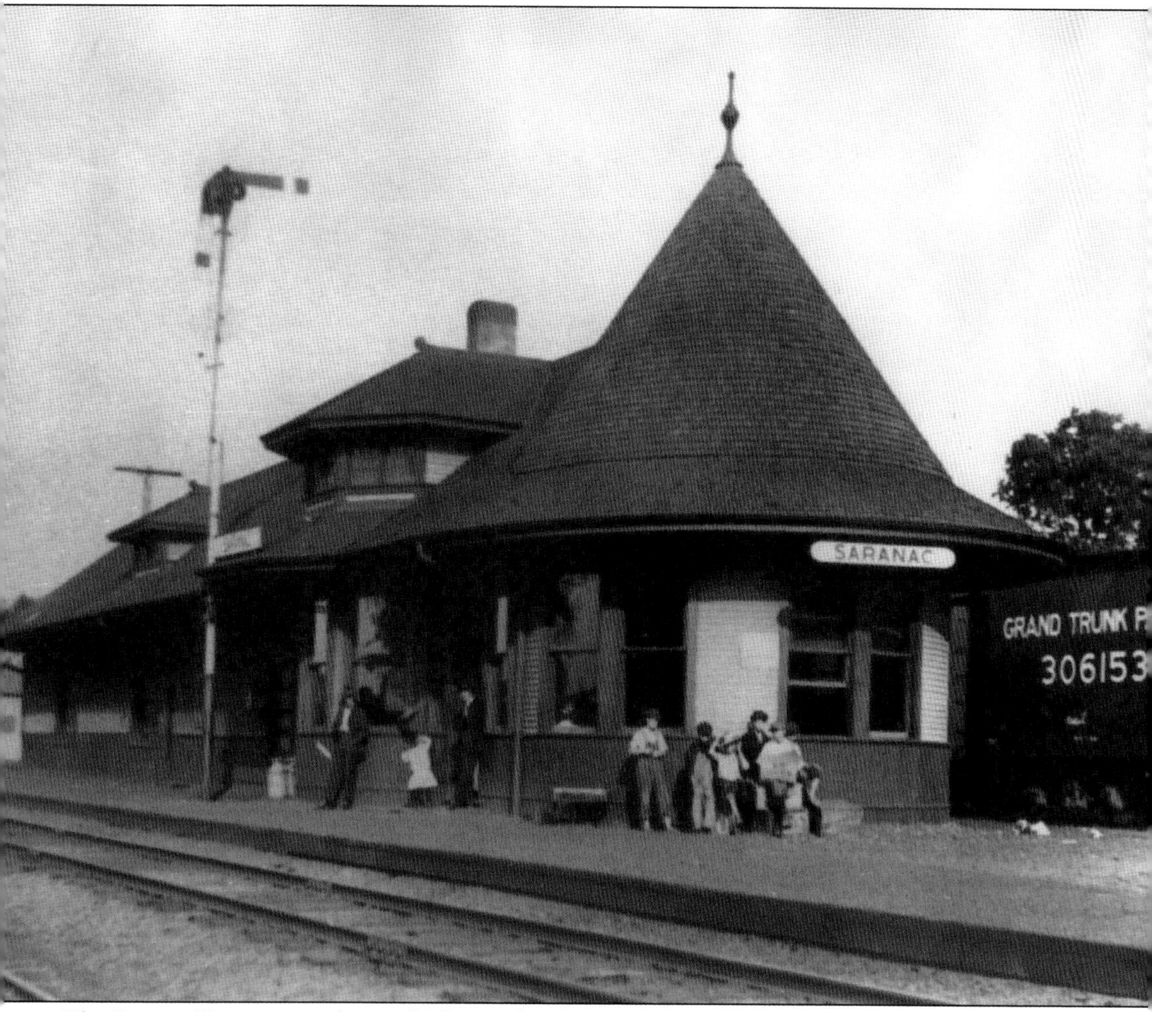

The Saranac Depot sports the witch's hat roof, a popular style when the building was constructed in 1907. The depot now houses the Boston-Saranac Museum and keeps the city's railroad history alive for children's groups and other visitors. (Courtesy of the Boston-Saranac Historical Society.)

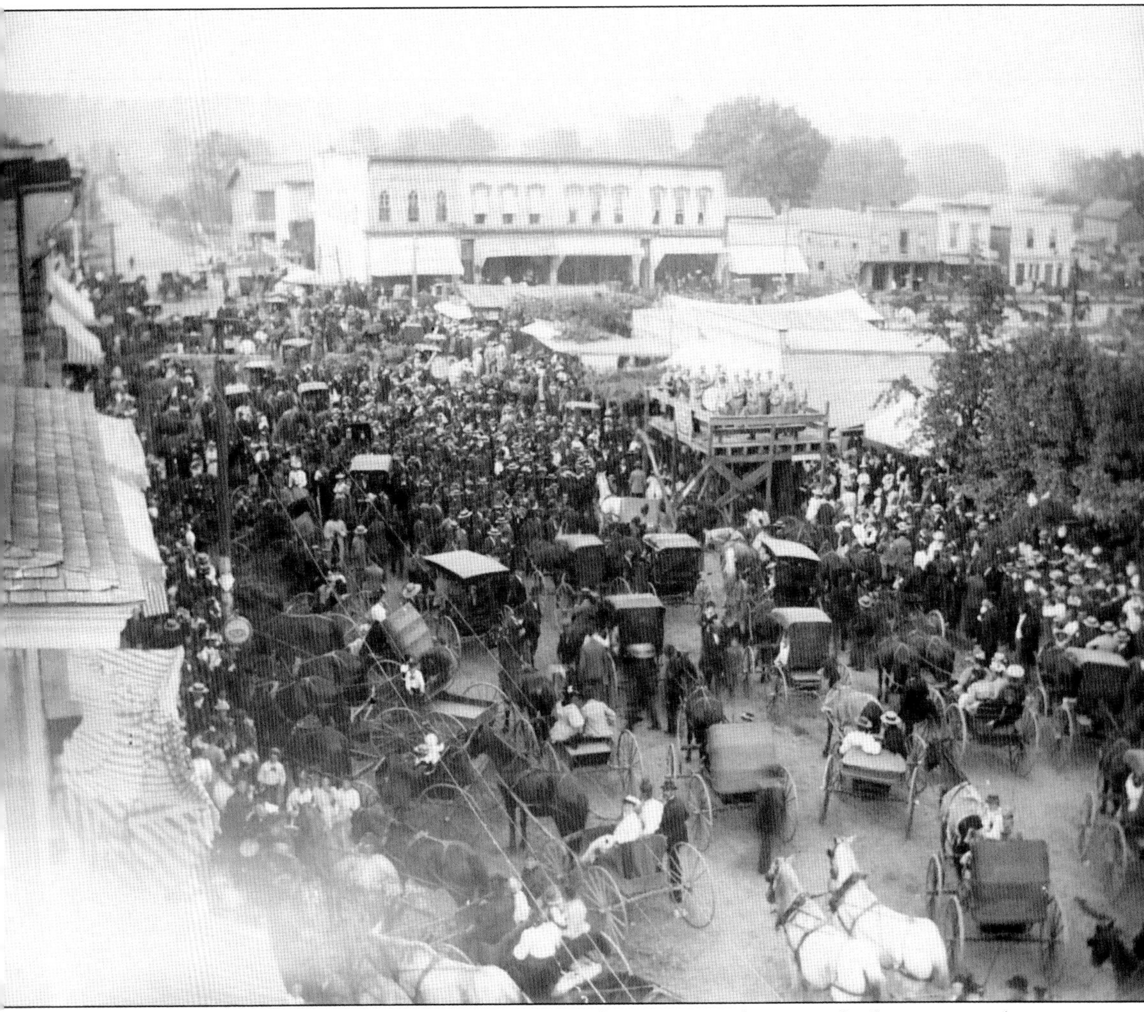

On August 15, 1894, Saranac hosted this large downtown gathering, which was a combination farmers' picnic and band tournament. The size of the crowd indicates it was a successful social event, and a good time was had by all. (Courtesy of the Boston-Saranac Historical Society.)

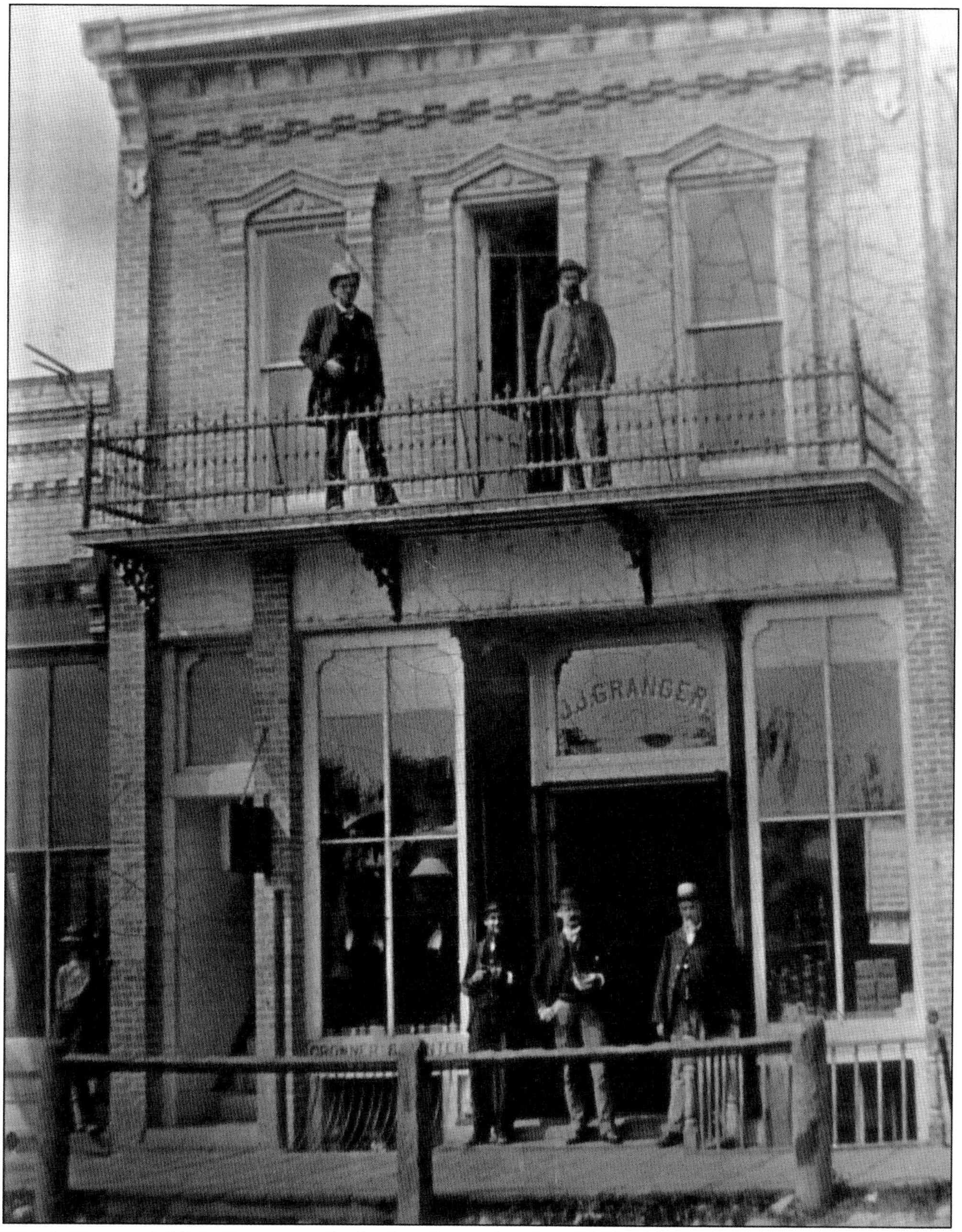

This is Saranac's Main Street as it looked in the mid-to-late 1800s, when these fellows were hanging out at the J.A. Granger building. It may have been the city's downtown, but that does not mean there were many entertainment options. (Courtesy of the Bentley Historical Society.)

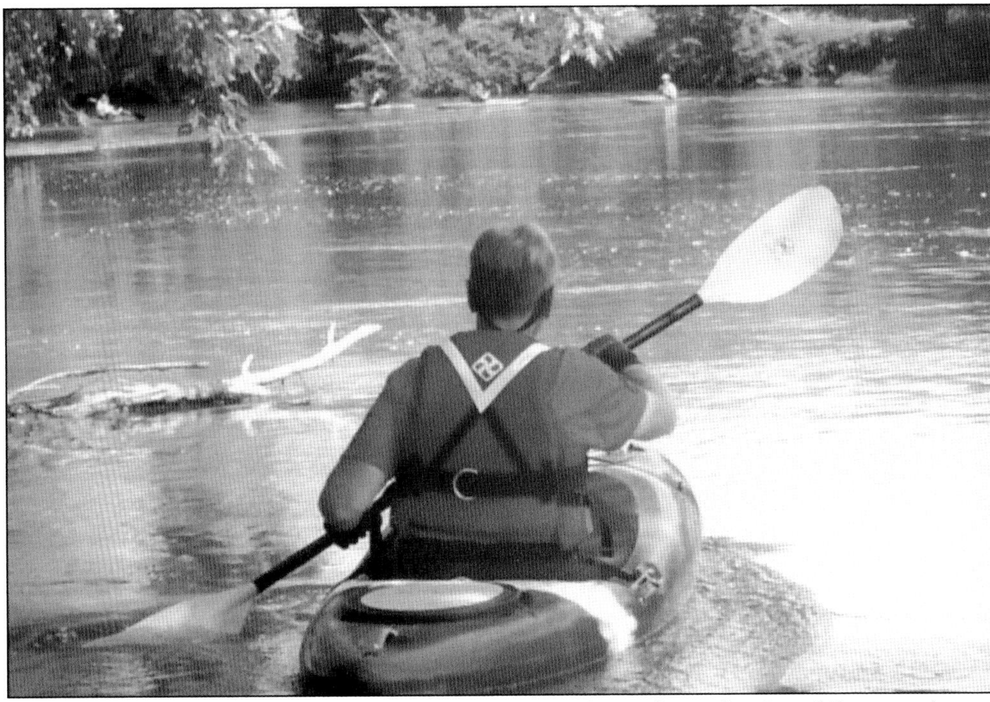

This kayaker is participating in the once-a-decade expedition down the Grand River to observe changes and check out the general health of the river. Those in the 2000 group pitched their tents overnight on the riverfront park at the museum. (Photograph by Pat Raimer.)

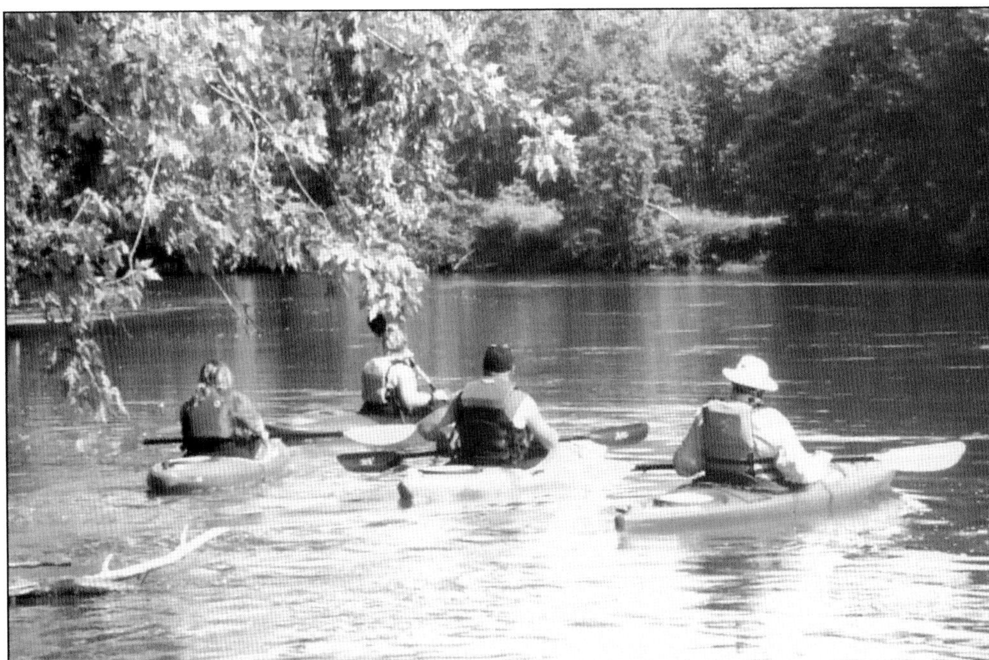

A few of the other expedition's members enjoy cruising down the river on a sunny day while doing the important job of assessing its heath. (Photograph by Pat Raimer.)

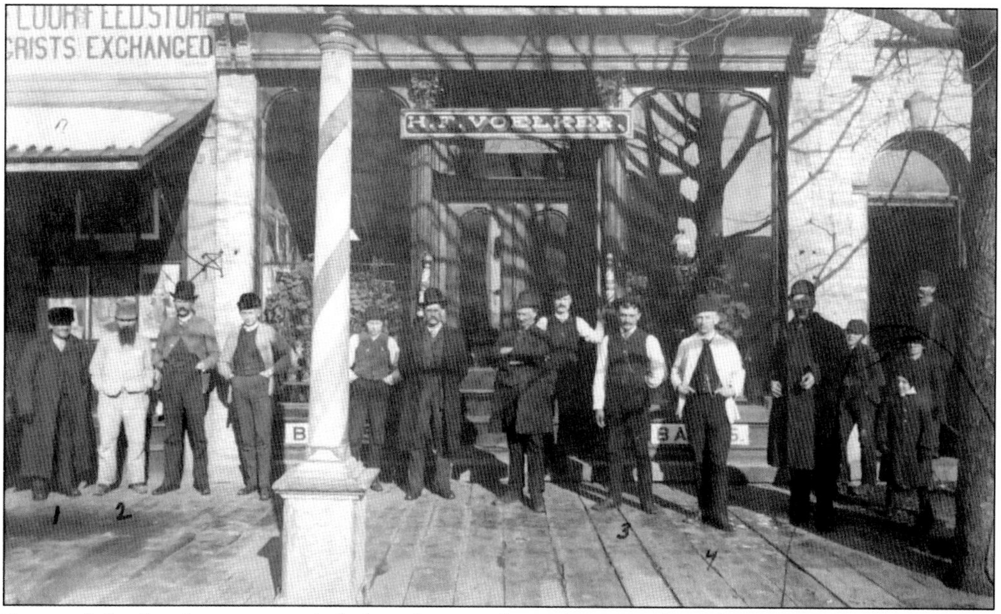

Some of the local movers and shakers line up for a photograph in front of Henry F. Voelker's barbershop. They are, from left to right, Abraham Desluck, William Steody, six unidentified, Henry Voelker, Fred Henrisch, two unidentified, and James Harvey Kidd standing behind his son, Fred. The Kidds were among the early families settling in Ionia. (Courtesy of the Bentley Historical Library, University of Michigan.)

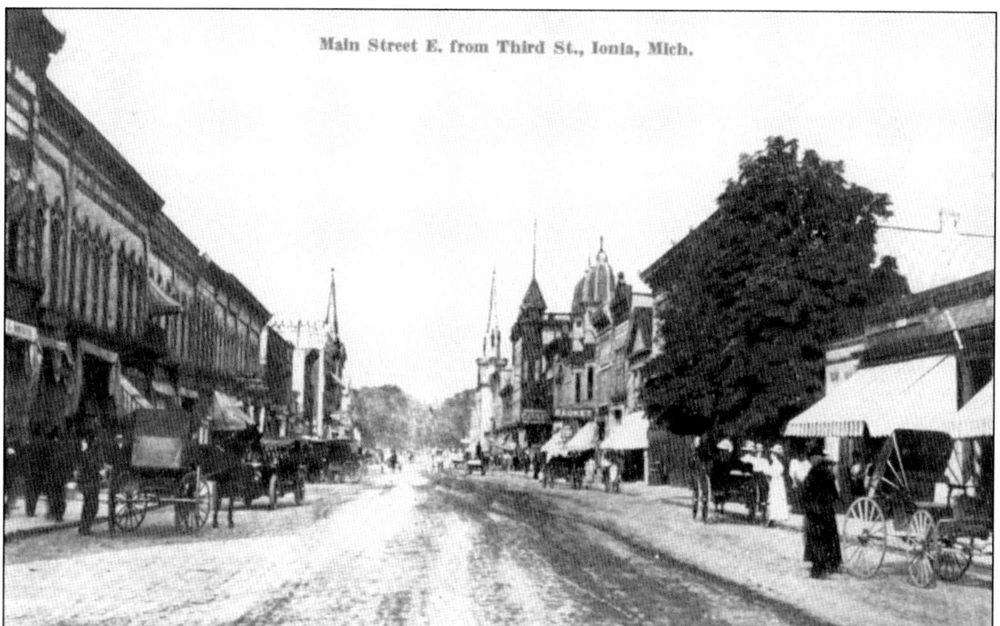

This c. 1913 postcard depicts Ionia's Main Street, in a view looking east from Third Avenue. It was, and is, a thriving community. (Courtesy of the Bentley Historical Library, University of Michigan.)

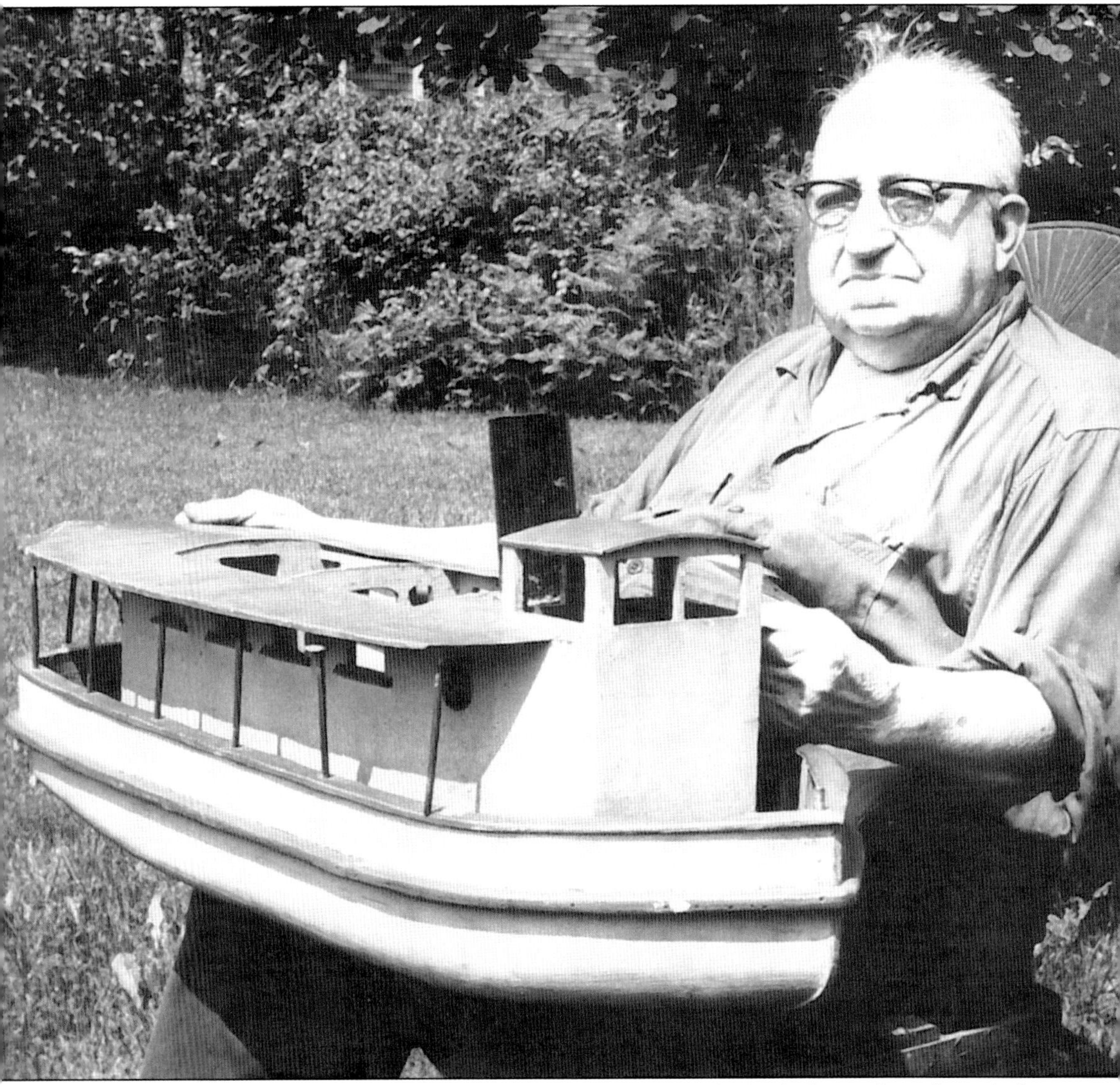

Harrie Morgan was a retired Ionia furniture craftsman when he built this scale replica of a boat he had piloted up and down the river 50 years earlier. He did not use a blueprint or write a plan. The boat on which the replica was based was destroyed when an icy stream overflowed, causing the craft to crash on the riverbank. (Courtesy of the Ionia Historical Society.)

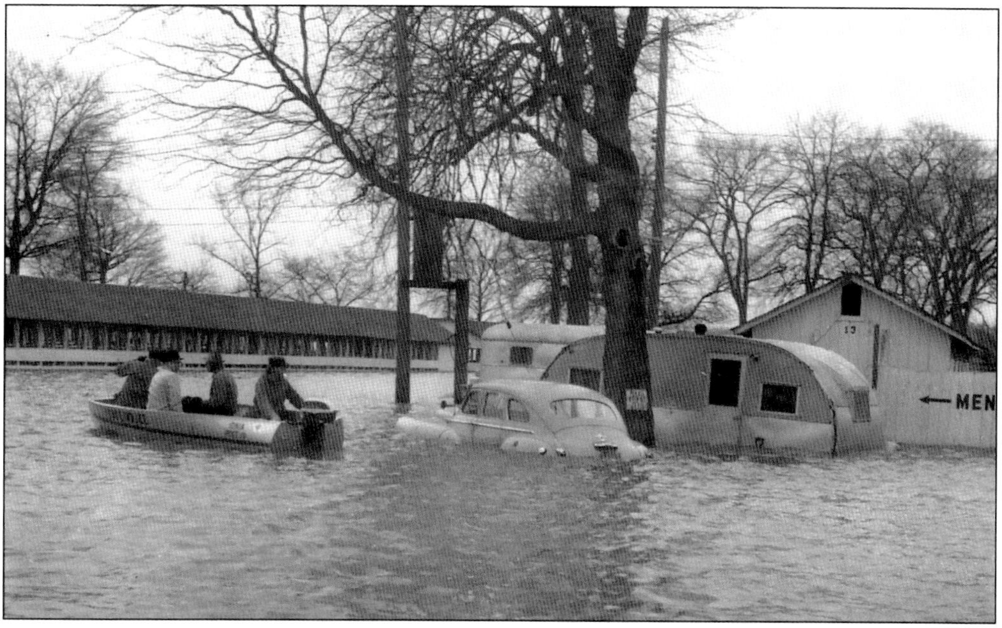

The Ionia Free Fair has drawn crowds each summer since 1867. Flooding is an ever-present danger in times of heavy rains or snowmelt, and on April 23, 1975, the fairgrounds were navigable only by rowboat. (Both, courtesy of the Ionia Historical Society.)

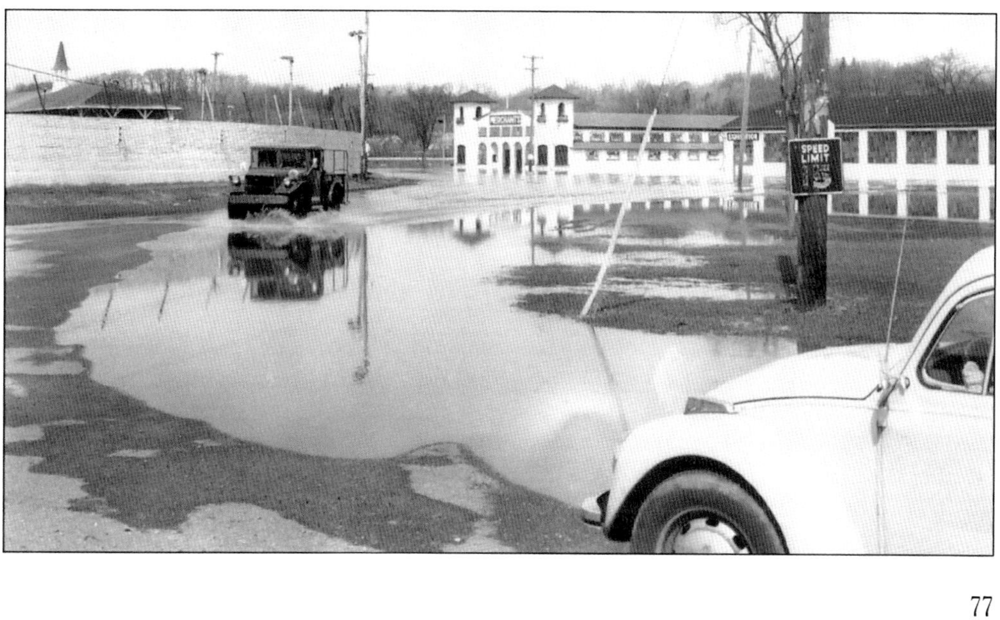

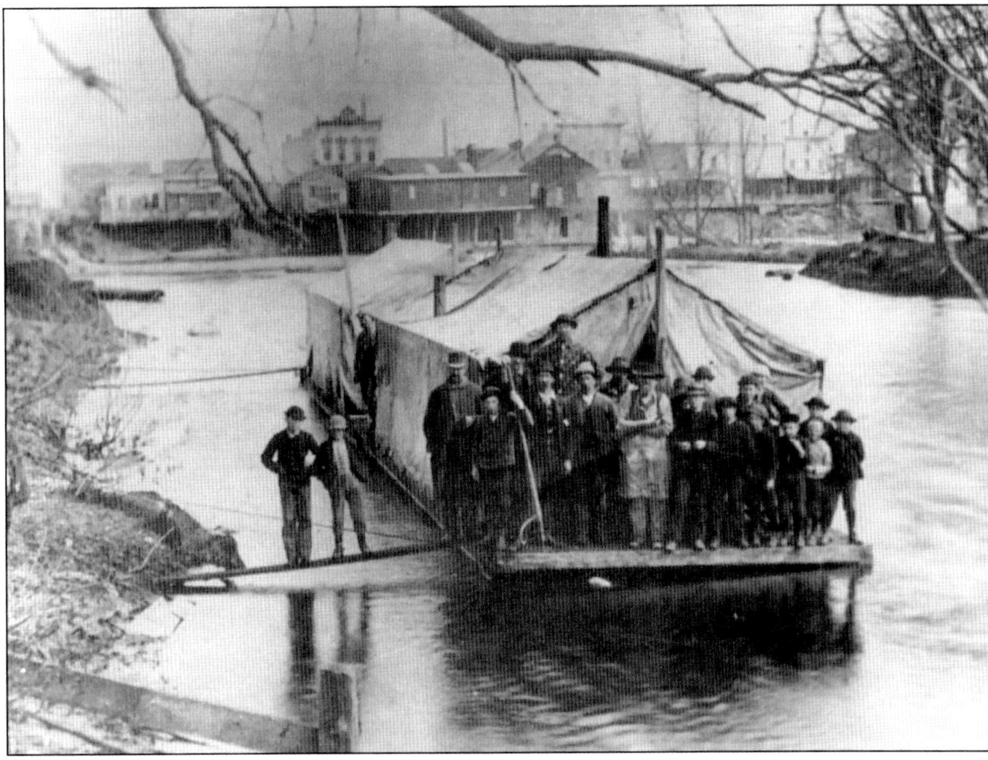

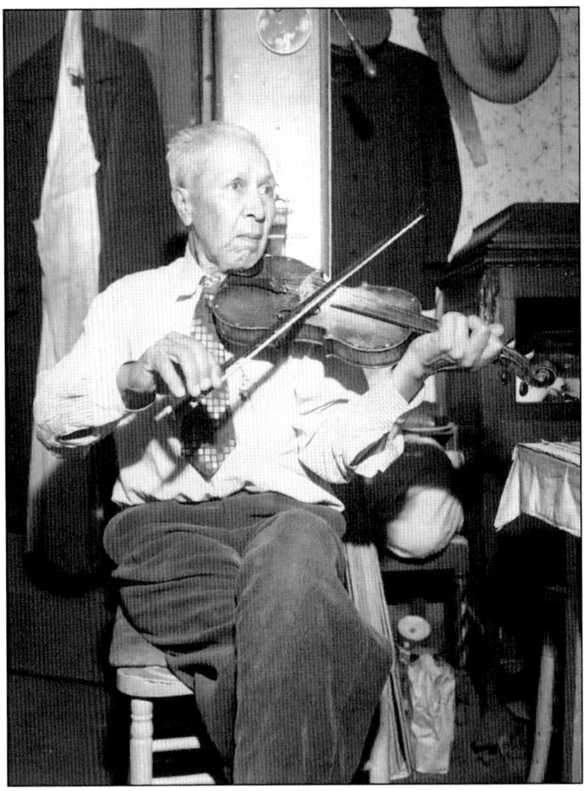

Lowell was another logging community on the Grand River and its Flat River tributary. Cooking shanties were essential, and this is the last one on the Flat River, marking the end of an era. (Courtesy of the Lowell Museum.)

Chief Cobmoosa and his people owned five huts and had already planted crops in the area that is now Ionia. When the Dexter party of 62 arrived, the men bartered with the chief for the huts and crops. He was an articulate speaker for the Odawa and was present for the signings of all three major treaties with the US government. This image was taken after he had settled in Grand Rapids. (Courtesy of the Grand Rapids Public Library.)

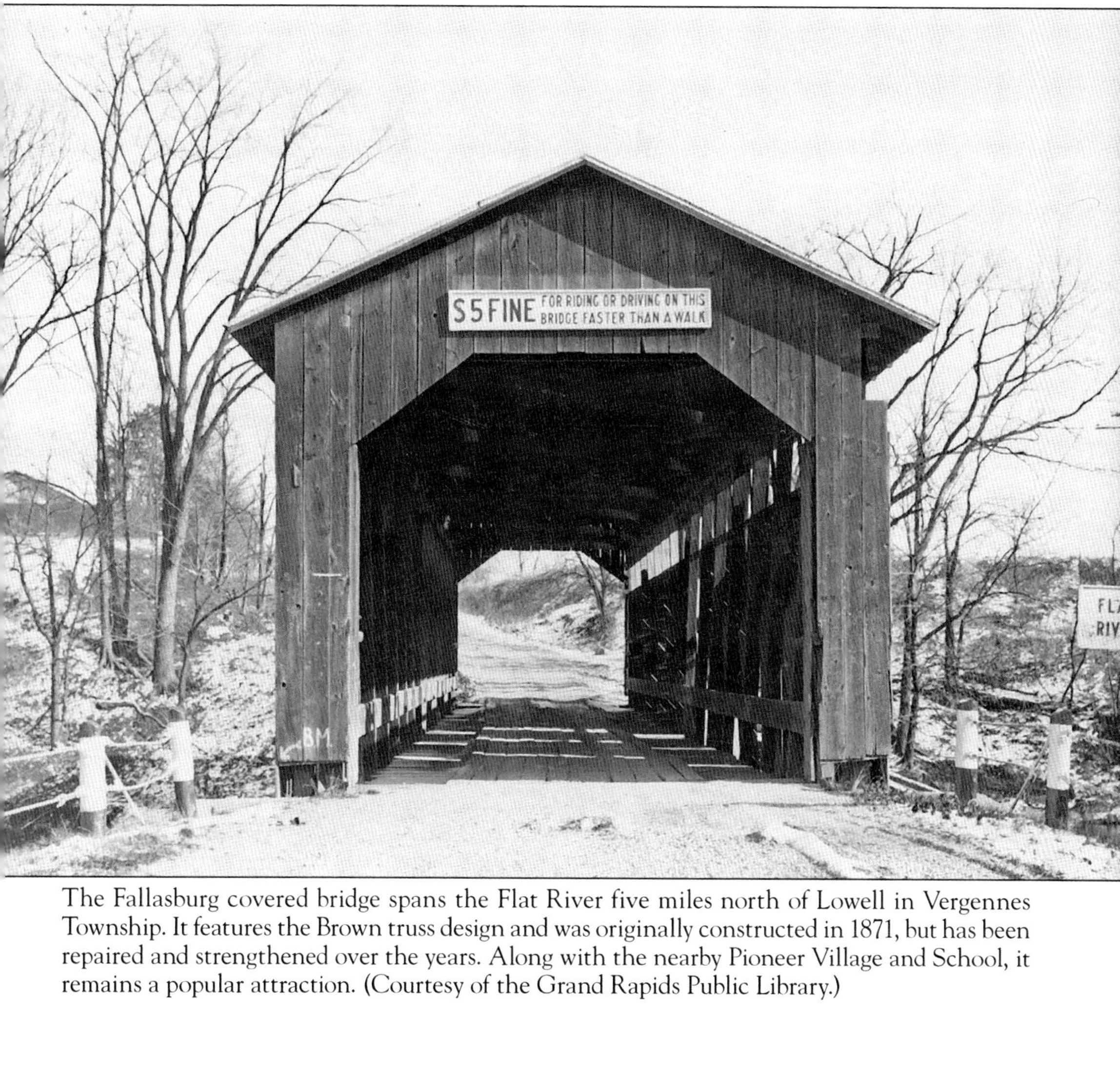

The Fallasburg covered bridge spans the Flat River five miles north of Lowell in Vergennes Township. It features the Brown truss design and was originally constructed in 1871, but has been repaired and strengthened over the years. Along with the nearby Pioneer Village and School, it remains a popular attraction. (Courtesy of the Grand Rapids Public Library.)

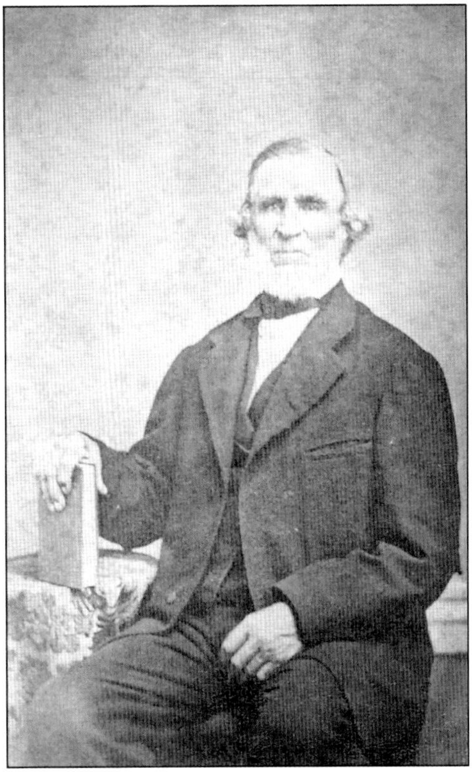

John Jacob Astor hired Rix Robinson (pictured) to manage a trading post in Ada near the confluence of the Grand and Thornapple Rivers. He spoke English, French, and the dialects of the American Indian tribes with whom he worked, and earned the respect and the trust of both the Indians and the trappers. (Courtesy of the Loutit District Library, Grand Haven.)

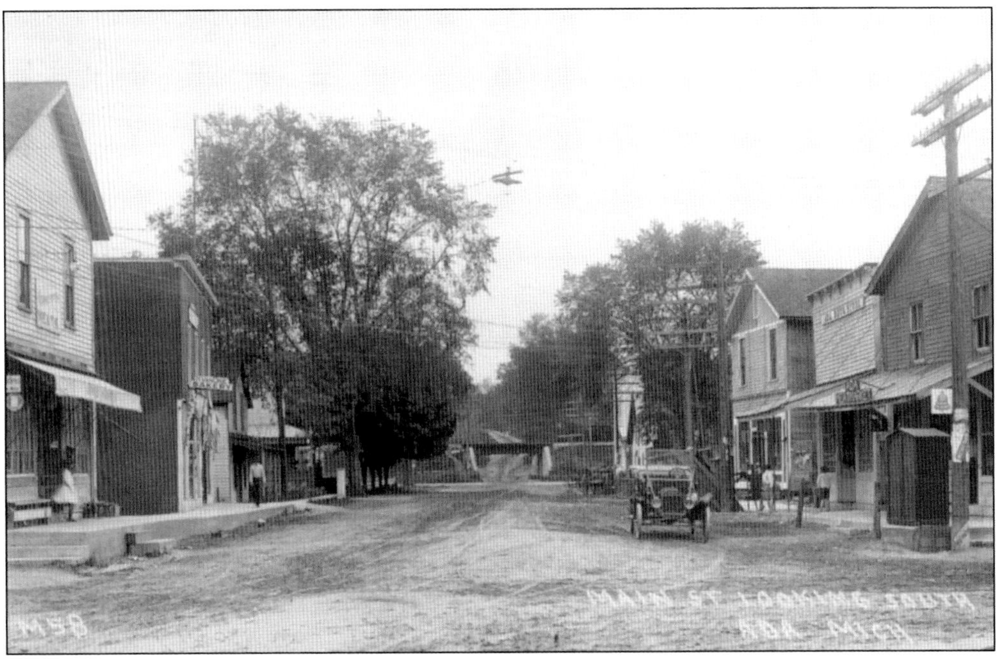

Ada's main street looked like this in 1910. Ada is on the bank of the Thornapple River, a tributary of the Grand. The township is best known today as the home of Amway's world headquarters. When fire destroyed Ada's historic covered bridge in 1978, Amway provided funds to build a replica. (Courtesy of the Hekman Library, Calvin College.)

Three

Grand Rapids to Grand Haven

Grand Rapids was another river location that started with a trading post. Louis Campeau set up shop to trade with the American Indian village that had been long established on the spot. He flourished until the bank he founded went bankrupt. Other pioneers opened businesses, and the city grew to become the second-largest in the state. For a century, it reigned as "Furniture City."

Immigrants came in droves, with the Dutch being the largest group. Their rock-solid work ethic made them reliable, and jobs were easy to find. The Poles followed, along with the Latvians, Germans, and Italians. Soon, nearly every nationality had a solid foothold.

Outside the city, the fertile Grand River Valley provided excellent growing conditions. Hudsonville is still called "Michigan's Salad Bowl," and fruit orchards thrived as well. In 1970, Grand Valley State University came to Allendale and the surrounding area has built up proportionately, but there is still ample room for the muck farms.

County parks along the way provide boat launching ease, and on any summer day people can be seen fishing from a boat in the river or simply dropping a line from the banks. It is almost just as it was in the old days, except now if the anglers come up empty, the nearest supermarket will solve the problem of dinner.

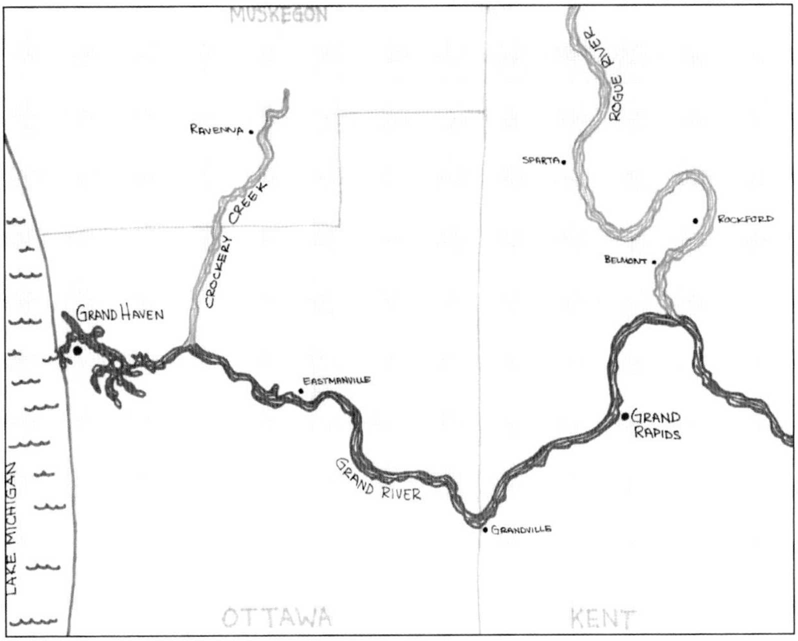

From Grand Rapids, the river completes its course to Grand Haven and Lake Michigan. (Map by Jillian Berry.)

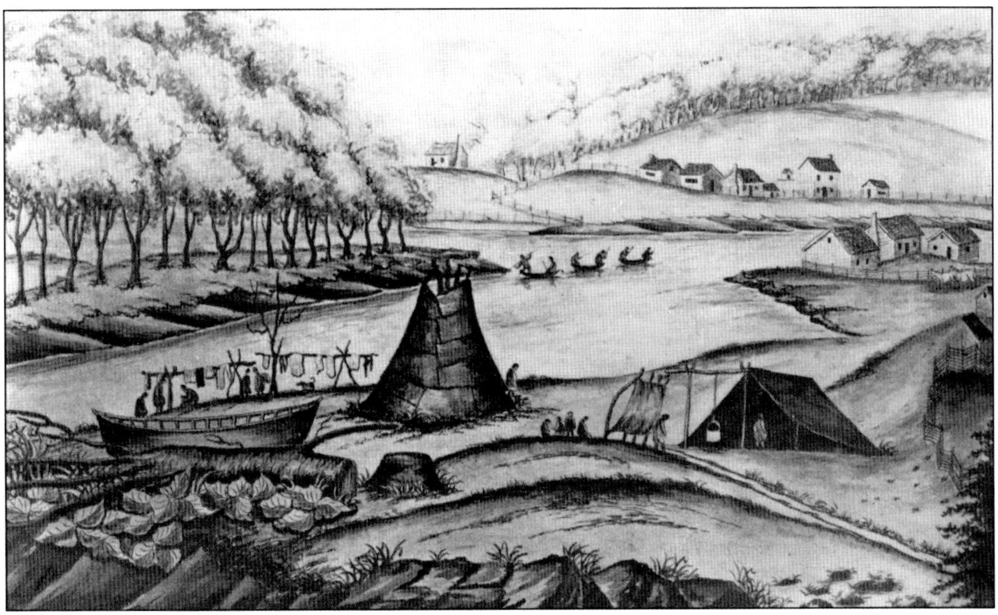

Rev. John Booth sketched this Grand Rapids scene in 1831. Behind the Ottawa chief Nawaquegeezhik's camp are Louis Campeau's cabin, blacksmith shop, and trading post. Across the river is the Rev. Isaac McCoy's Baptist mission. Today, the site of Campeau's buildings is occupied by the Grand Rapids Civic Auditorium. The Gerald Ford Presidential Museum and Ah-Nab-Awen Park are across the river, where the mission used to be. (Courtesy of the Grand Rapids Public Library.)

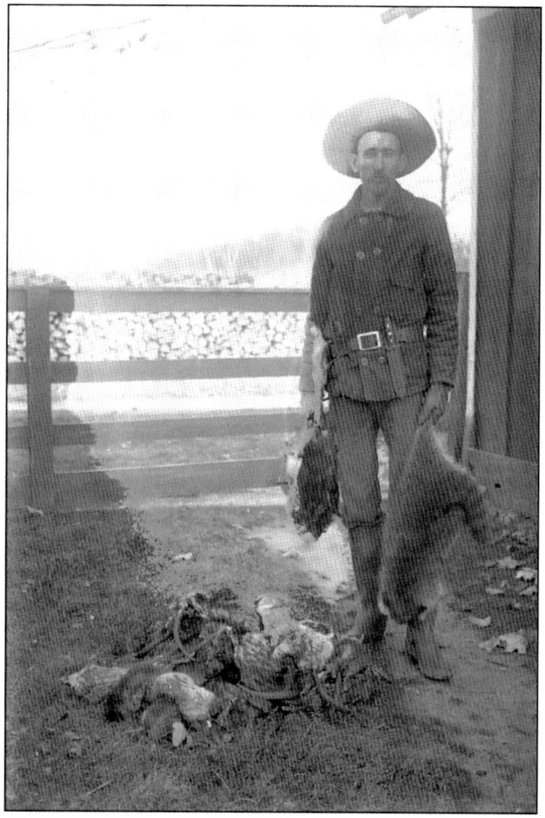

Fur trappers made good use of the river in trading their pelts to the Indian villages scattered along the banks. Some were the French Canadian voyageurs; others were adventurers with a romantic notion of life in the wilderness. They had to learn to communicate with other cultures and respect the different lifestyles of the villagers and the trading post operators. (Both, courtesy of the Grand Rapids Public Library.)

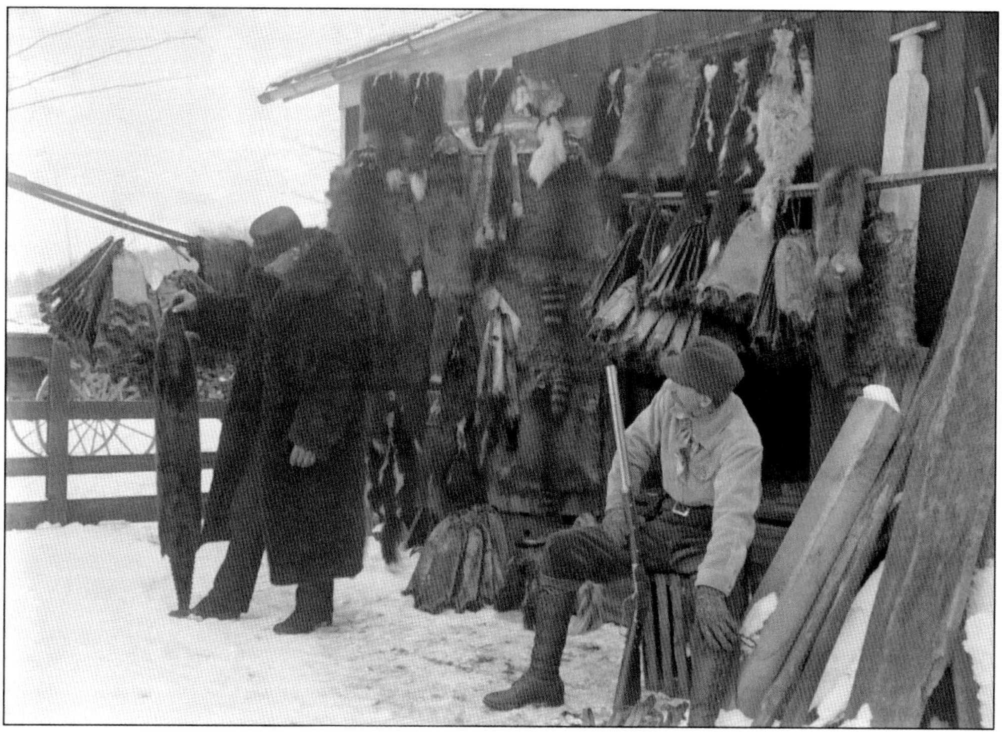

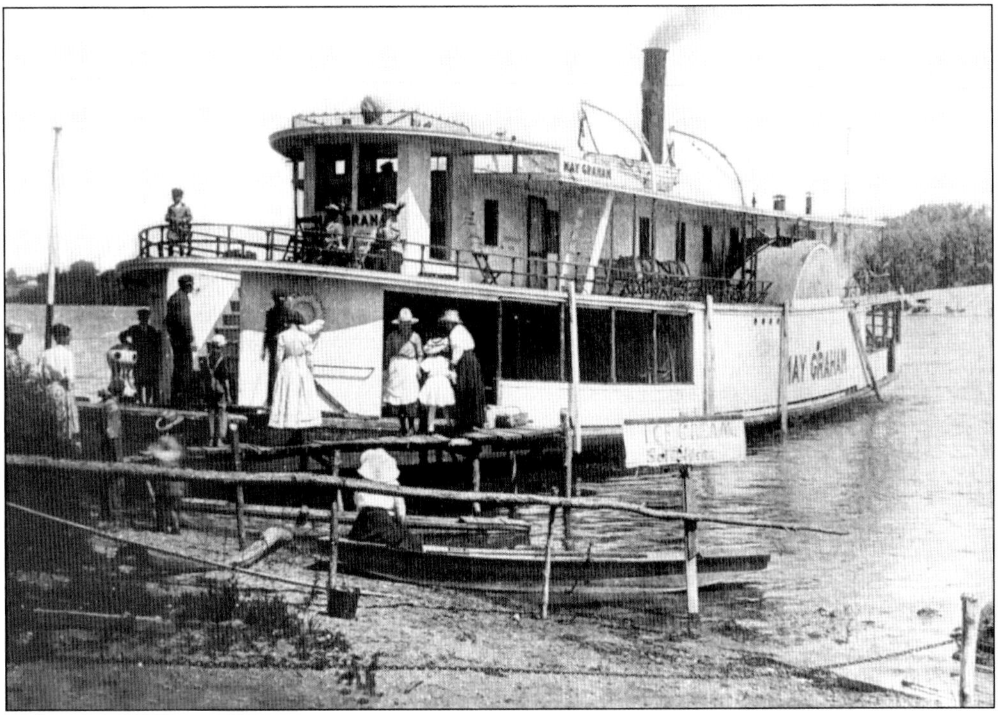

In 1836, the river was deemed safe for steamboats. Shown here in 1912, excursion passengers aboard the *May Graham* pose near Grandville. The boat did a brisk business transporting both goods and passengers. Most of the river traffic was between Grand Rapids and Grand Haven. (Courtesy of the Hekman Library, Calvin College.)

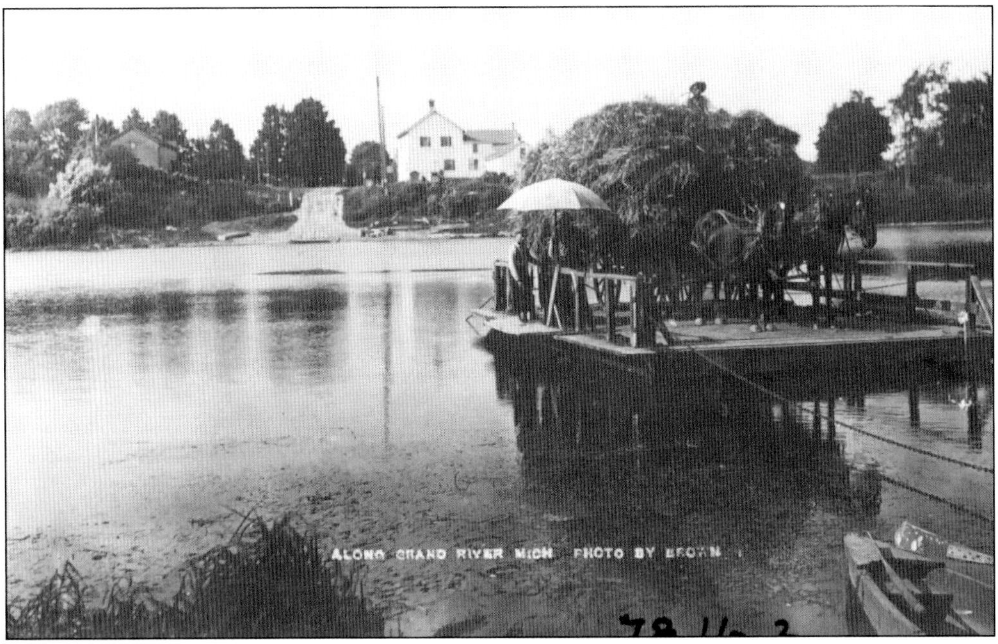

The Bridge Street ferry was just one of many crossing the Grand River with both passengers and goods that needed to get to the other side. (Courtesy of the Grand Rapids Public Library.)

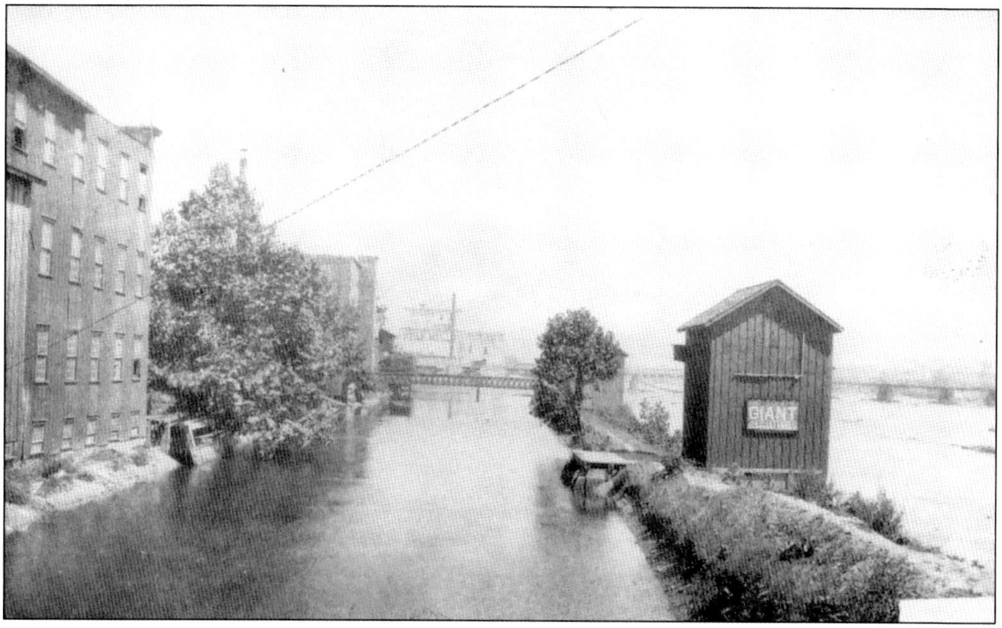

Grand Rapids had islands in the river, but unlike the resorts found at Grand Ledge, here they had more utilitarian uses. There were three islands, and one served as the city jail. (Courtesy of the Grand Rapids Public Library.)

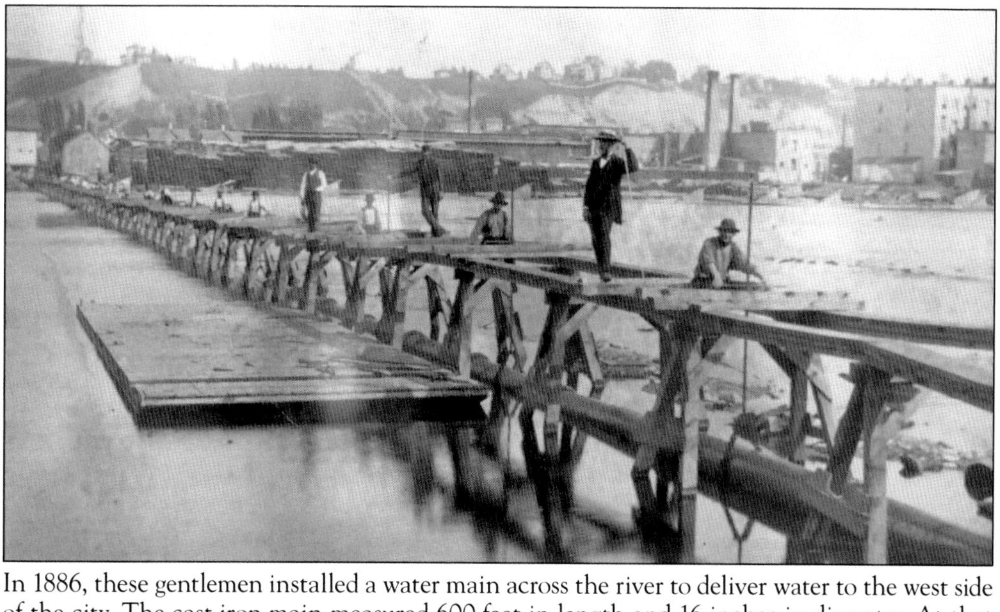

In 1886, these gentlemen installed a water main across the river to deliver water to the west side of the city. The cast iron main measured 600 feet in length and 16 inches in diameter. At that time, such a project was considered a remarkable engineering accomplishment. (Courtesy of the Hekman Library, Calvin College.)

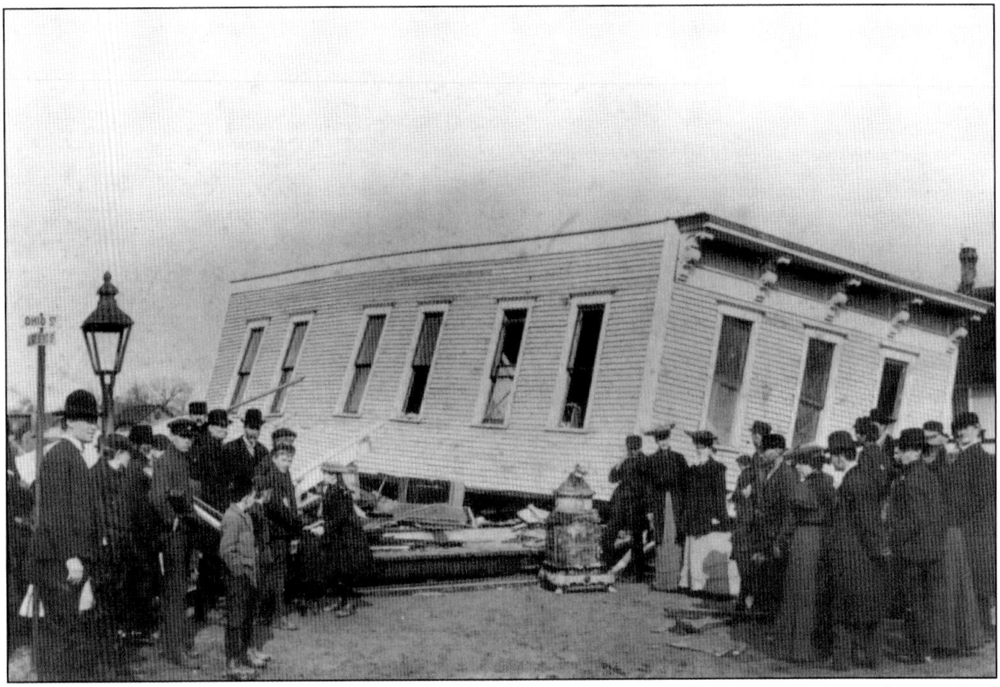

A massive flood was not the only thing that destroyed property in 1904. A tornado touched down on the corner of Temple and Ohio Streets and lifted this grocery store off its foundation. (Courtesy of the Hekman Library, Calvin College.)

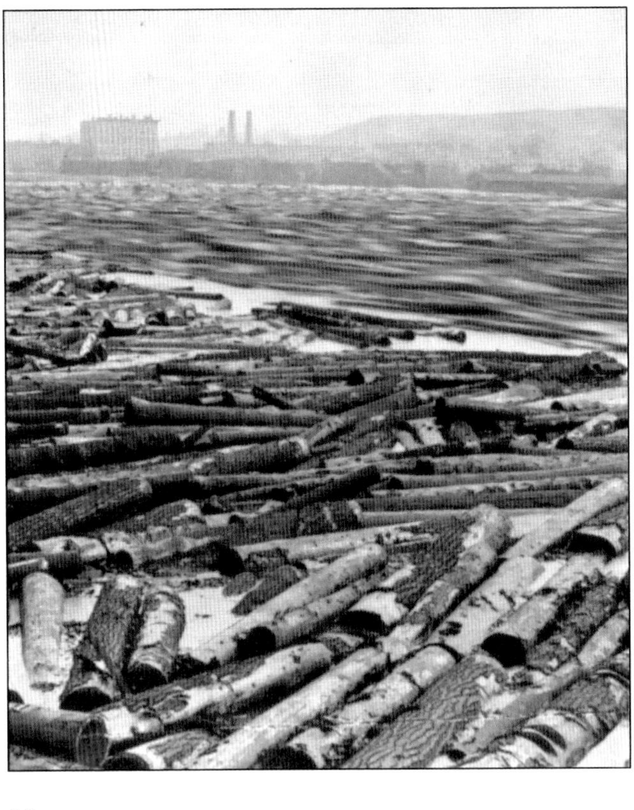

The river made it possible to flourish in the cities dotting its banks. But the great logjam of 1893 is an extreme example of how quickly those early entrepreneurs could see their luck turn sour. Even bridges were destroyed by the jam, which was estimated to be 33 feet deep and 27 miles long. (Courtesy of the Grand Rapids Public Library.)

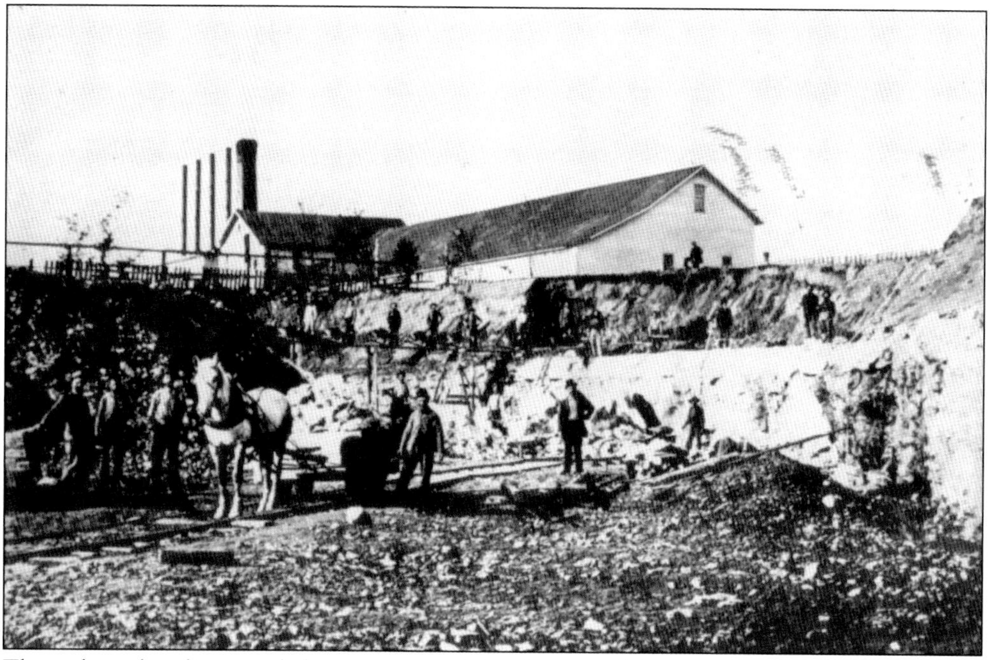

The early settlers discovered plaster mines, making that one of the first industries. The Alabastine mine shown here was under where Grand Rapids and the city of Wyoming meet today. They have all closed except for one located in Wyoming, which is now used for cold storage. (Courtesy of the Hekman Library, Calvin College.)

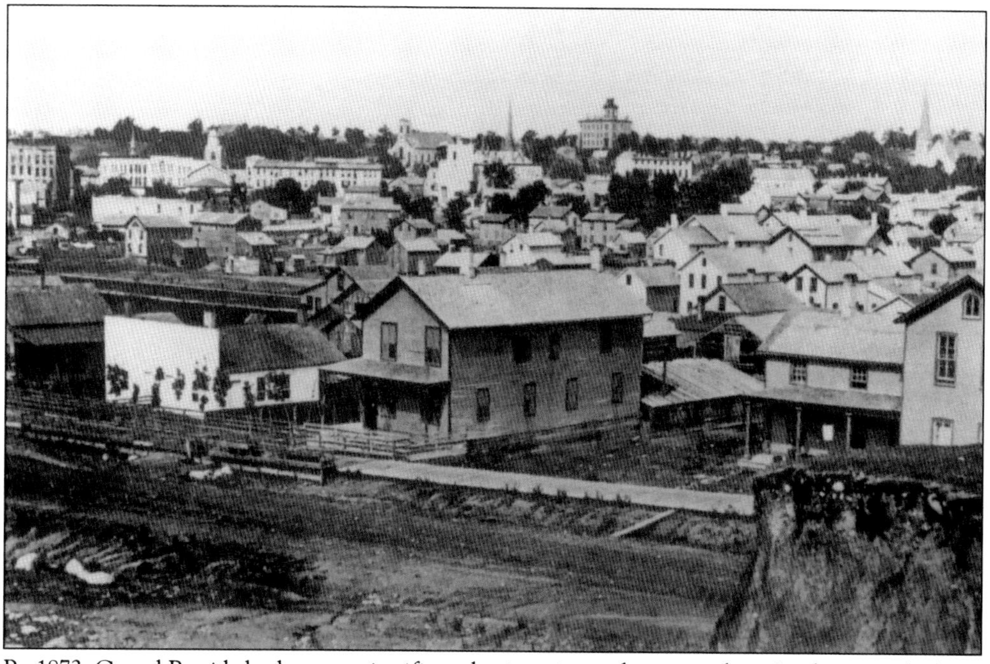

By 1873, Grand Rapids had grown significantly since its trading post days. In this view looking southwest toward the river, wooden bridges can be seen in the background. On April 13, 1873, just weeks after this photograph was taken, fire destroyed many of the buildings in the foreground. Most were soon rebuilt. (Courtesy of the Grand Rapids Public Library.)

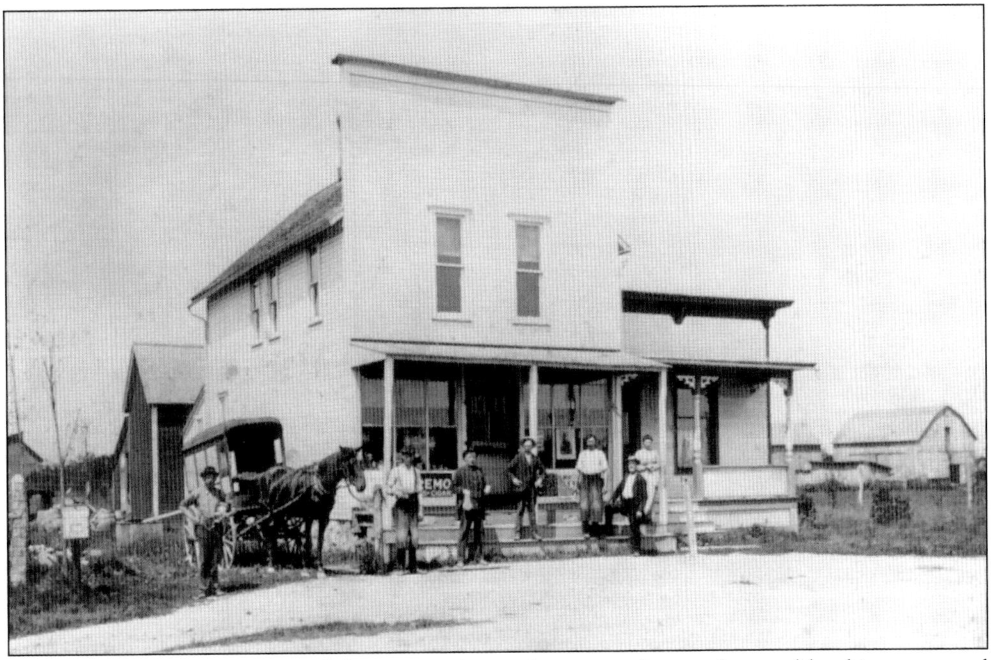

In the late 1880s, there were still farms in and near the city, and general stores like this one served residents basic needs; they only had to go downtown for major shopping excursions. The Schuling family lived in the city at 214 Morrison Street. Pictured, from left to right, are Mr. Schuling, Abe, Will, Henry, and Mrs. Schuling. (Above, courtesy of the Grand Rapids Public Library; below, courtesy of the Hekman Library, Calvin College.)

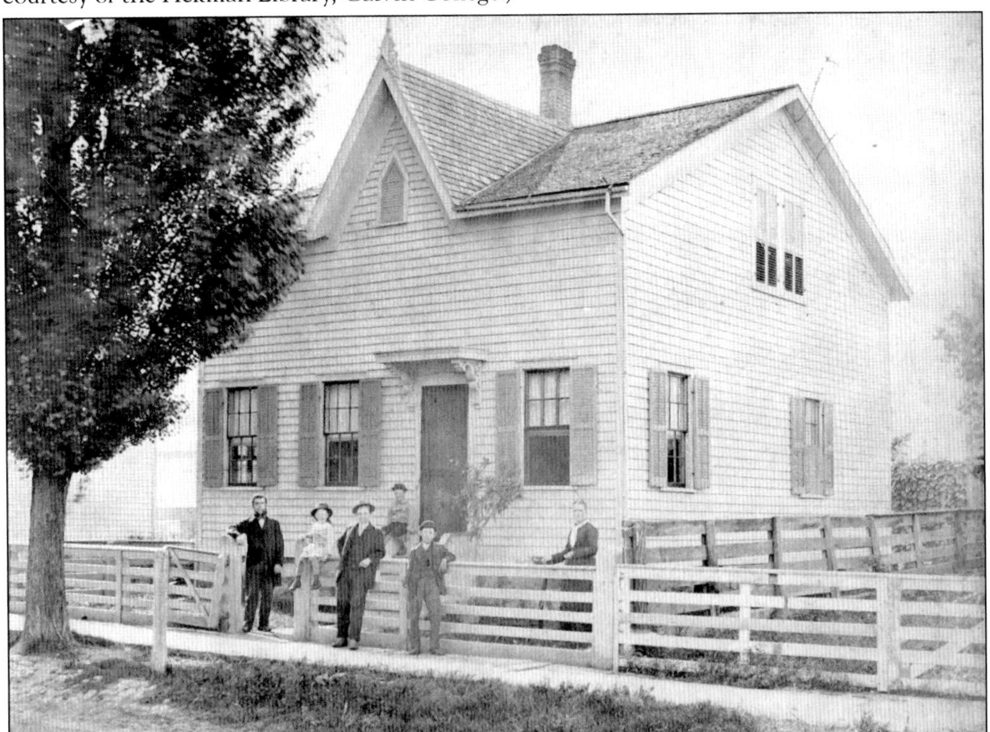

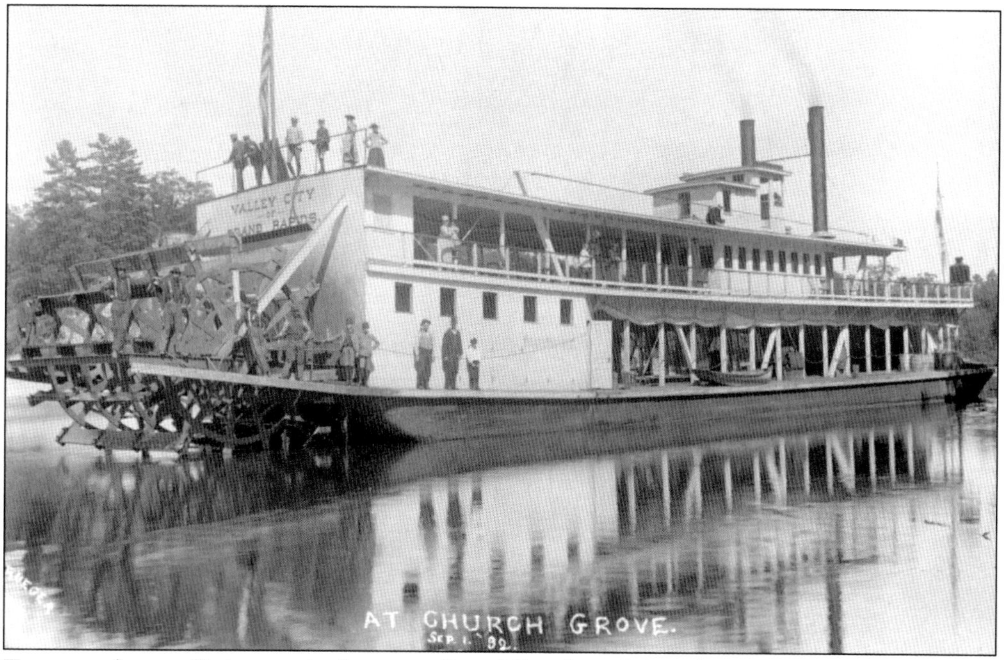

Two steamboats offering service between Grand Rapids and Grand Haven were the *Valley City*, pictured above docked at Church Grove Landing on September 1, 1892, and the *W.H. Barrett*, seen below. The band on the top level indicates a special occasion is in progress in this undated image. (Both, courtesy of the Grand Rapids Public Library.)

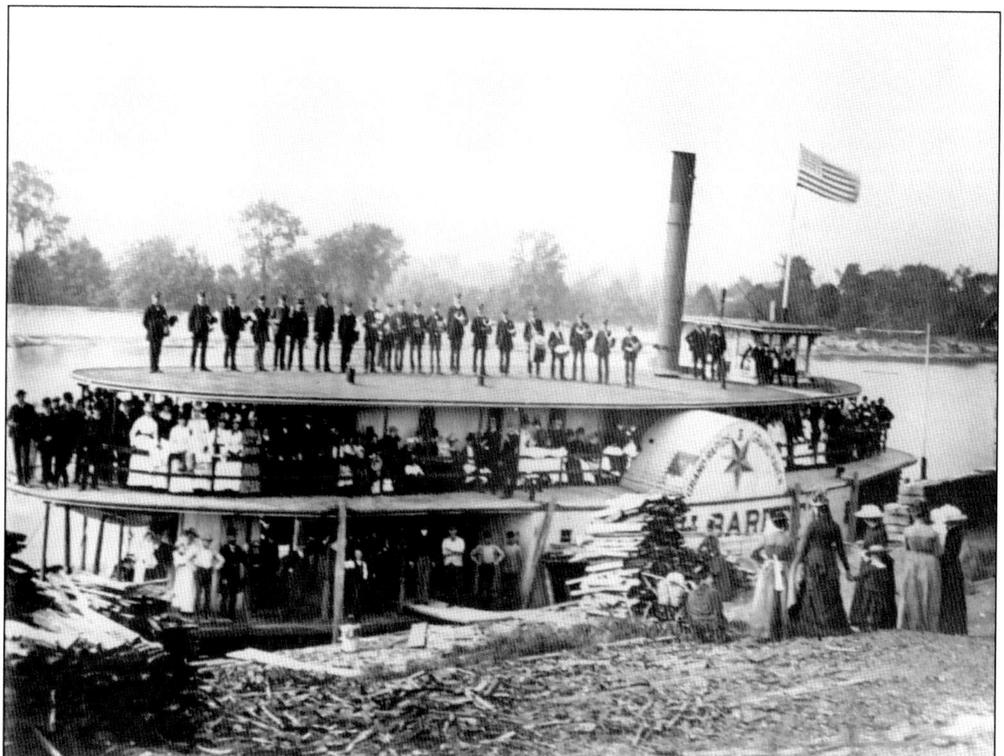

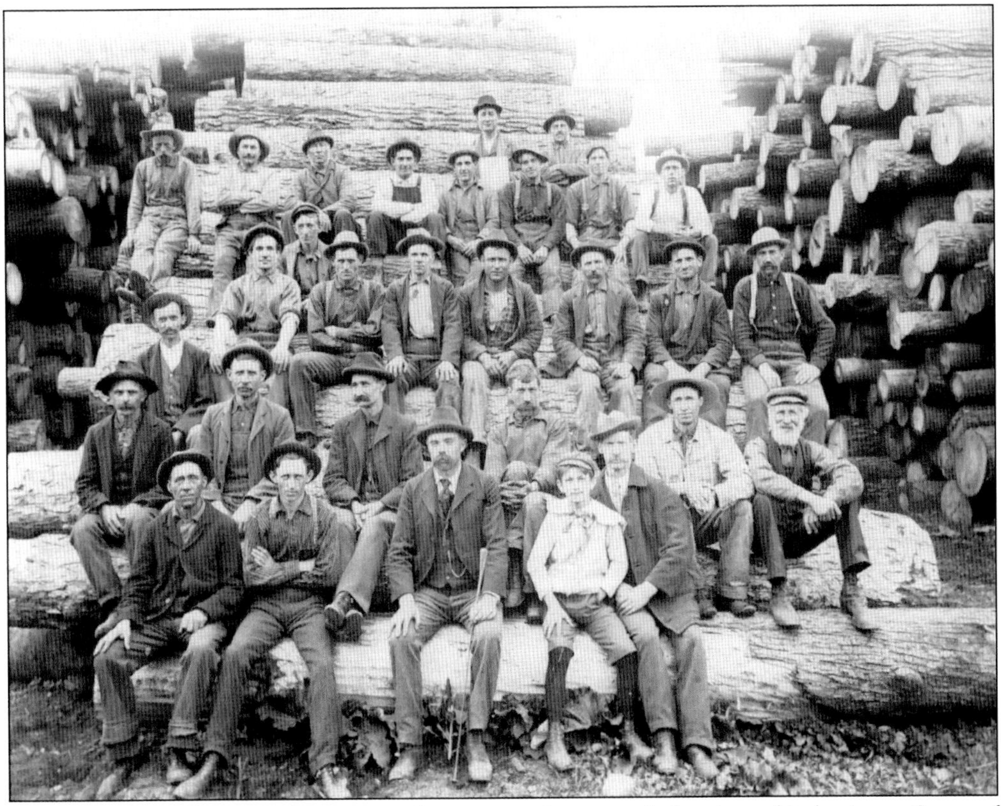

The area's dense forests and a growing furniture industry made logging a big business. Some of the logs were used locally, and others were transported from Grand Haven to Chicago via Lake Michigan. Logging led to the lumber business, which boomed during the early days as more and more people moved to the city. A growing need for lumberyards and sawmills created opportunities for entrepreneurs like the Holladays. (Both, courtesy of the Grand Rapids Public Library.)

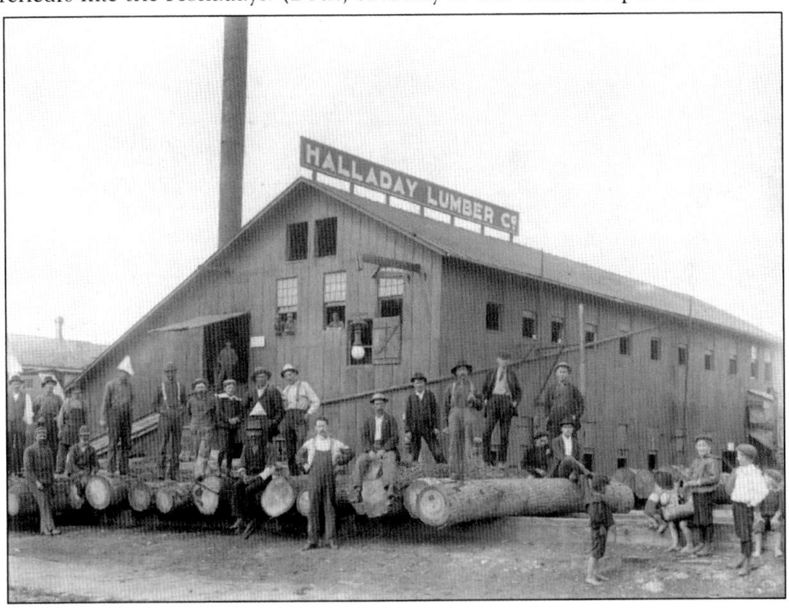

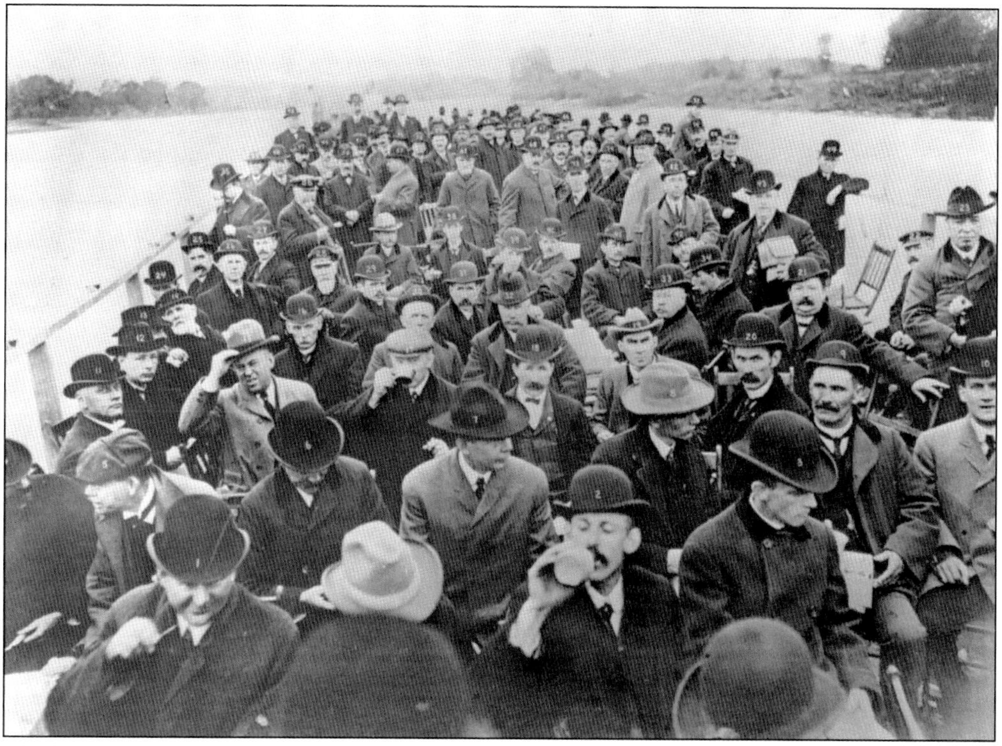

The board of trade members looked forward to an annual river outing. Congressman T.E. Burton was invited to join this 1905 excursion to Claybanks, 10 miles below Grand Rapids, so he could see firsthand the need for a government dredging project to enable larger vessels to navigate the river. (Courtesy of the Grand Rapids Public Library.)

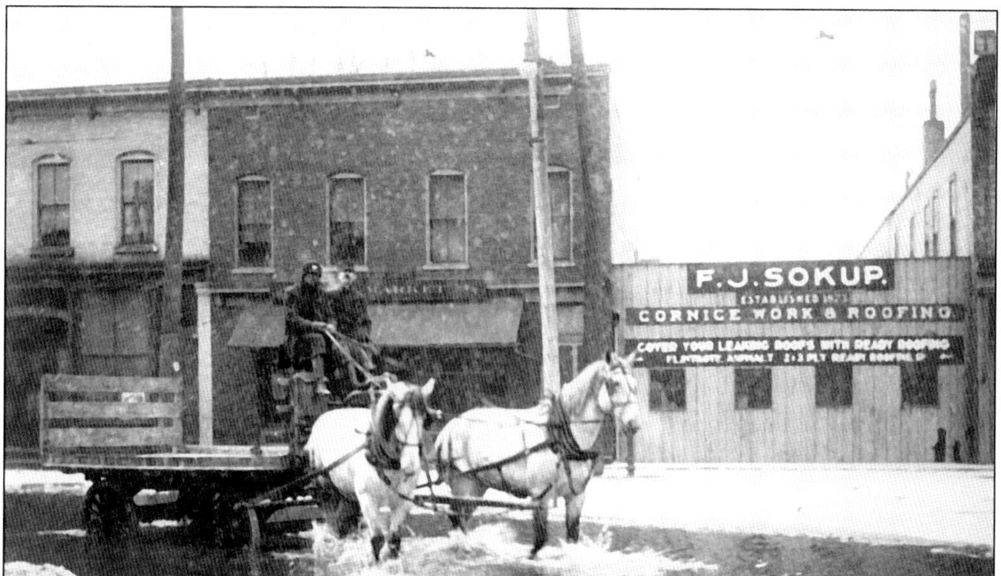

The infamous flood of 1904 wreaked havoc in downtown Grand Rapids. While some people were traveling by rowboat, this man sits high and dry while his horses splash through floodwater near the corner of Pearl Street and Front Avenue. (Courtesy of the Grand Rapids Public Library.)

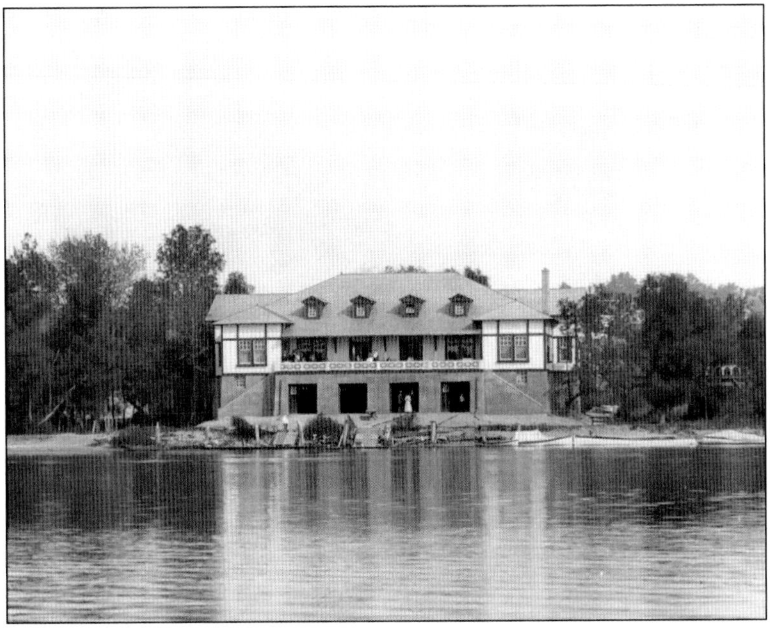

The Grand Rapids Boat and Canoe Club seen here from the eastern bank of the river was located just north of the North Park Bridge. The date is unknown. (Courtesy of the Grand Rapids Public Library.)

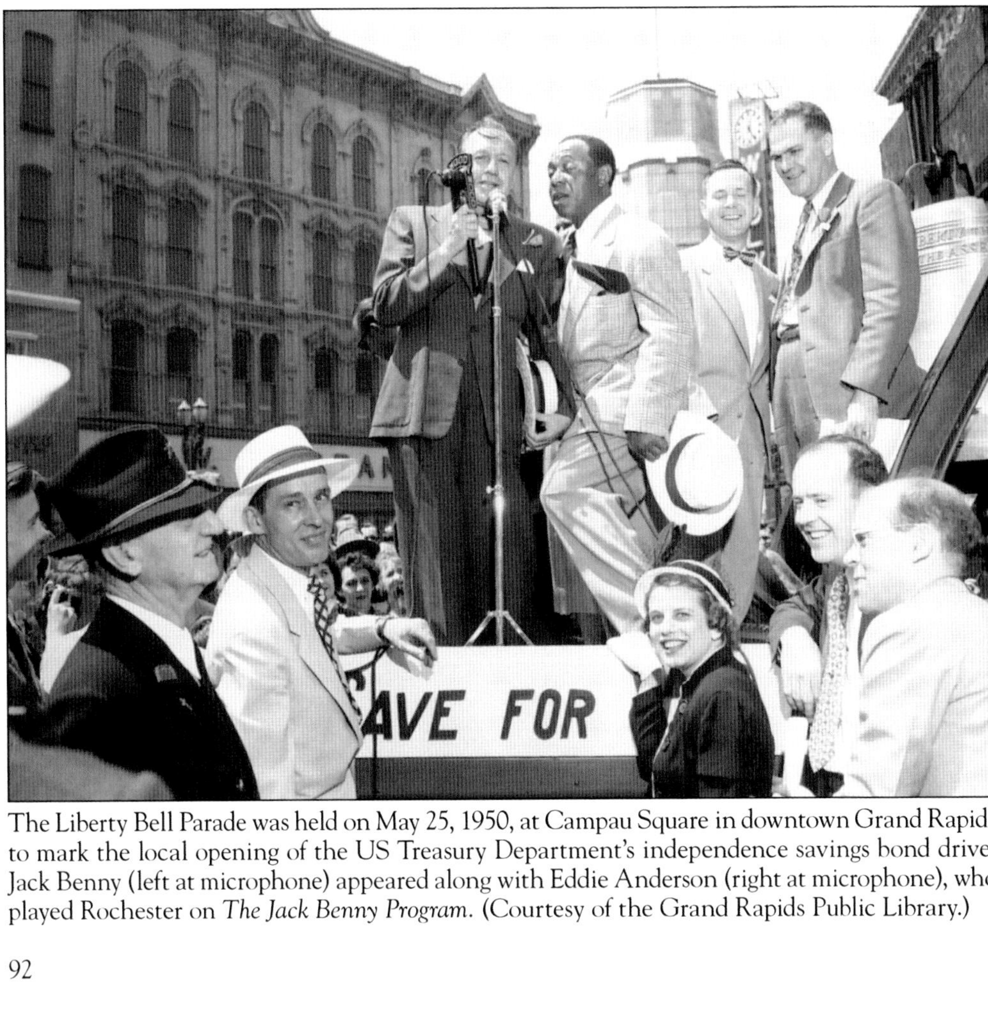

The Liberty Bell Parade was held on May 25, 1950, at Campau Square in downtown Grand Rapids to mark the local opening of the US Treasury Department's independence savings bond drive. Jack Benny (left at microphone) appeared along with Eddie Anderson (right at microphone), who played Rochester on *The Jack Benny Program*. (Courtesy of the Grand Rapids Public Library.)

Grand Rapids is still home to many Native Americans, and in 1954 the Human Relations Commission of Grand Rapids was founded to protect the rights of all citizens and eliminate discrimination. Native Americans serving on the commission in 1971 are, from left to right, George Bennett, Chet Eagleman, and John R. Winchester. (Courtesy of the Grand Rapids Public Library.)

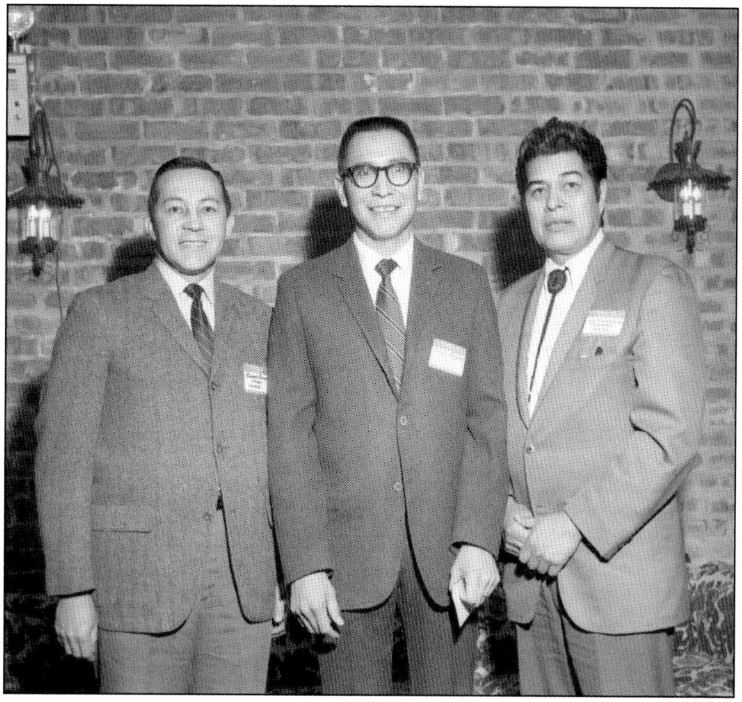

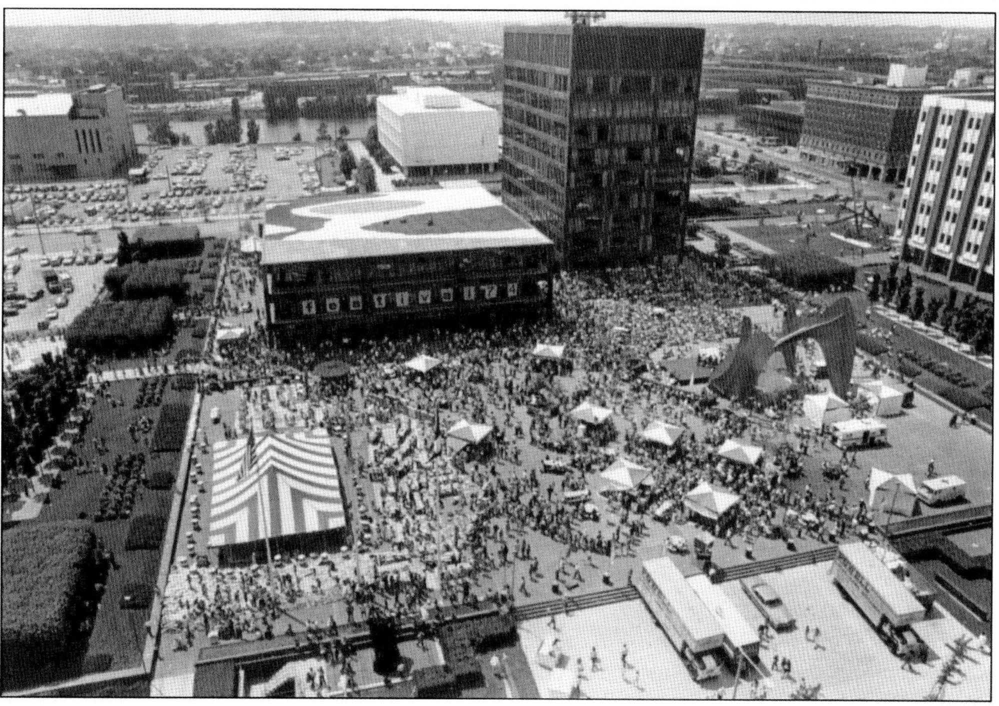

Michigan winters are long and cold, so summers are savored. The first weekend in June brings the Festival of the Arts to Calder Square and other downtown locations. The 1974 festival brought more than 100,000 people out to enjoy live music, dance, cinema, art exhibits, food, and more. The first festival was held in 1970, and it keeps getting bigger and better. (Courtesy of the Grand Rapids Public Library.)

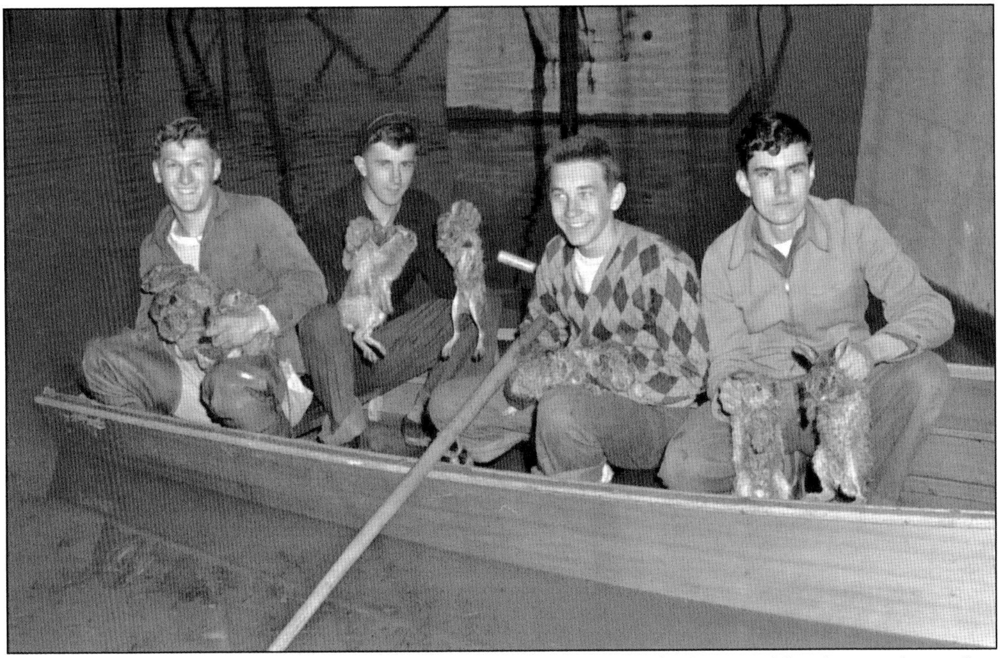

More than fish have been pulled out of the river. The bunnies look more like drowned rats, but going swimming must have seemed like a good idea at the time. The alligator may be the only one of his species rescued from a river in Grand Rapids, Michigan. (Both, courtesy of the Grand Rapids Public Library.)

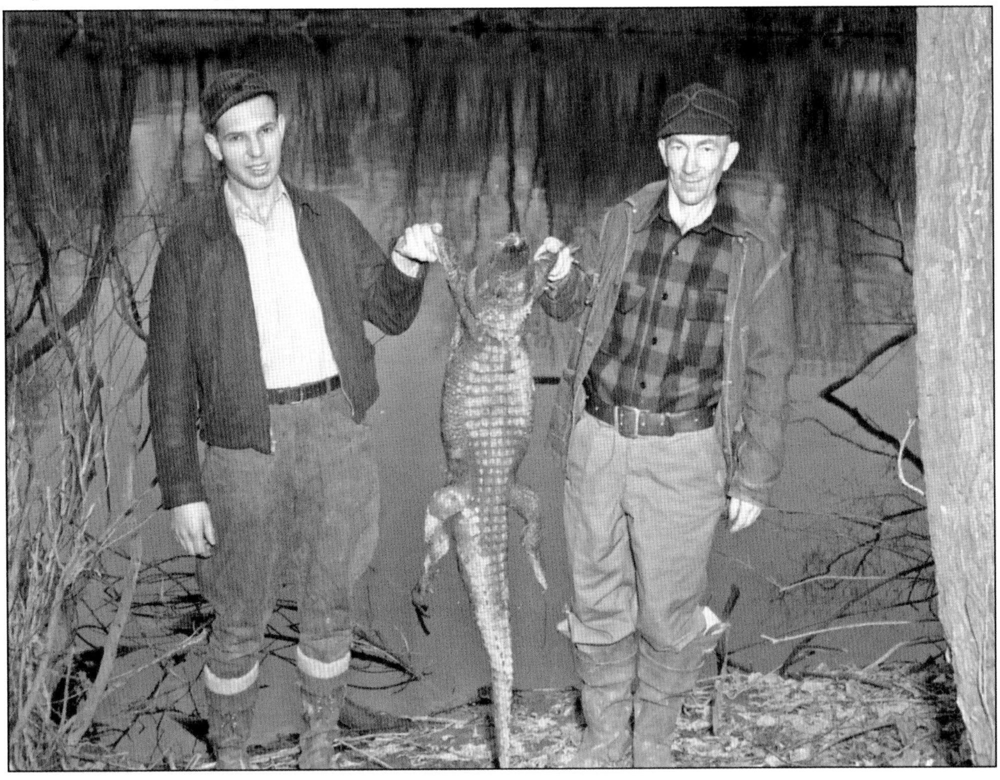

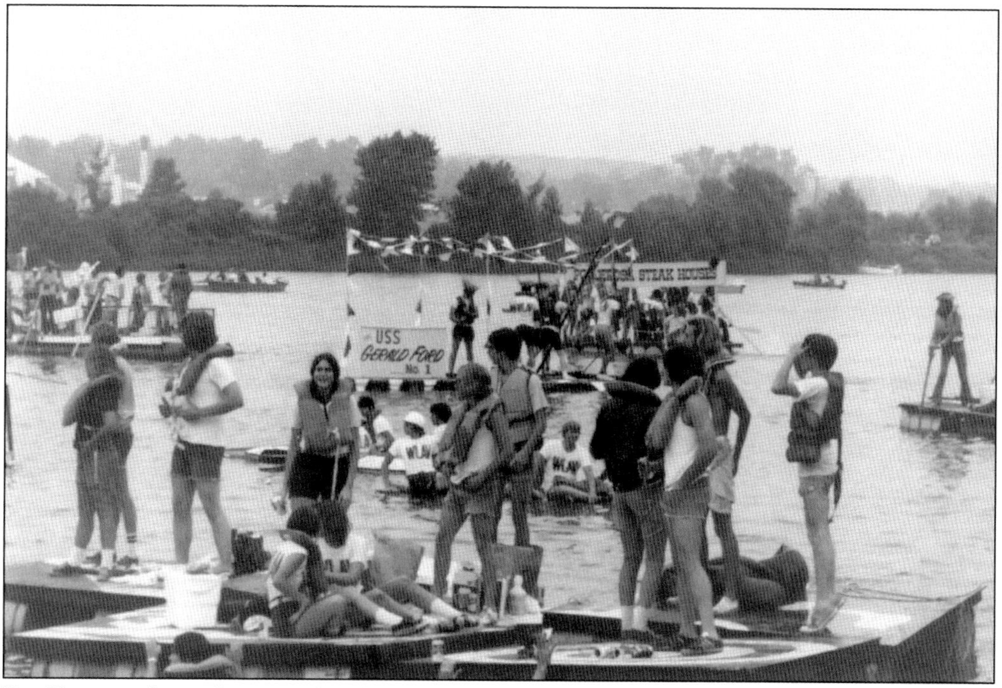

For 12 years, the rock station WLAV sponsored a raft race on the river. Because the 1974 race happened shortly after Gerald Ford became president, it was only fitting that one raft would be named the USS *Gerald Ford* (above). When he received newspaper clippings and photographs, Ford wrote back thanking the sender for sharing information about "an event that seems well on the way to becoming a tradition in my hometown!" (Both, courtesy of the Grand Rapids Public Library.)

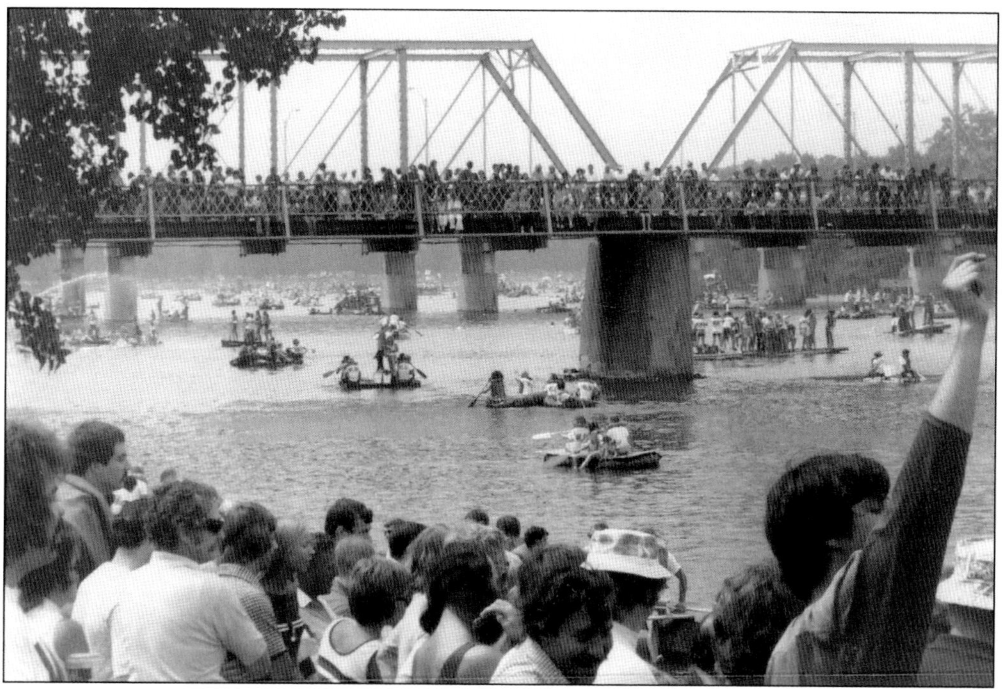

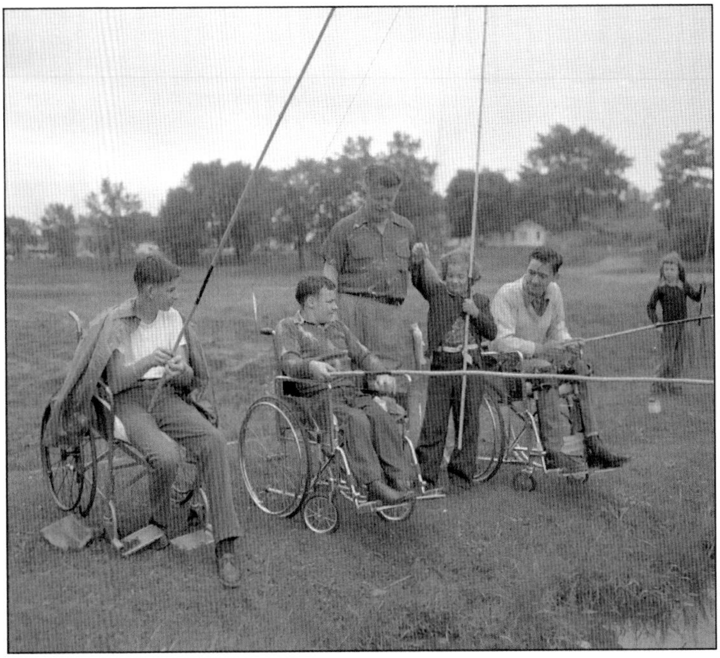

The fact that these fishermen use wheelchairs does not stop them from fishing. The Grand Rapids Jaycees periodically arranged outings for rehabilitation patients at Mary Free Bed Hospital and others in need of outdoor recreation. (Courtesy of the Grand Rapids Public Library.)

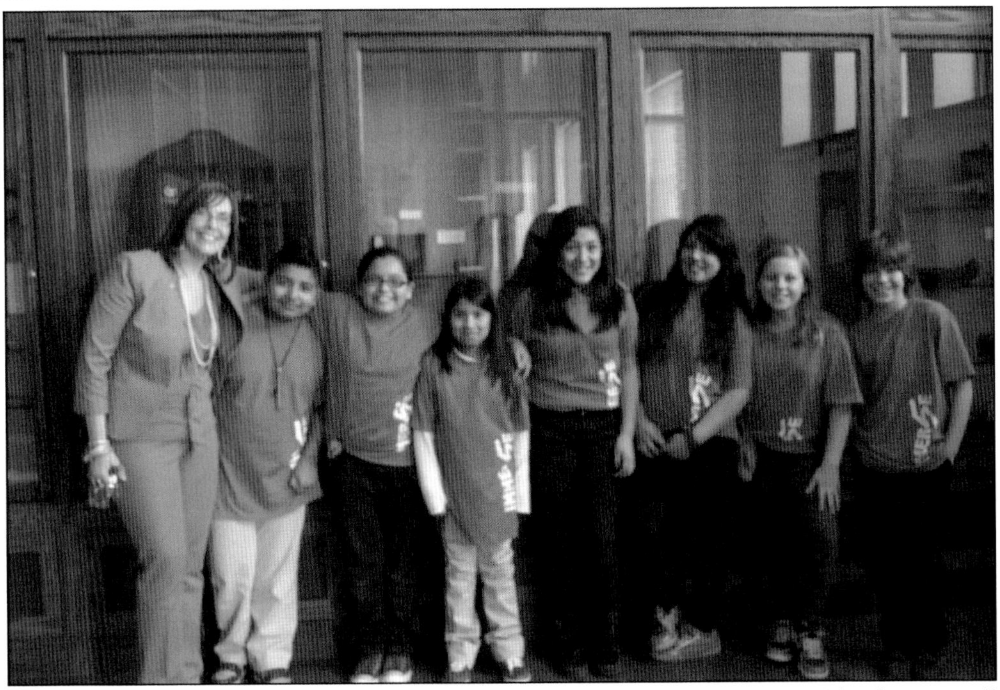

Abbie Marr's fifth-grade Harrison Elementary class studied the river in 2013. After learning all they could in the classroom, students selected artifacts from the Grand Rapids Public Museum pertaining to the earliest natives and settlers. They created a Grand River museum in the school showcases that remained in place until the close of the school year. Some of the rightfully proud curators at the opening reception are, from left to right, teacher Abbie Marr, Jordi Rodruguez-Zurita, Marly Secundino-Rodriguez, Jahira Vargas, Tania Bedolla-Ortiz, Gisela Calderon-Gomez, Lacie Moore, and Jesse Laster. (Photograph by Shelby Ayers.)

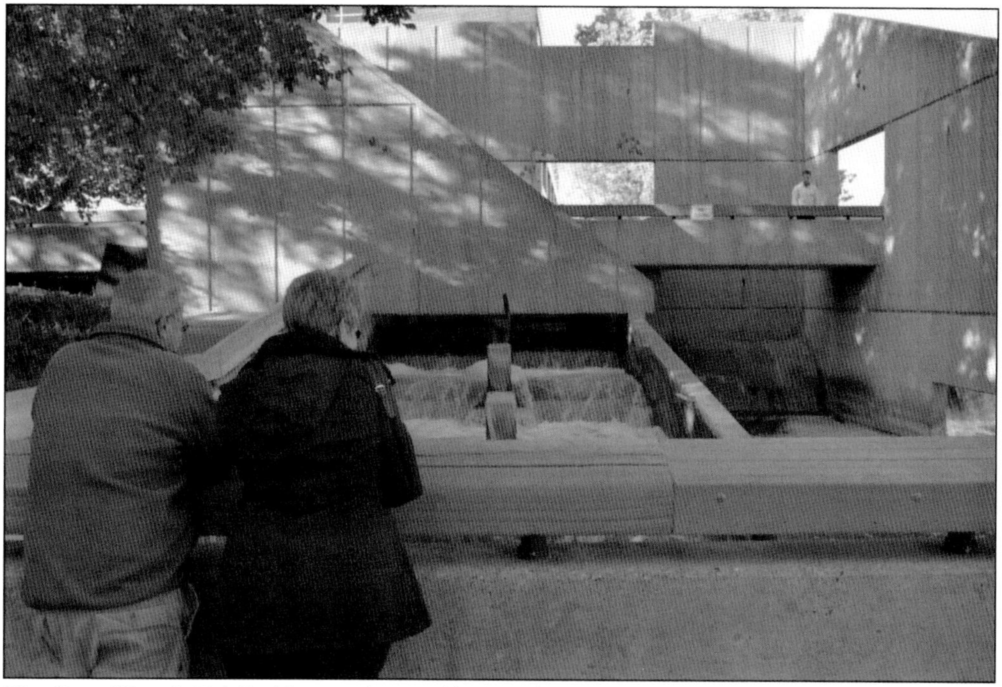

The Grand Rapids Fish Ladder was designed by Joseph Kinnebrew IV and was built to assist salmon in their uphill struggles to reach their spawning grounds. Fish Ladder Park is downtown off Front Street and serves as an attraction for residents and visitors alike. (Photograph by Shelby Ayers.)

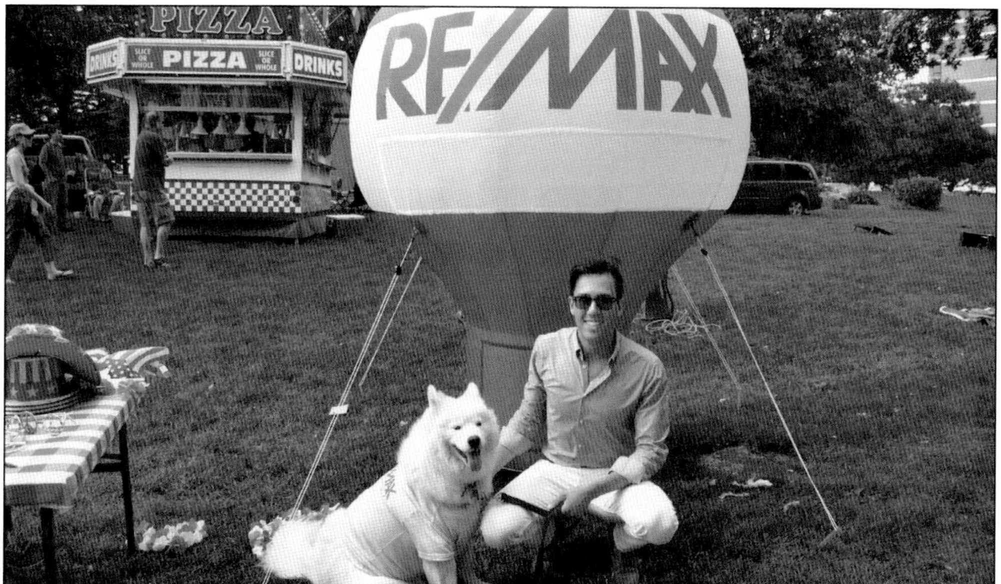

Celebration on the Grand is an annual Grand Rapids event that includes music, games, food, and more. Remax Real Estate is one of the sponsors. Here, agent Jake Theoret poses with his dog Jules. On this day, she is serving as mascot for Remax, but Theoret is training her for the important career of therapy dog. He expects Jules to be ready for work in spring 2015. (Photograph by Shelby Ayers.)

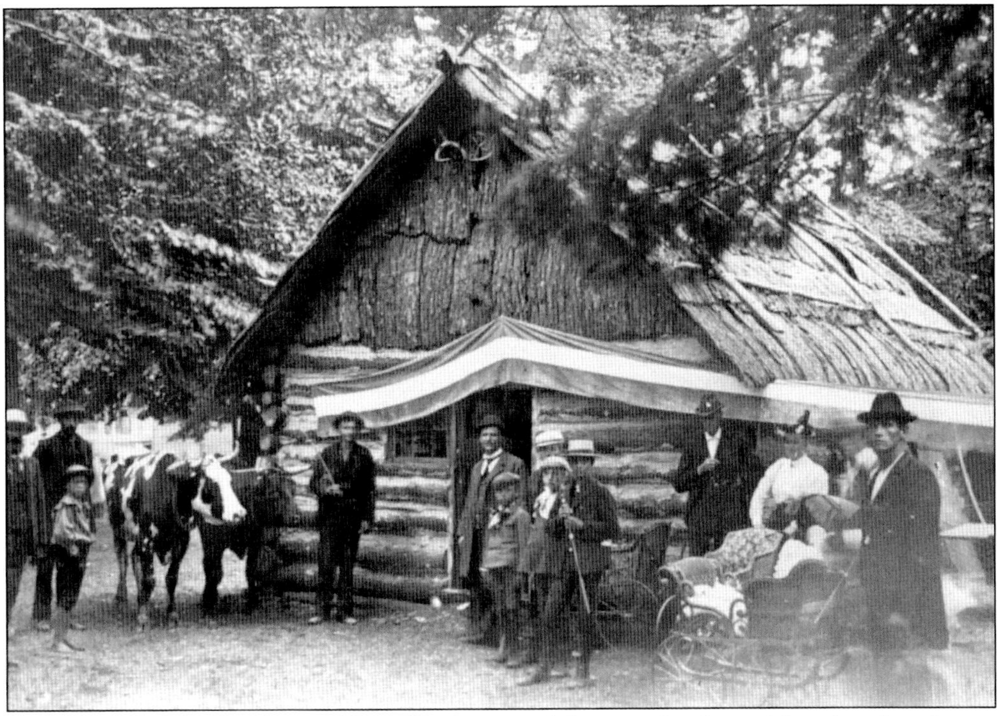

Grandville, southwest of Grand Rapids, was one of the river landings. The abundant forests provided logs for the early settlers to build cabins like this one, pictured here at the end of the 19th century. (Courtesy of the Hekman Library, Calvin College.)

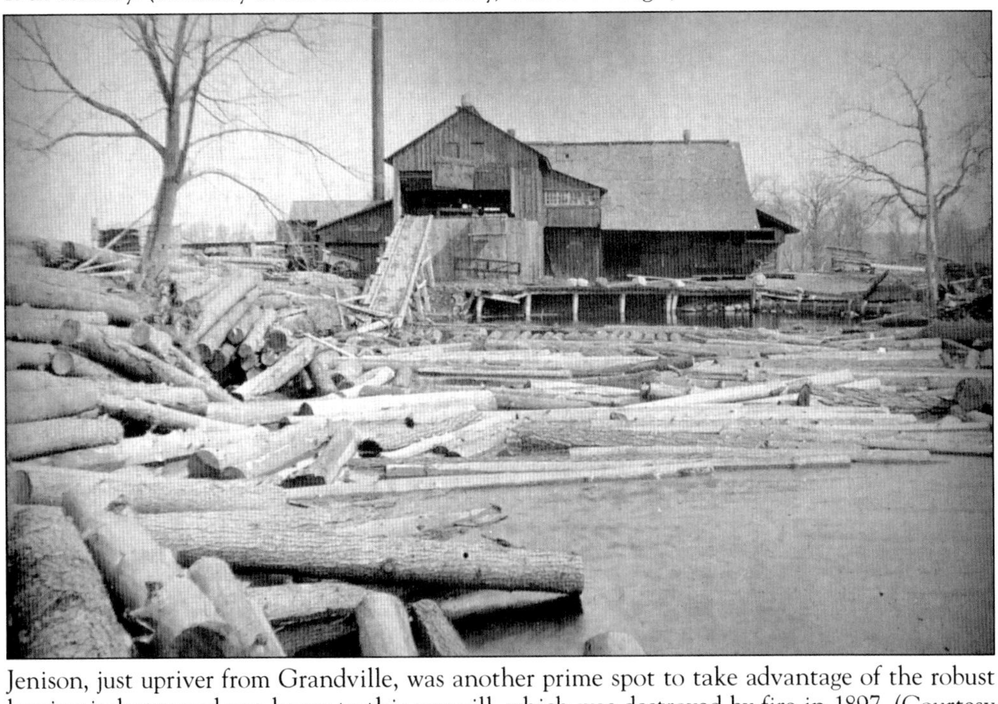

Jenison, just upriver from Grandville, was another prime spot to take advantage of the robust logging industry and was home to this sawmill, which was destroyed by fire in 1897. (Courtesy of the Grand Rapids Public Library.)

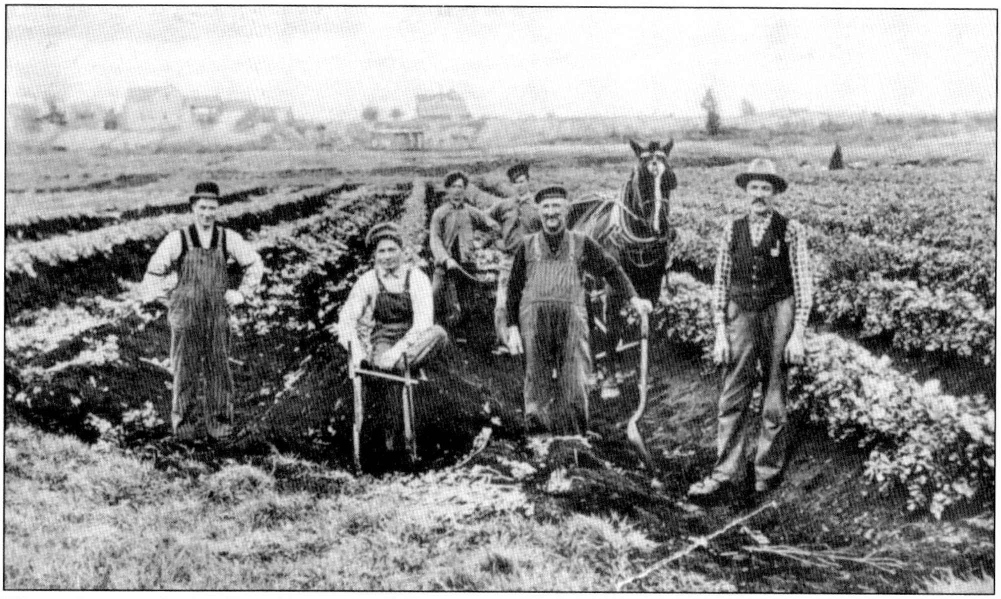

These farmworkers take advantage of the perfect growing conditions on one of the many muck farms located in the Grand River Valley. This farm is near Zeeland, and the photograph was taken during the early 1920s; the crops are celery and other vegetables. (Courtesy of the Hekman Library, Calvin College.)

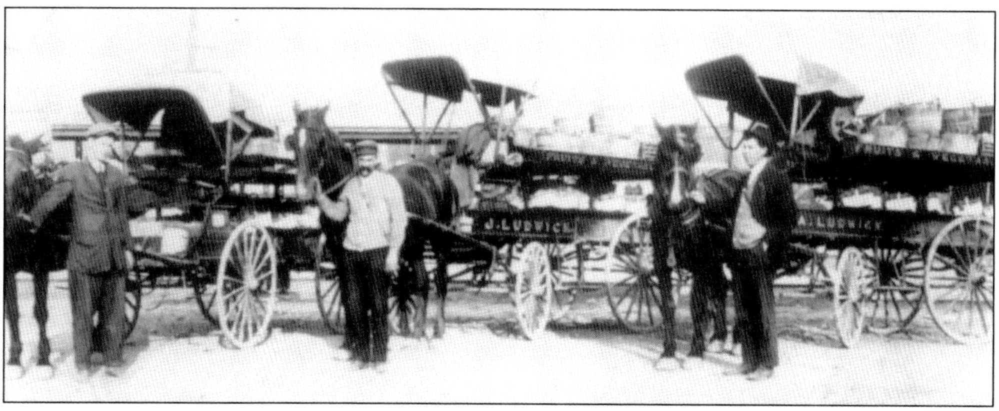

Farmers found ready buyers for their produce in the Grand Rapids markets and sold ripe, still-sun-warmed tomatoes, celery, corn, and berries from the backs of their wagons. The Ludwig brothers shown here were regular sellers at the Westside Vegetable Market. (Courtesy of the Hekman Library, Calvin College.)

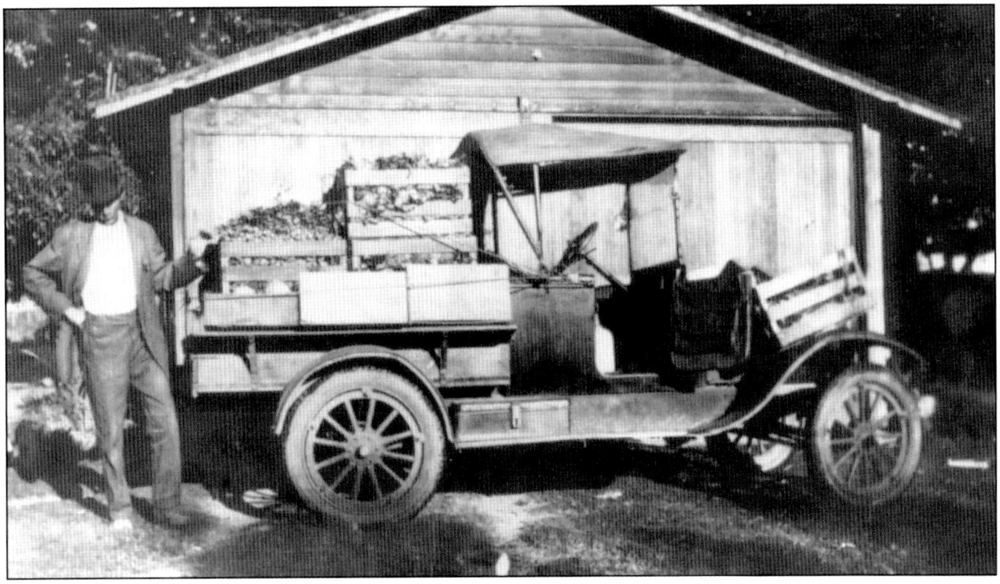

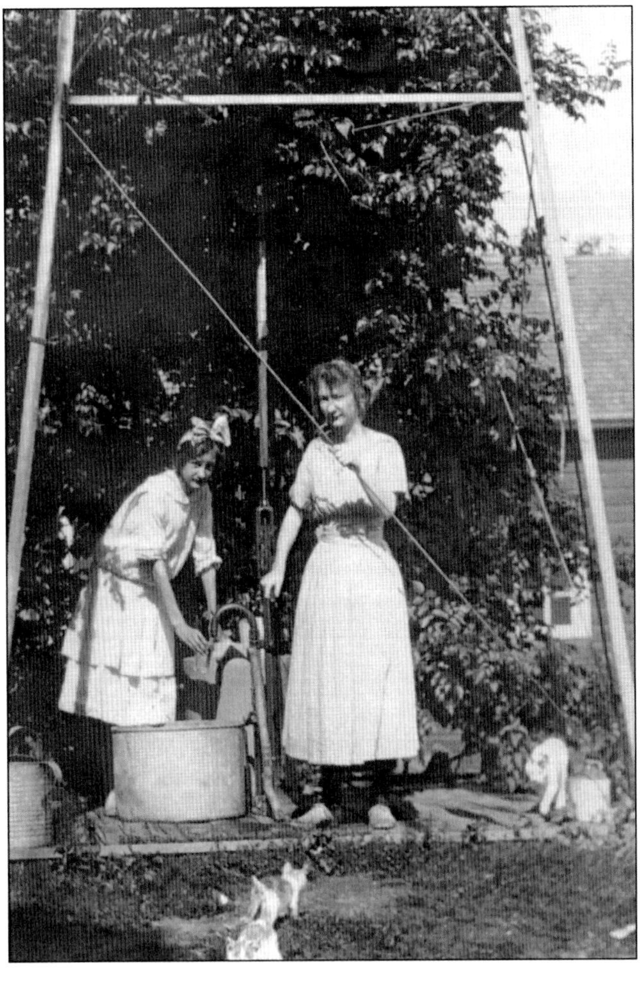

Byron Center, now a thriving Grand Rapids suburb, was once primarily a farming community taking advantage of the superior Grand River Valley growing conditions. An unidentified farmer stands beside his produce truck around 1910. (Courtesy of the Hekman Library, Calvin College.)

Women's work really was never done in the so-called good old days. Imagine having to pump water for laundry, dishwashing, and even bathing. (Courtesy of the Gary Byker Memorial Library, Hudsonville.)

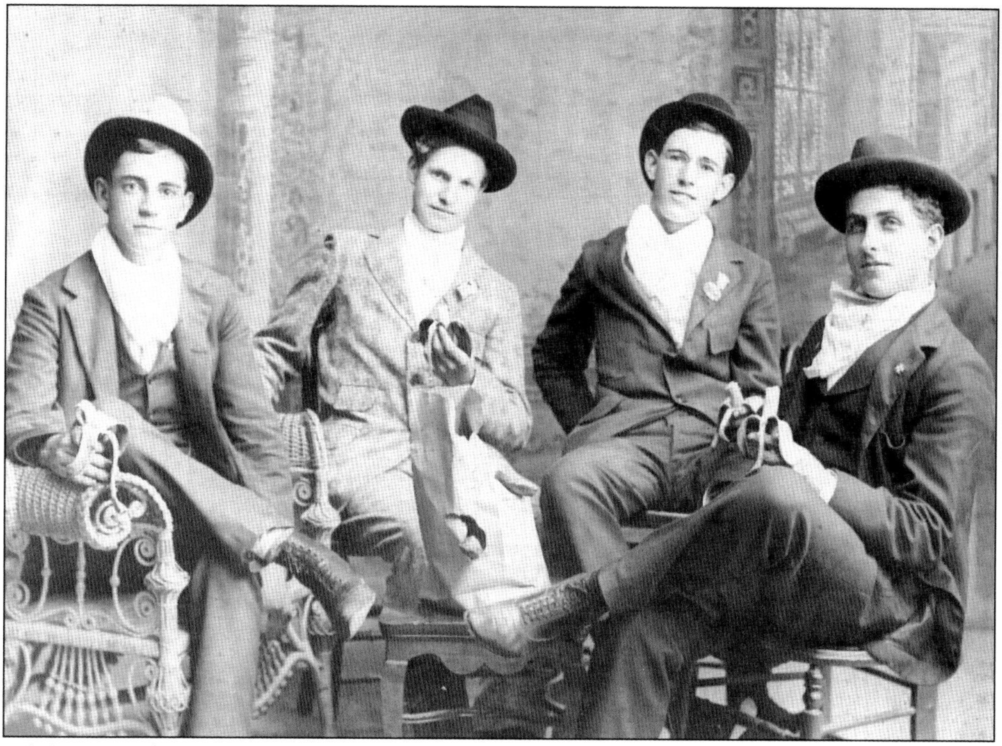

While it is not known why these four young men are holding partially eaten bananas, one can guess that after a lifetime of the lush berries and other fruits grown in the area, bananas were probably considered deliciously exotic. (Courtesy of the Gary Byker Memorial Library, Hudsonville.)

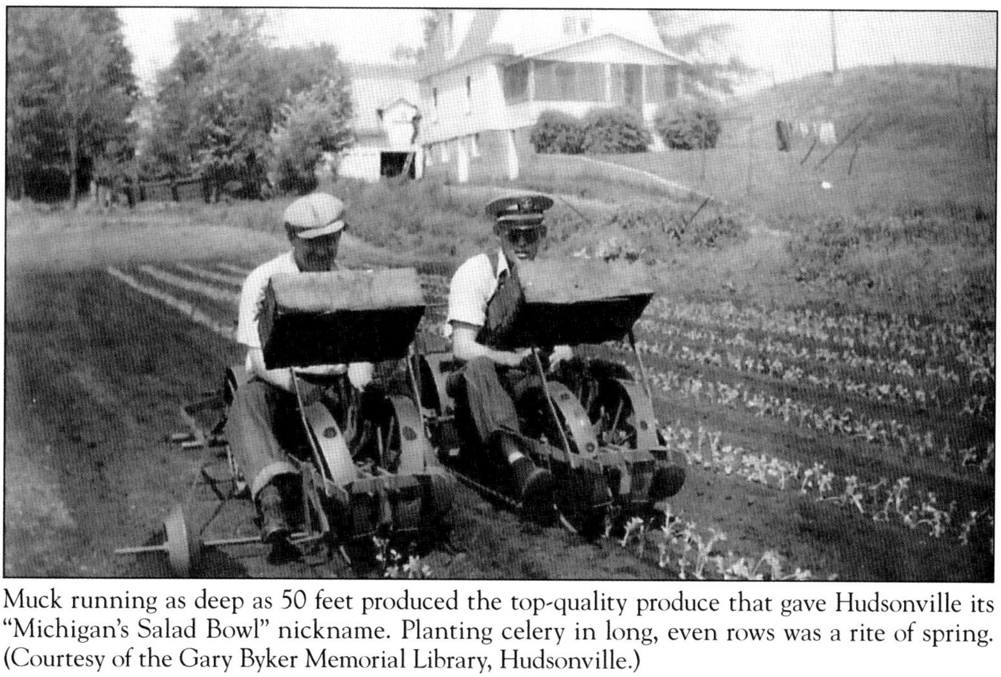

Muck running as deep as 50 feet produced the top-quality produce that gave Hudsonville its "Michigan's Salad Bowl" nickname. Planting celery in long, even rows was a rite of spring. (Courtesy of the Gary Byker Memorial Library, Hudsonville.)

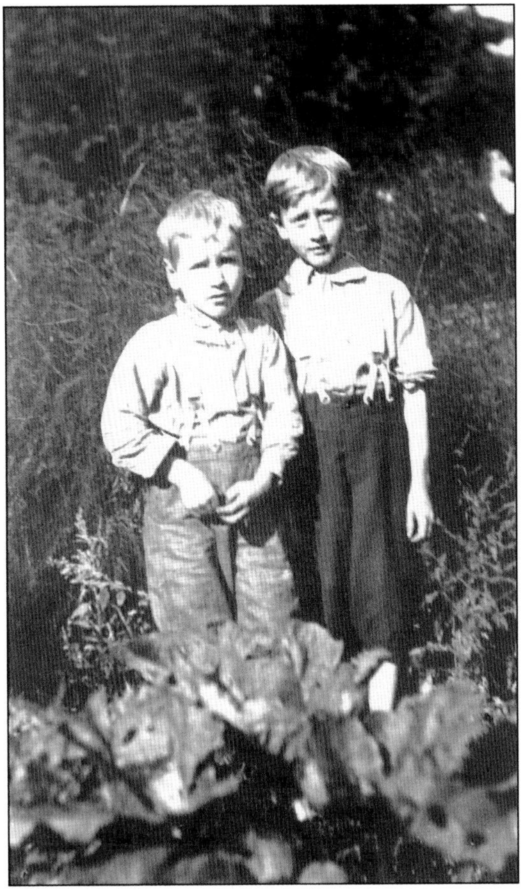

These brothers are out checking the crops. Early experience gave them a leg up when it came time to work their own farms. (Courtesy of the Gary Byker Memorial Library, Hudsonville.)

Here are five generations of the Edson family, longtime Grand River Valley residents and farmers. Pictured in 1941 are, from left to right, Guy Edson (father of Doris), Doris Edson Nyhuis, Phillip Allen Nyhuis (son of Edson), Edson J. Nyhuis (son of Doris), and Orin Edson (father of Guy). (Courtesy of the Gary Byker Memorial Library, Hudsonville.)

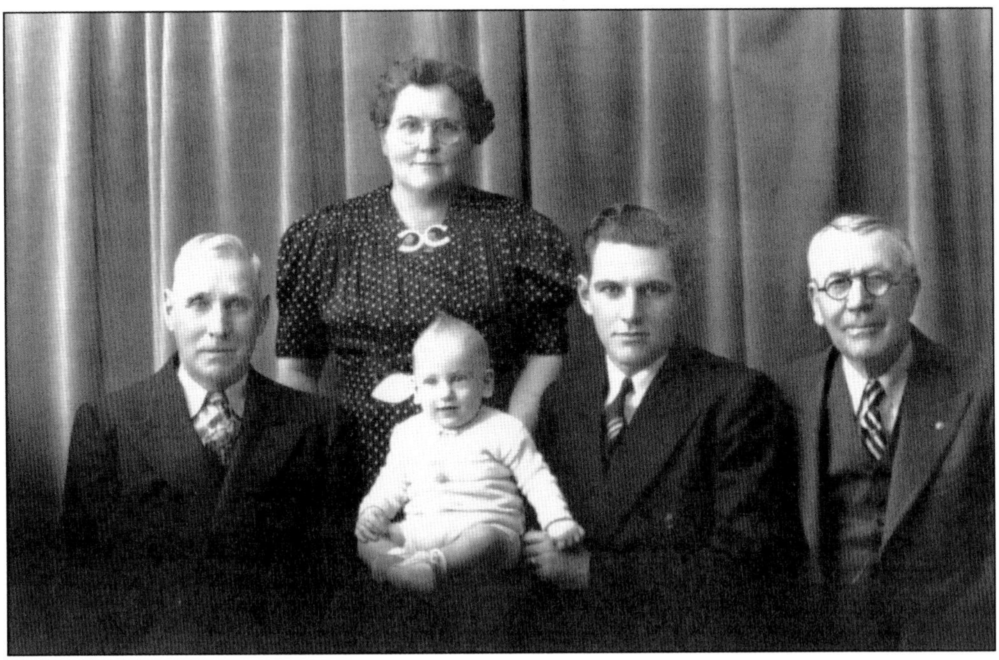

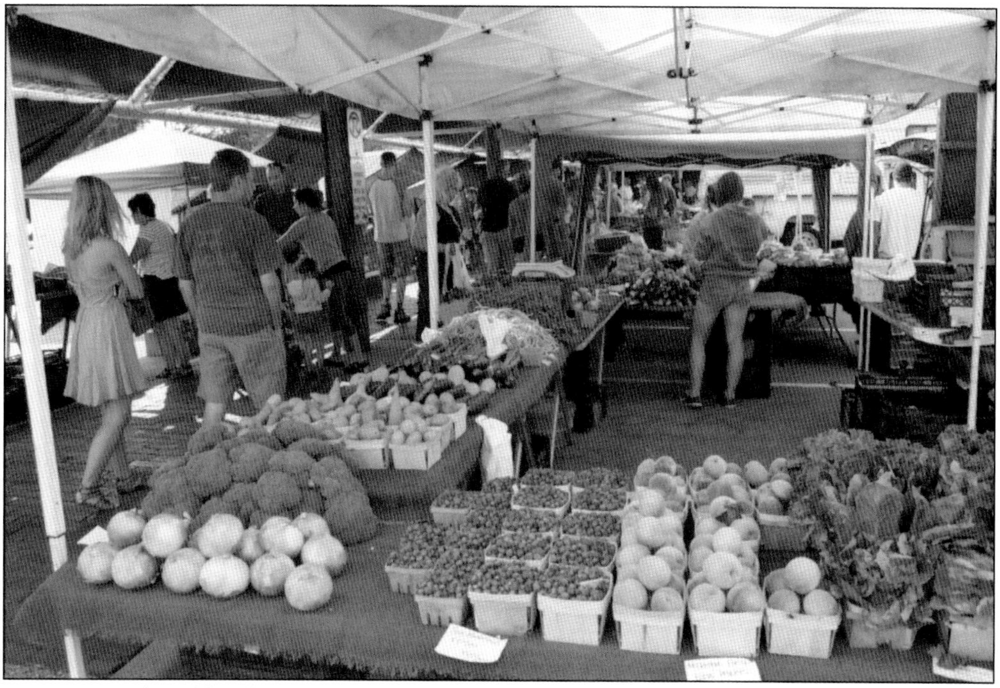

Farmers' markets like this one in Grand Haven are well attended because people know they will be getting produce from local farms such as the Ter Avest family farm in Hudsonville. The blueberries and Red Haven peaches in the center front are regional favorites. (Photograph by Shelby Ayers.)

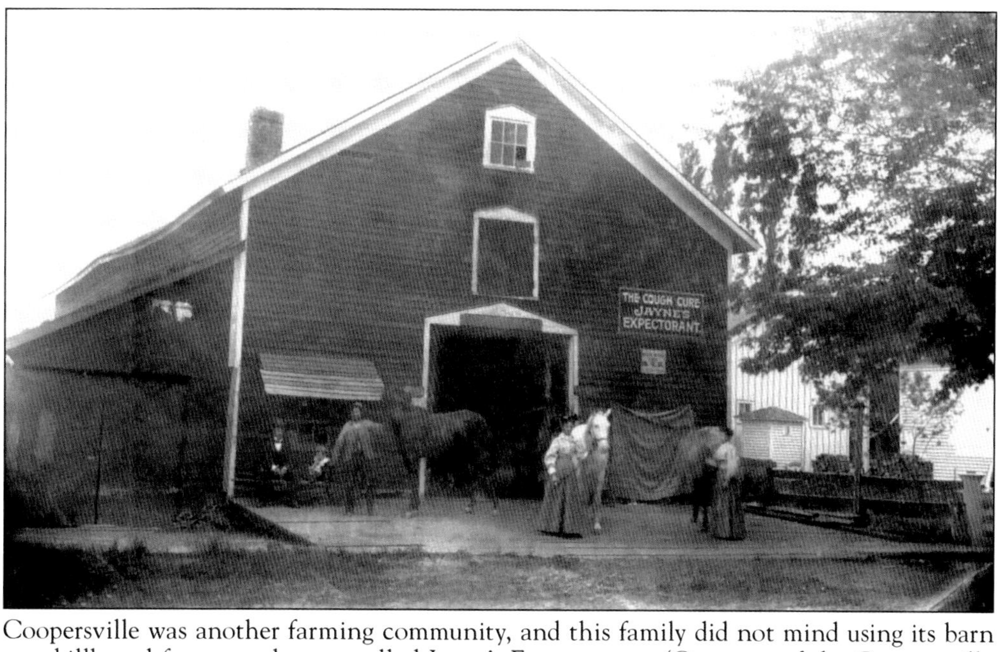

Coopersville was another farming community, and this family did not mind using its barn as a billboard for a cough cure called Jayne's Expectorant. (Courtesy of the Coopersville Historical Museum.)

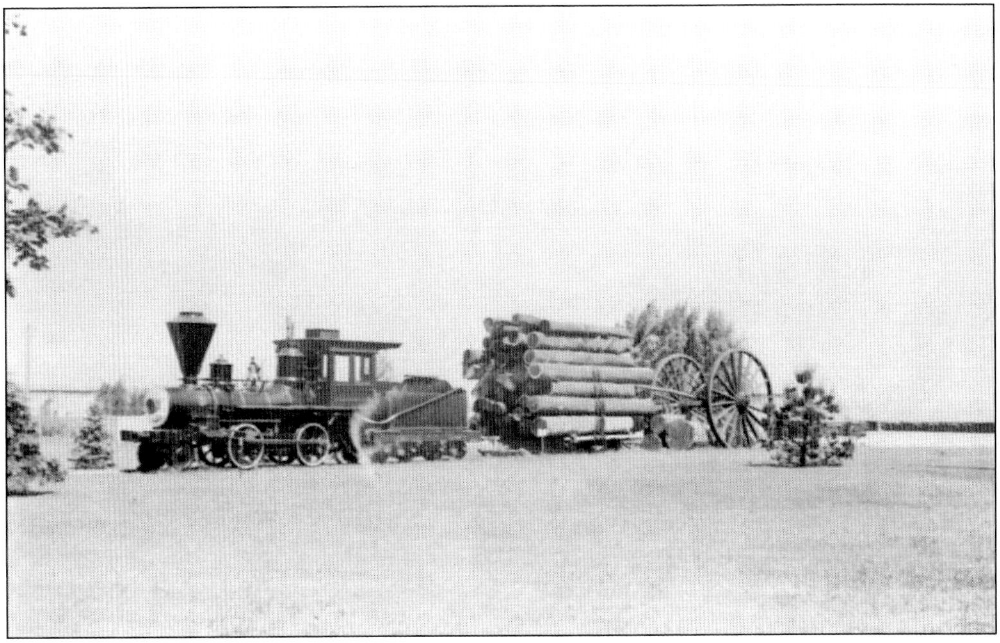

Logging, farming, and the Grand Rapids, Grand Haven & Muskegon Railway (interurban) make up much of Coopersville's history. Logs were either floated down the river for transport via Lake Michigan or taken to local sawmills. Sometimes, portable saws like this one were used to cut logs on-site rather than having them moved to sawmills. (Both, courtesy of the Coopersville Historical Museum.)

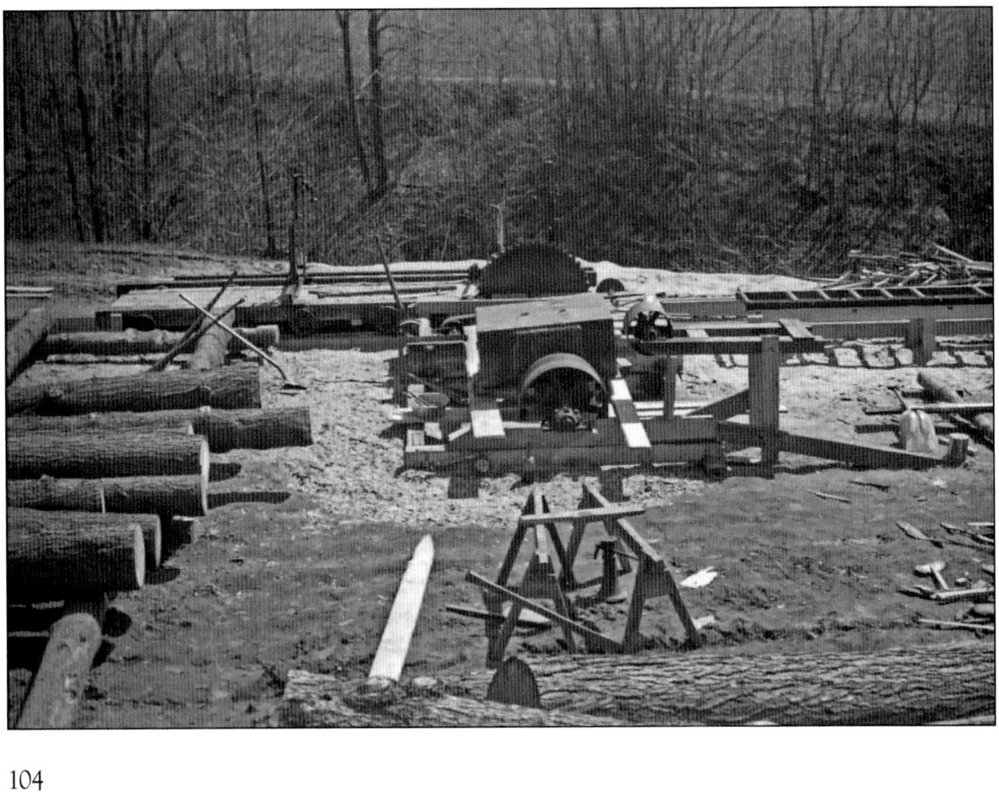

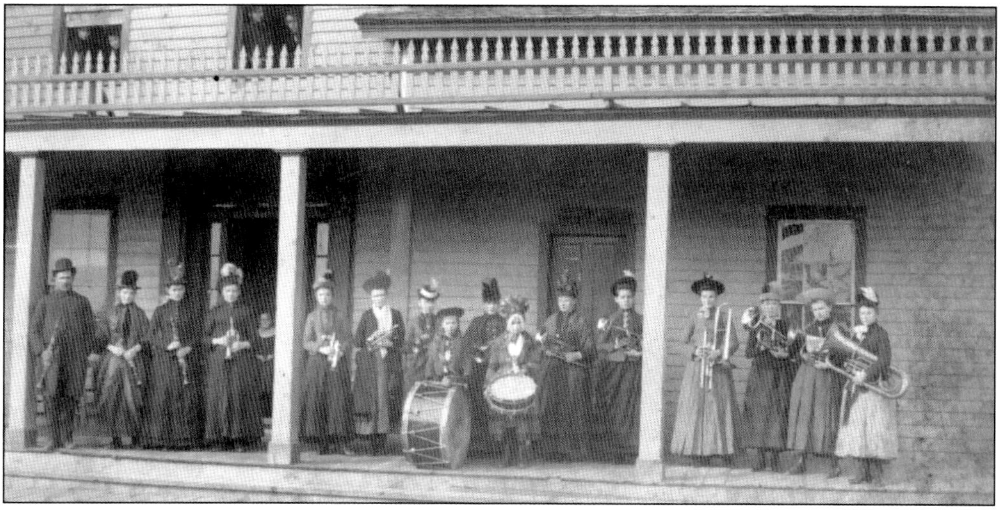

Some Coopersville women decided to take a little time from their labors to practice their musical talent and started this band in the 1890s. (Courtesy of the Coopersville Historical Museum.)

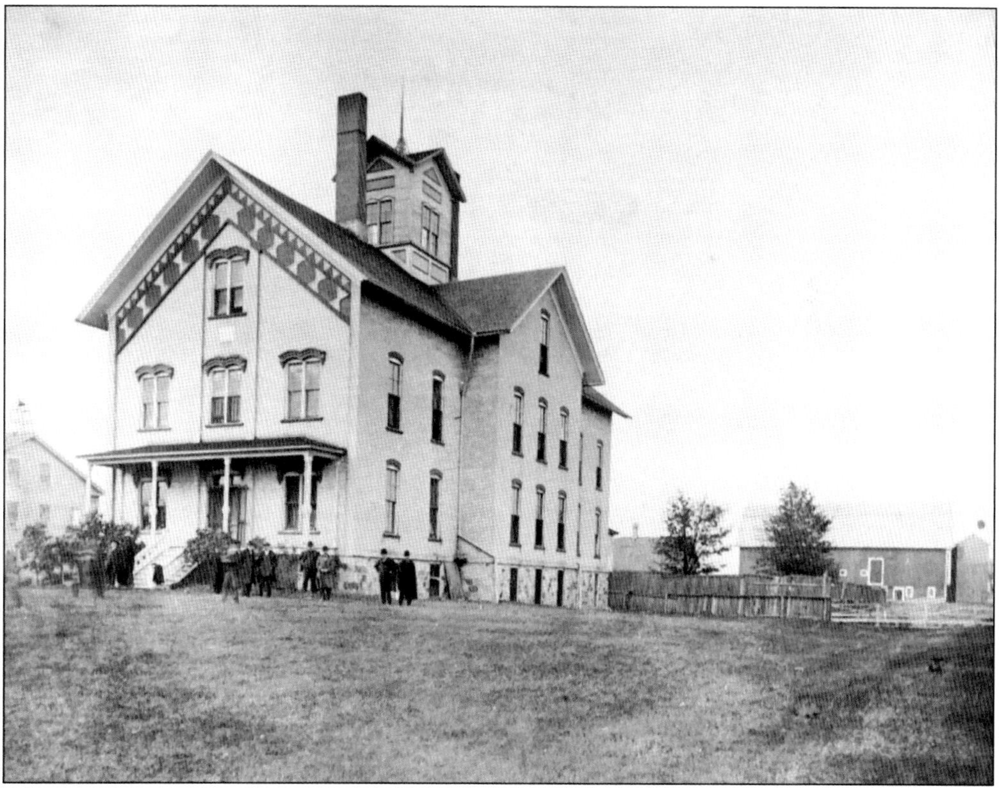

In the days before welfare and government aid, the poor had no choice but the poorhouse. These were often widows with children. The Coopersville poorhouse was a farm worked by the residents, allowing them to retain some of their dignity. The keeper of the facility earned from $460 to $600 a month, depending on experience. (Courtesy of the Coopersville Historical Museum.)

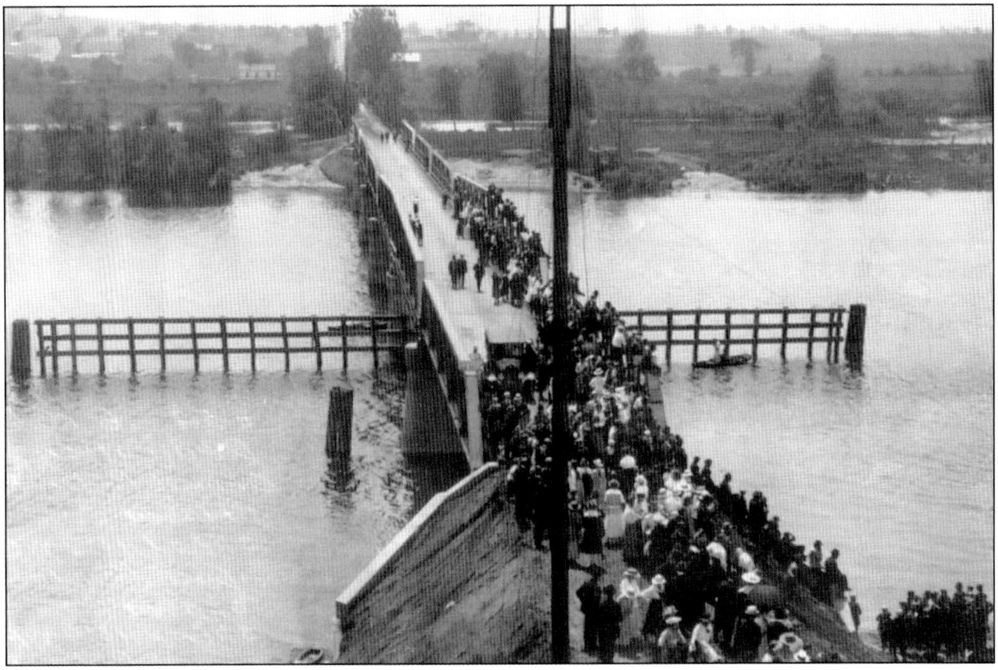

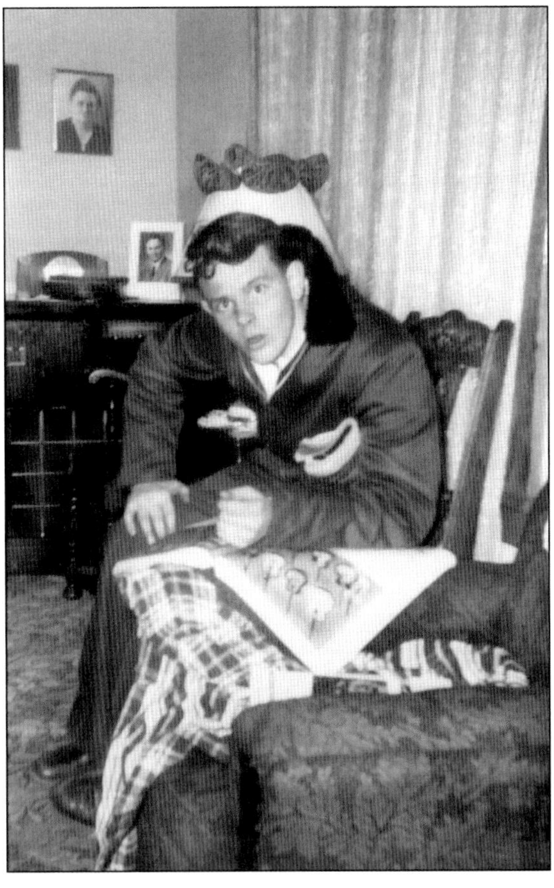

When the long-awaited Eastmanville Bridge opened, it was met with great enthusiasm. No longer would people have to depend on ferry service to cross the river. (Courtesy of the Coopersville Historical Museum.)

Coopersville may be known today for its farming and railroad history, but it has another claim to fame in Charles "Chuck" Westover, who was born in Grand Rapids and grew up in Coopersville. Chuck loved guitars and music and made a name for himself as Del Shannon. His hit song "Runaway" made him a sensation. He was also popular in Great Britain, where an up-and-coming group called the Beatles were his opening act. (Courtesy of the Coopersville Historical Museum.)

Architects from the firm of Meathe, Kessler & Associates are working on the new university's layout. (Courtesy of the Grand Valley State University Library.)

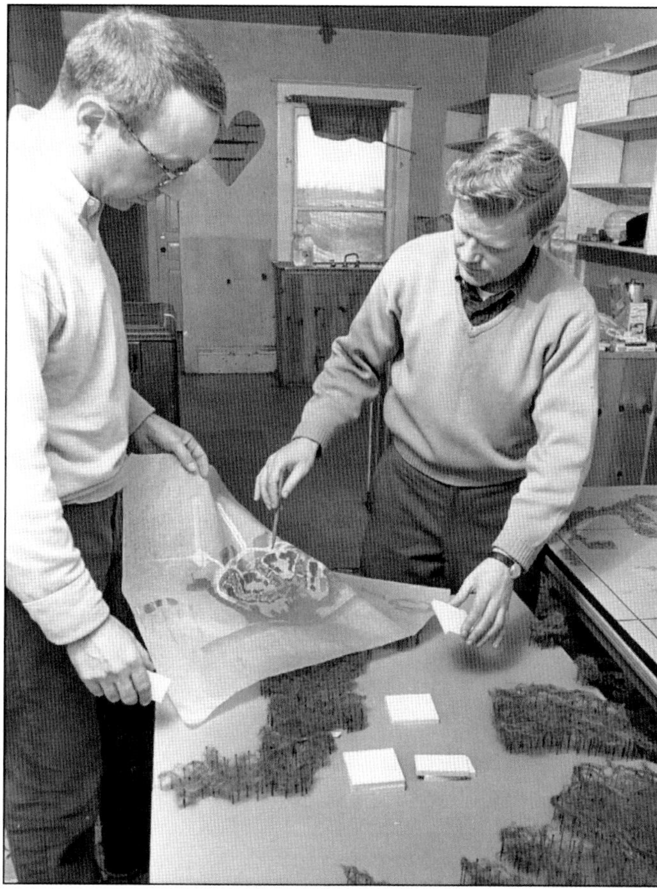

The cows in the road next to the field house illustrate the fact that the school was built in the Grand Valley farmlands. Though the area around the university has become more commercial, there are still many farms. (Courtesy of the Grand Valley State University Library.)

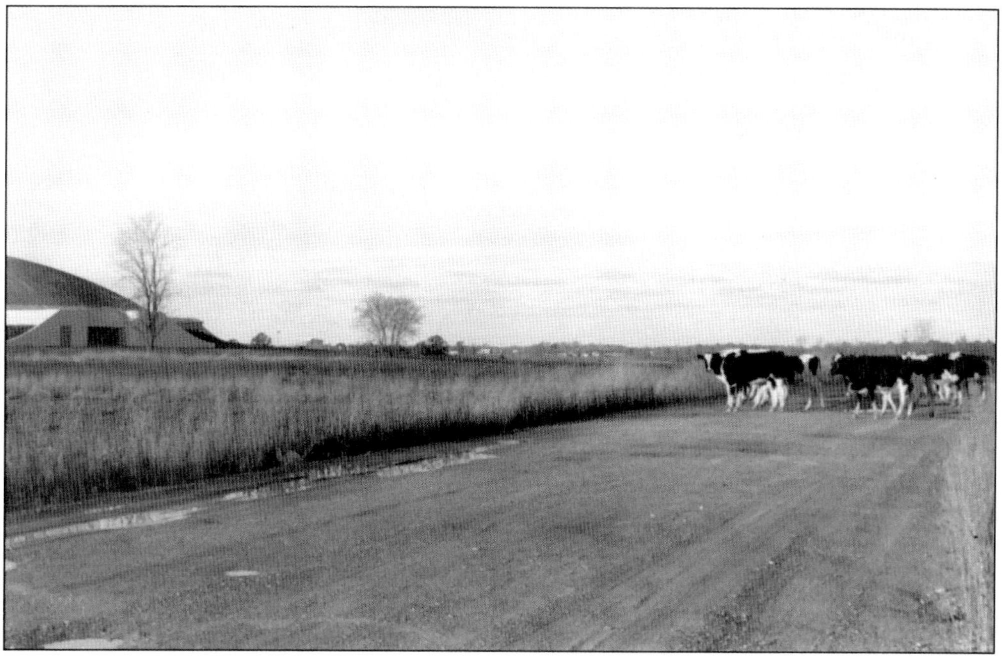

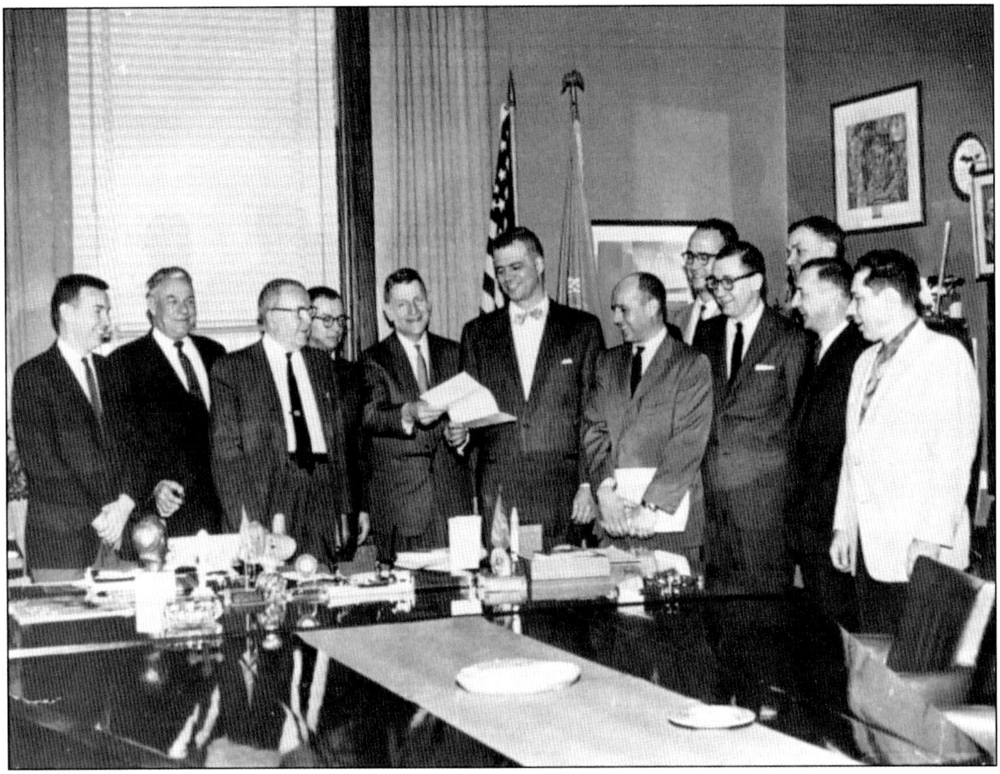

Gov. G. Mennen Williams (wearing bow tie) reviews a bill proposing establishment of GVSU. The bill was introduced by state representative Thomas Whinery on February 22, 1960. Whinery is holding the document, and the first GVSU president, Dr. James H. Zumberge, is standing at the governor's right. (Courtesy of the Grand Valley State University Library.)

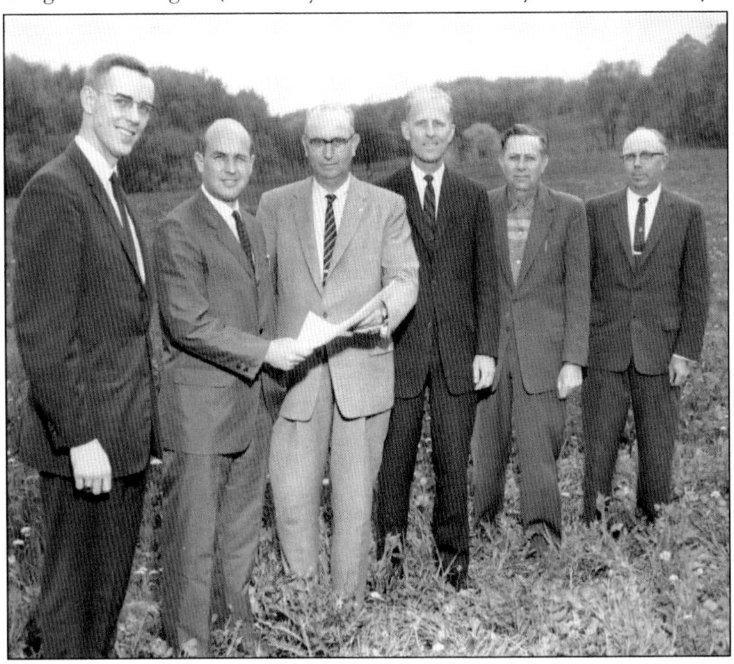

Dr. Zumberge meets with Allendale businessmen before construction began in 1970. (Courtesy of the Grand Valley State University Library.)

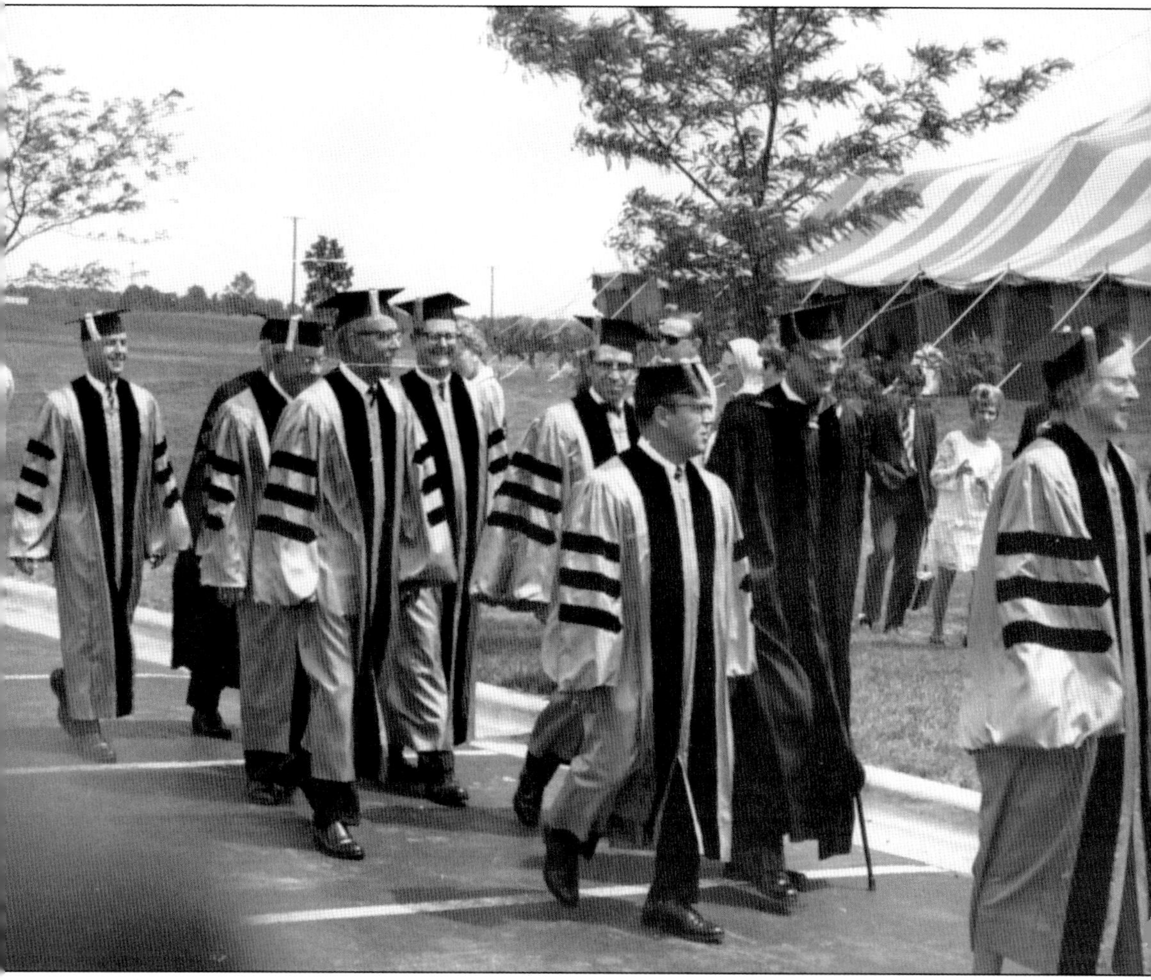

Grand Valley State University's first commencement was held in a tent on June 18, 1967. The class consisted of 138 students. By fall 2014, more than 25,000 undergraduates were enrolled. (Courtesy of the Grand Valley State University Library.)

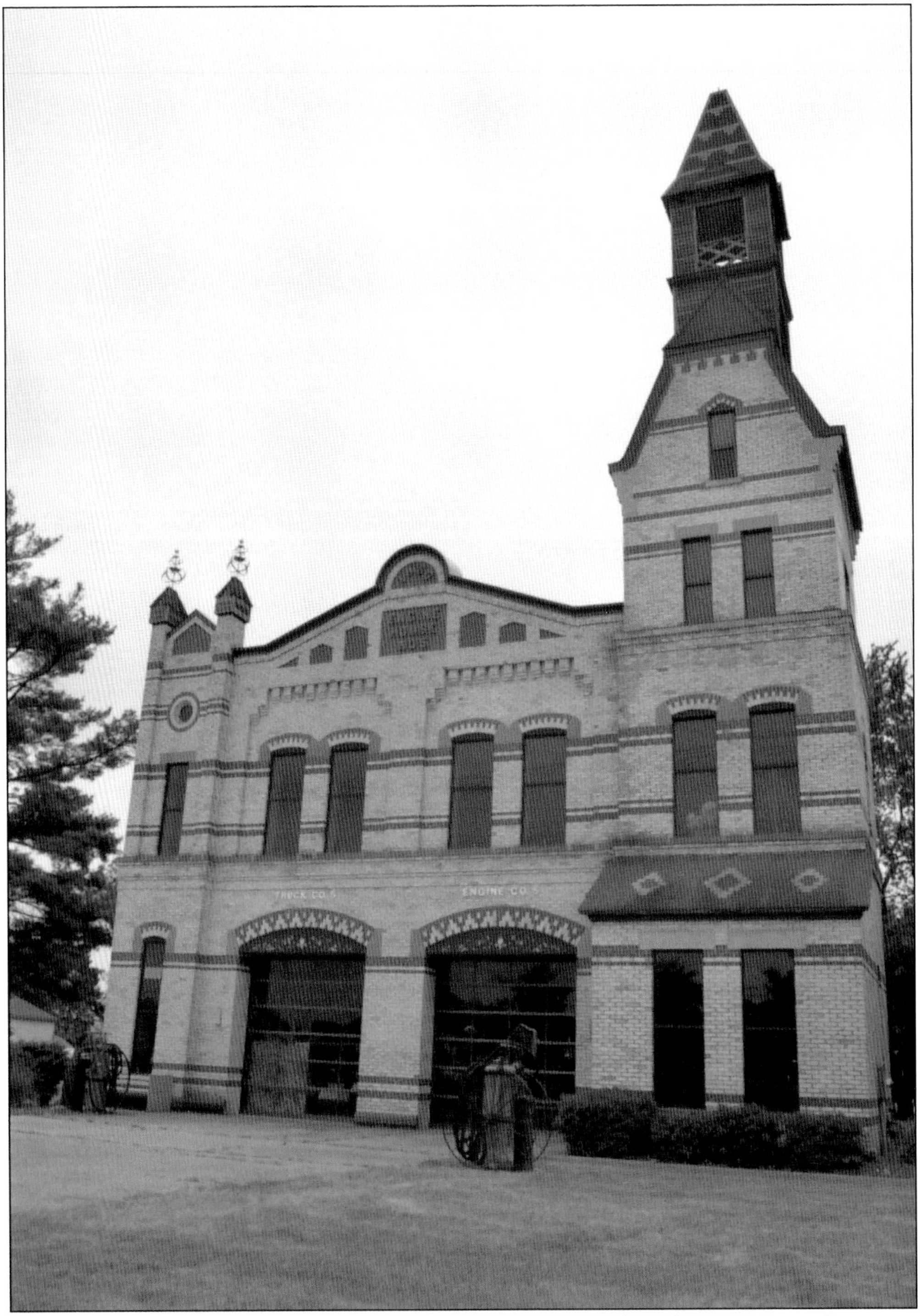

Engine House No. 5 was constructed in 1880 and stood on the north bank of the river in downtown Grand Rapids. In 1980, when it was announced that the building would be razed, the City of Allendale bought it, took it apart, and reconstructed it brick by brick. Five years later, it opened to the public in its new role as a fire museum. (Photograph by Shelby Ayers.)

Four

THE TRI-CITIES

William Montague Ferry is given credit for founding the area, but Rix Robinson was instrumental as well. Reverend Ferry, a Presbyterian, had been serving the mission at Mackinac Island in northern Michigan, and Robinson ran the Ada, Michigan, trading post before both men arrived at the mouth of river at nearly the same time. Robinson named it Grand Haven. A year later, four of his brothers settled on the river at what is now Robinson Townshsip. Ferrysburg is named for the Reverend Ferry.

The two men were friends and business partners, and when Ferry started the First Presbyterian Church, he preached his first sermon in Robinson's cabin. With Robert Stuart, they formed the Grand Haven Company and bought forested land on which they cut timber and brought the logs to their Grand Haven sawmills. Soon, area factories produced everything from farm machinery to pianos. Those jobs brought more people here.

The US Life-Saving Service established a station on the channel, which from the start was an important part of the community. Children in the beachfront Highland Park neighborhood recalled being taught to swim by crew members who held them over the side of a boat by their legs. When the Coast Guard cutter *Escanaba* went down in World War II, Grand Haven residents took it personally. This was its home port, and they raised more than $1 million to build a new ship. The city still holds an annual memorial service to honor the 101 men lost. The annual Coast Guard Festival is now the largest summer event.

During the 1960s, as more and more local industries closed or moved away, it was decided to turn to the obvious solution and promote tourism. That idea was a winner, as it would be hard to find a better place to vacation or have a second home. Between the Grand River, Spring Lake with all its bayous, and Lake Michigan, it is a water lover's dream destination. The downtown area was revitalized, and exudes quaint charm.

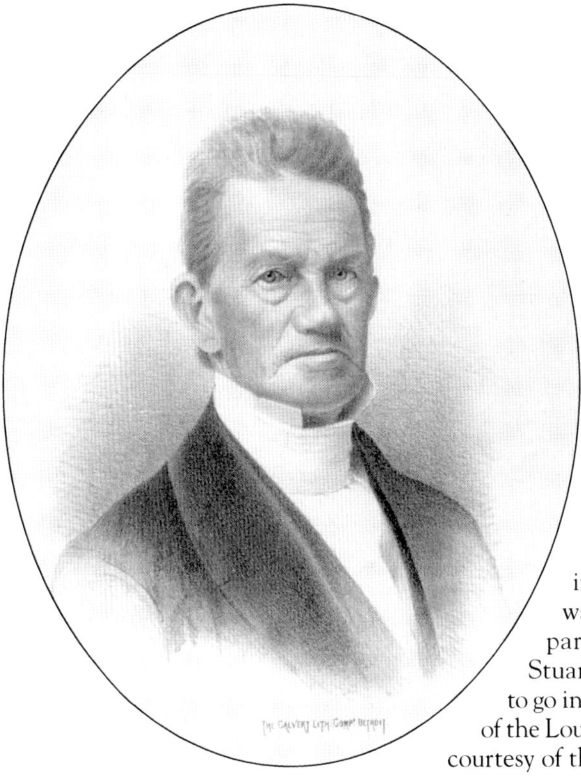

Rev. William Montague Ferry and his wife, Amanda, came to the area in 1834, and he founded the First Presbyterian Church. He preached his first sermon in Rix Robinson's cabin. Reverend Ferry was also an astute businessman and, in partnership with Robinson and Robert Stuart, formed the Grand Haven Company to go into the lumbering business. (Left, courtesy of the Loutit District Library, Grand Haven; below, courtesy of the Tri-Cities Museum, Grand Haven.)

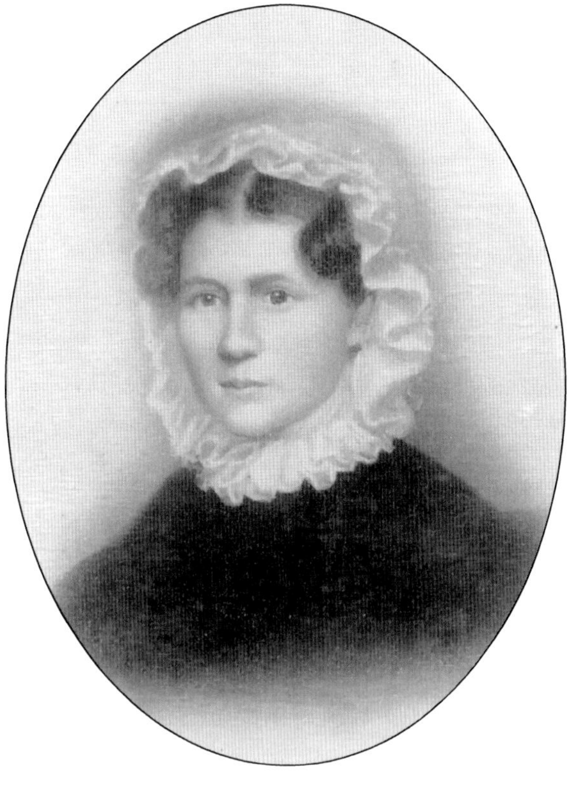

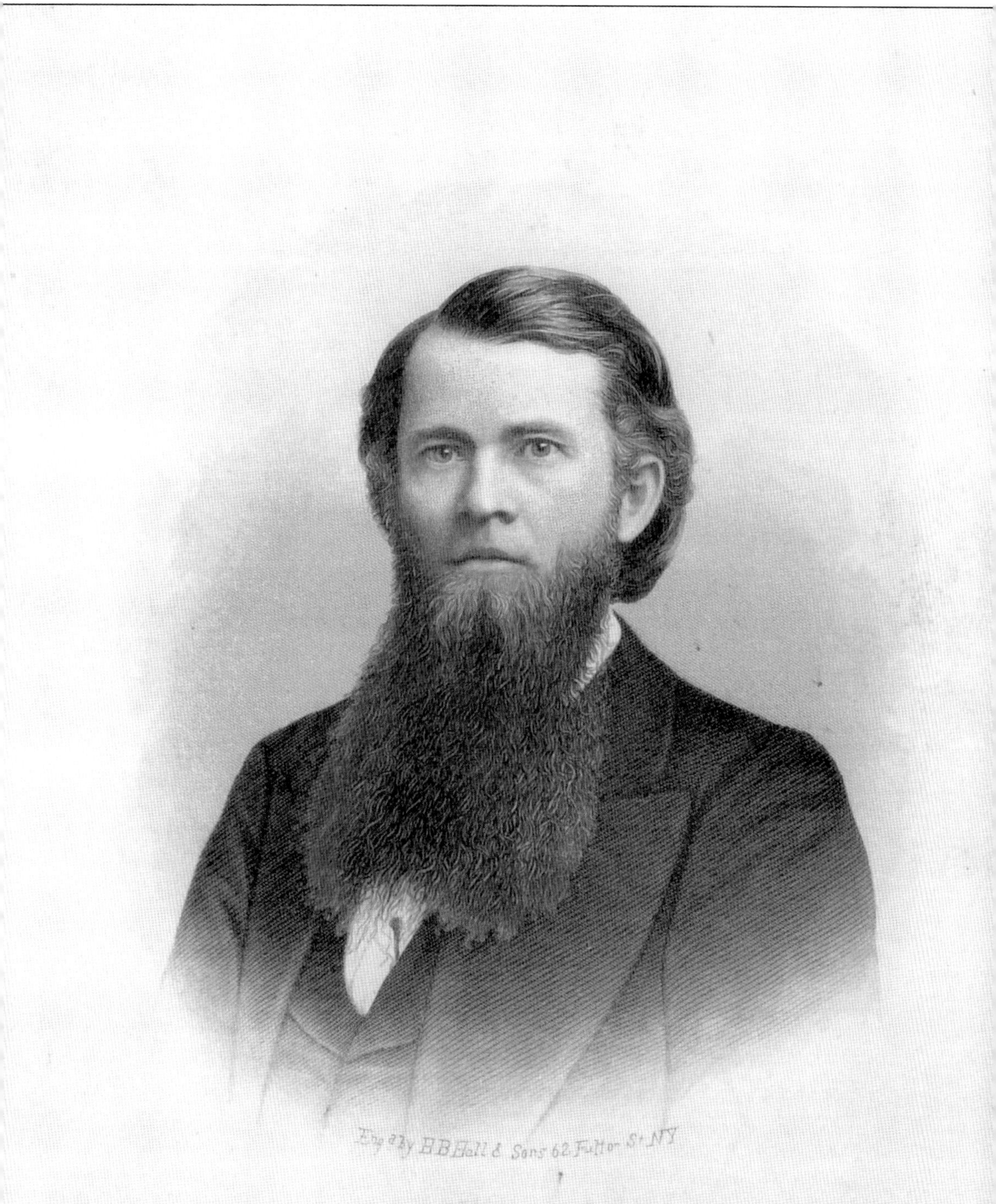

William and Amanda's son, Thomas White Ferry, was elected to the US House of Representatives and served from 1865 until 1871, when he became a US senator. Thomas Ferry was the first person from Michigan to serve in both houses of Congress. (Courtesy of the Loutit District Library, Grand Haven.)

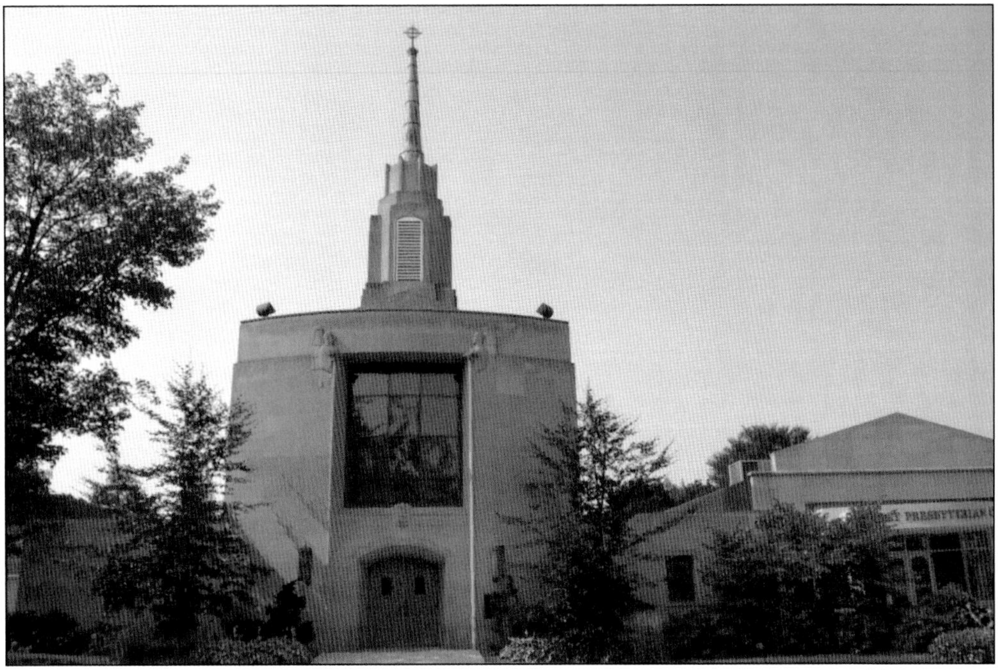

Reverend Ferry's First Presbyterian Church is still going strong at its present 508 Franklin Avenue location, and the congregation is now led by senior pastor and head of staff Rev. Dr. Tom Cook. A plaque honors the Reverend Ferry's role in the history of the church and the city. (Both, photograph by Shelby Ayers.)

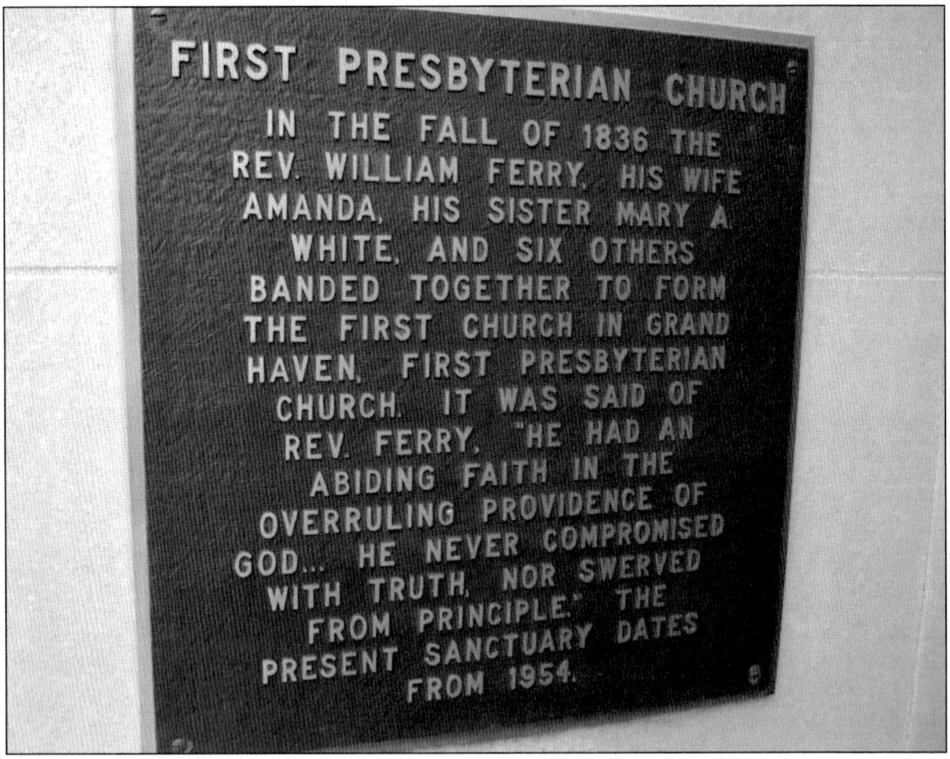

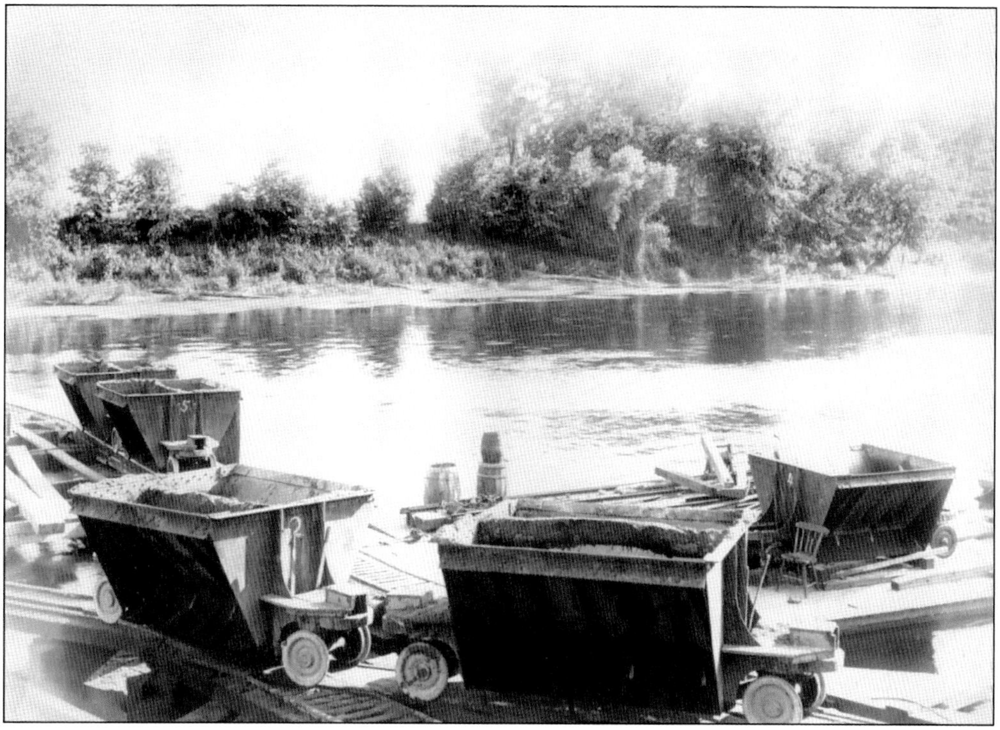

A wing dam, a barrier that extends only partway into the stream, was constructed for better navigability. In the image below, pile driver Tom Johnson of Grand Haven is using a wing dam pole to probe the water. Diggings from the channel were loaded in metal railcars on a small-gauge track to be dumped in the wing dam as fill. (Both, courtesy of the Loutit District Library, Grand Haven.)

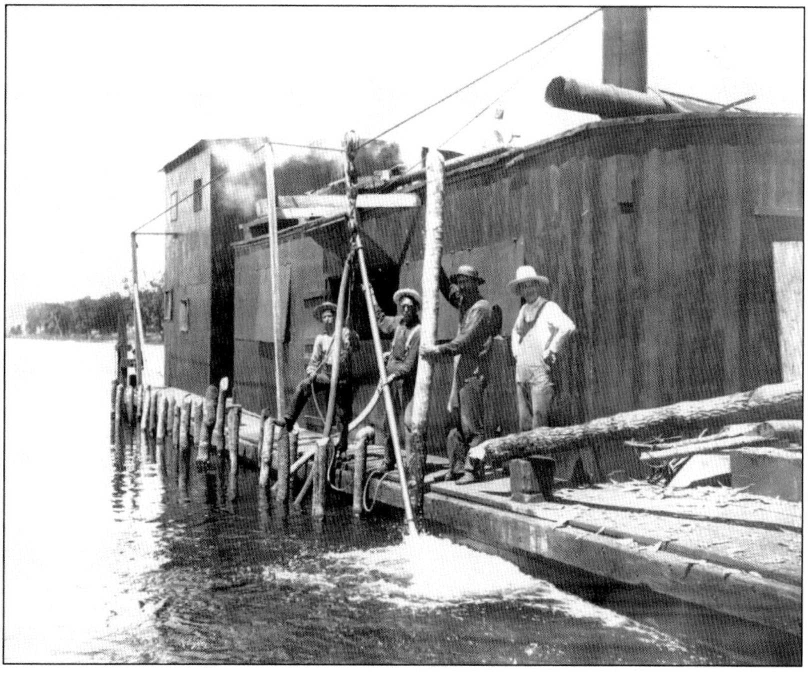

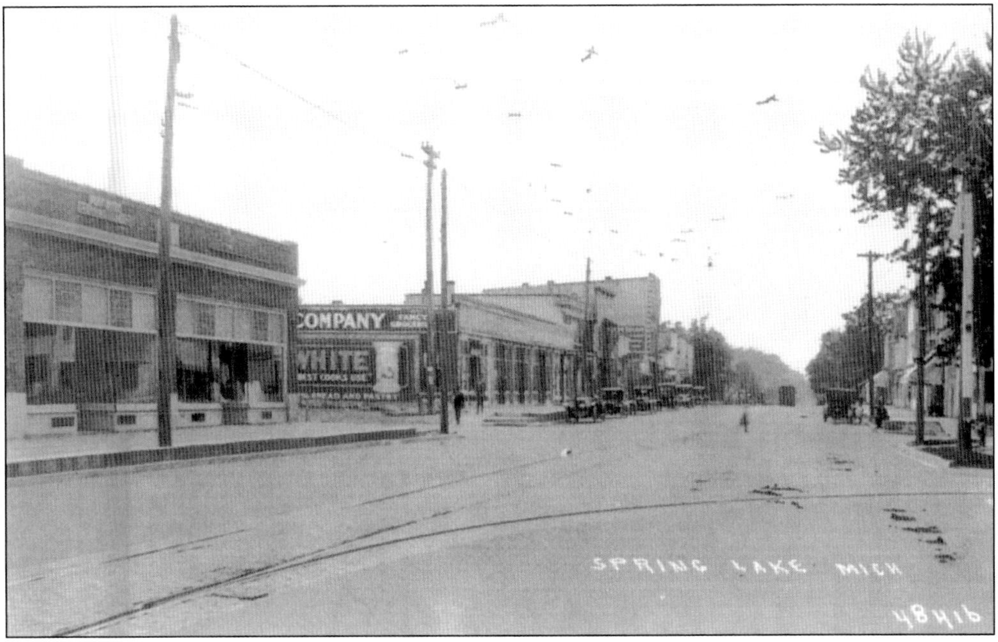

Spring Lake's Savidge Street looked like this around 1910, when residents were just beginning to discover the joys of automobile ownership. (Courtesy of Joyce Howard.)

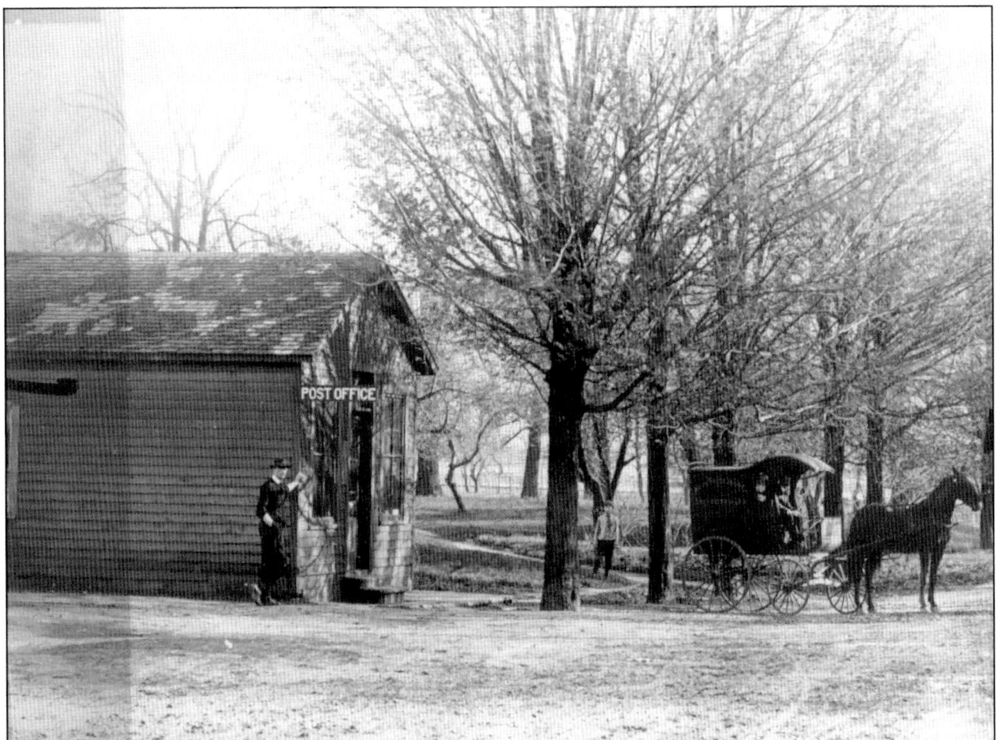

By the end of the 19th century, the tri-cities area was well established and provided all the necessary services. Here, an unidentified man driving a horse and buggy is stopped outside the Ferrysburg post office. (Courtesy of the Hekman Library, Calvin College.)

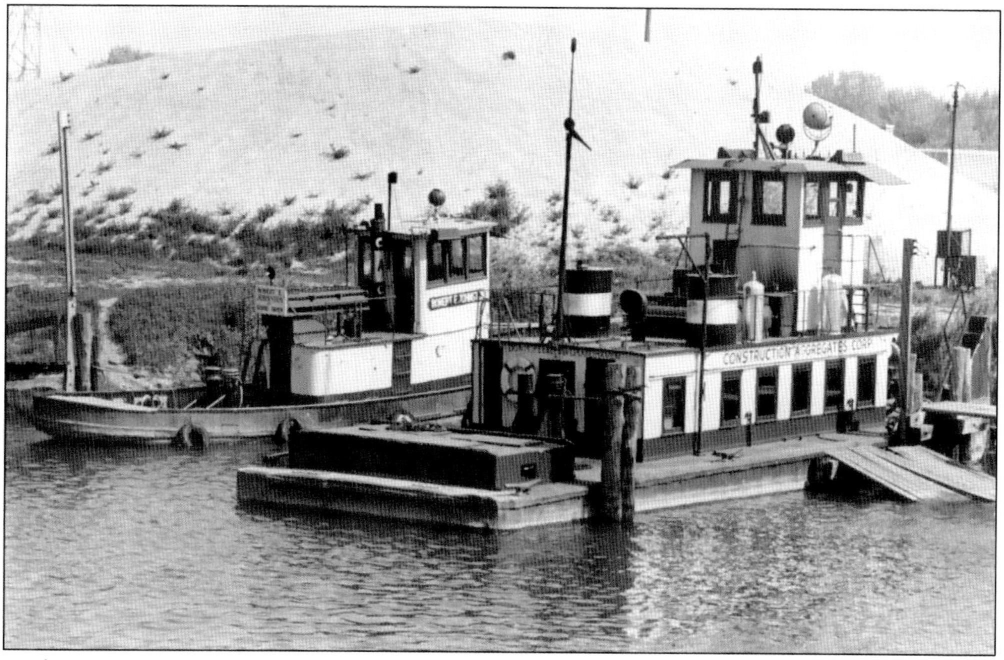

Tugboats were a common sight in the channel to Lake Michigan. These two are in front of Dewey Hill. This is the spot where boaters now drop anchor to watch the musical fountain or listen to the many concerts held during the summer months. (Courtesy of the Loutit District Library, Grand Haven.)

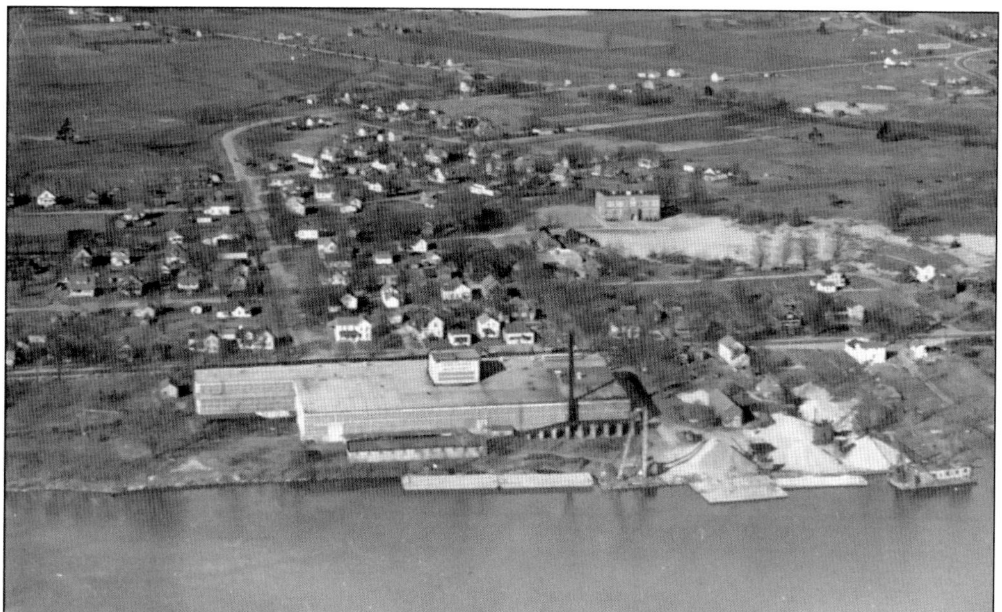

When Willard Sheldon discovered mineral springs in Grand Haven, he did what others on the river had done and opened a resort, the Magnetic Mineral Hot Springs. Sheldon's establishment included croquet and other outdoor games and other upscale extras. Like the other mineral water resorts on the river, it closed permanently when the fad ran its course. (Courtesy of the Loutit District Library, Grand Haven.)

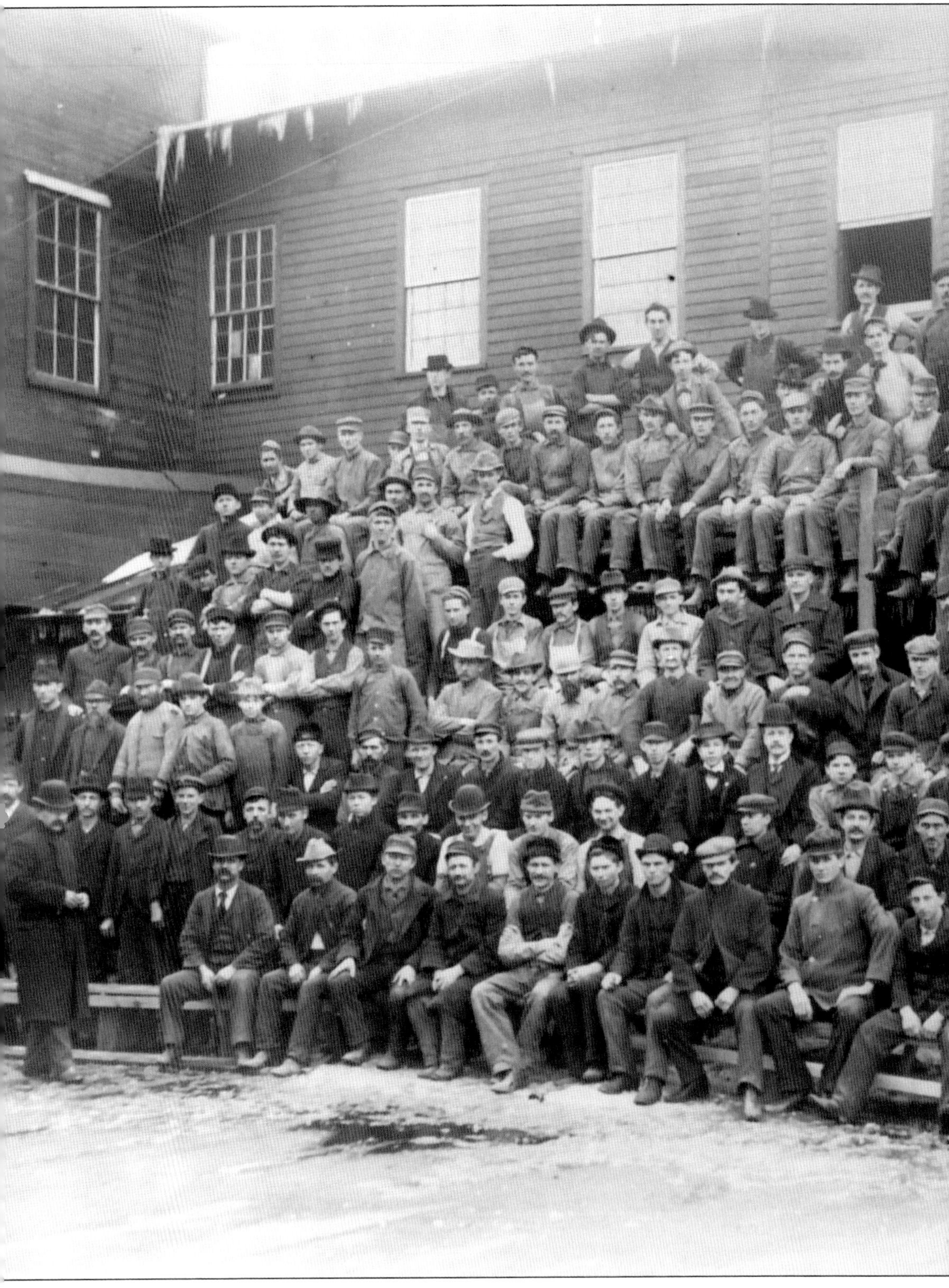

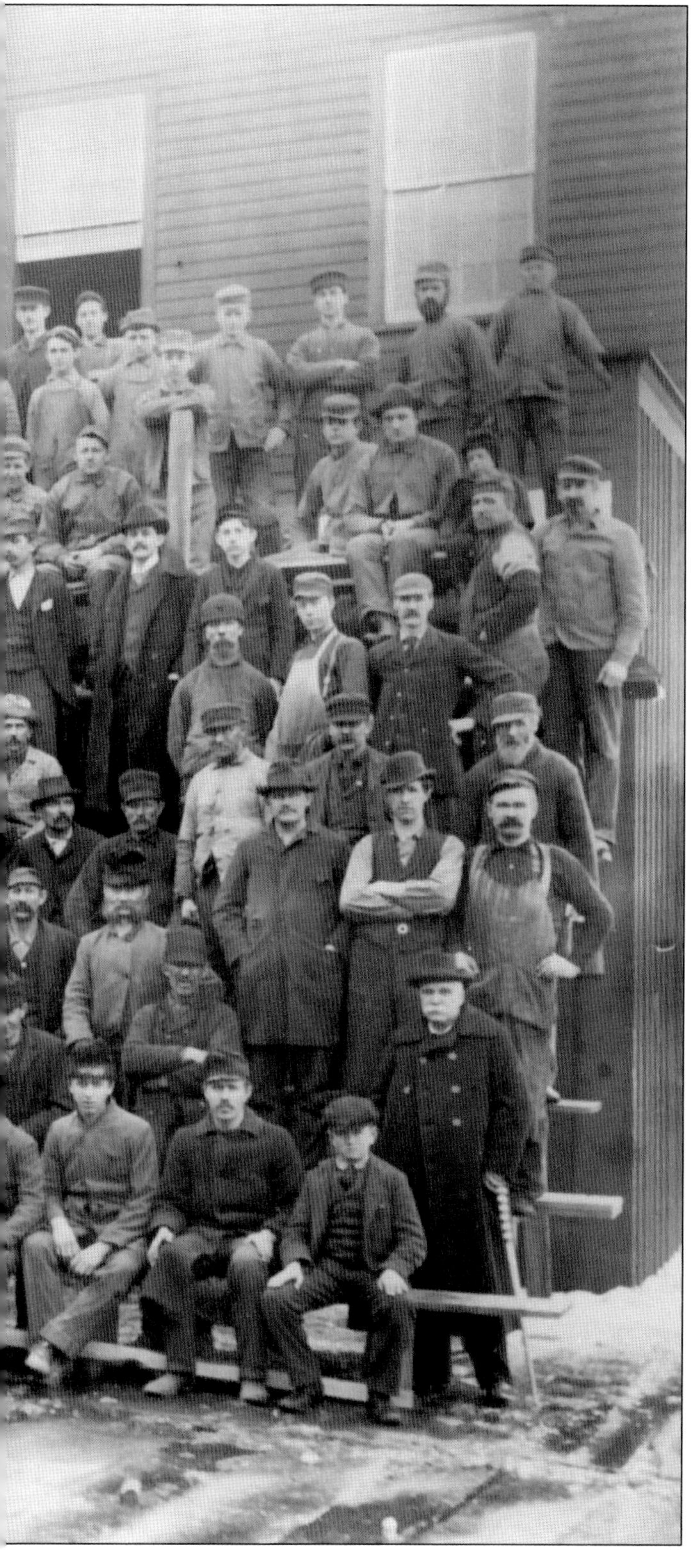

The Challenge Corn Planter Works began producing corn planting machines and refrigerators in 1883 and soon became one of Grand Haven's largest employers. The company's products were sold all across the United States. By 1912, the factory was spread over 20 acres and had at least 10 buildings. (Courtesy of the Loutit District Library, Grand Haven.)

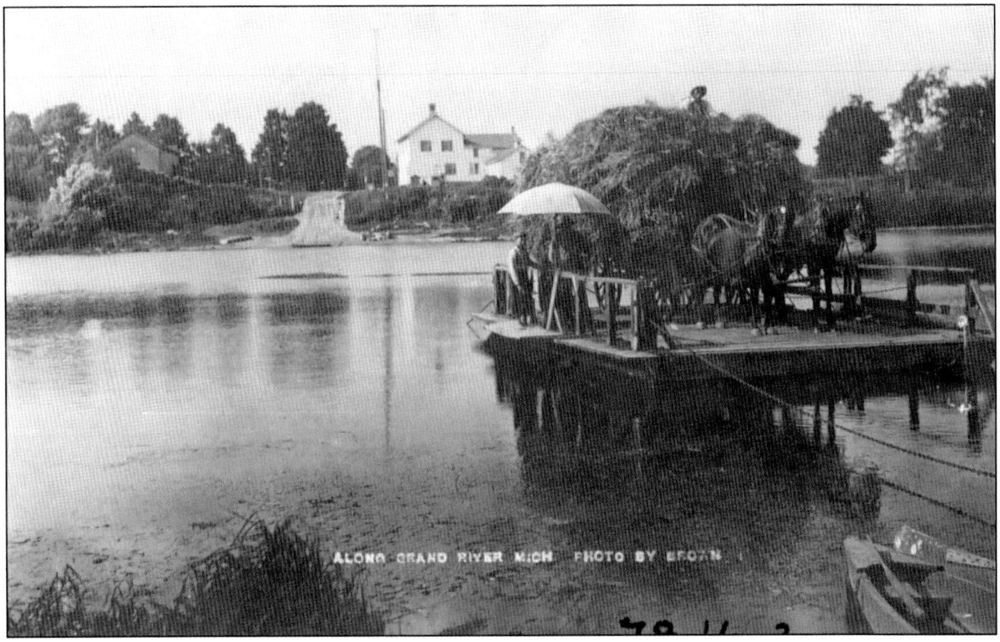

Two of the many ferries crossing the Grand River before bridges were constructed to meet the growing need. The ferry above operated east of Spoonville, near Crockery Creek. The early automobile industry increased the demand for bridges. (Both, courtesy of the Tri-Cities Museum, Grand Haven.)

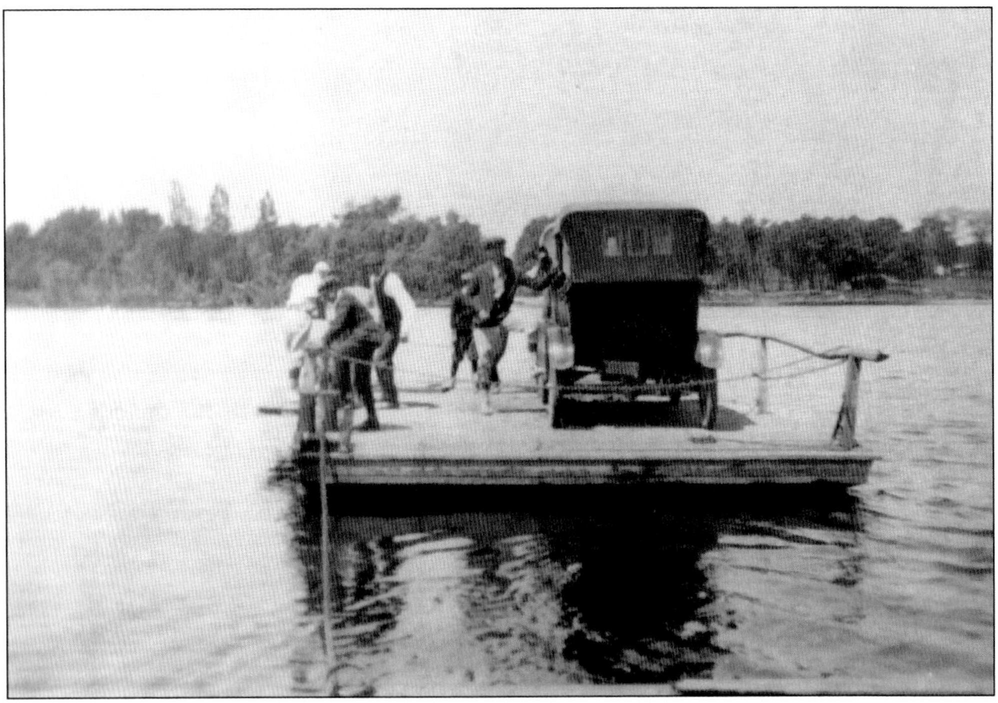

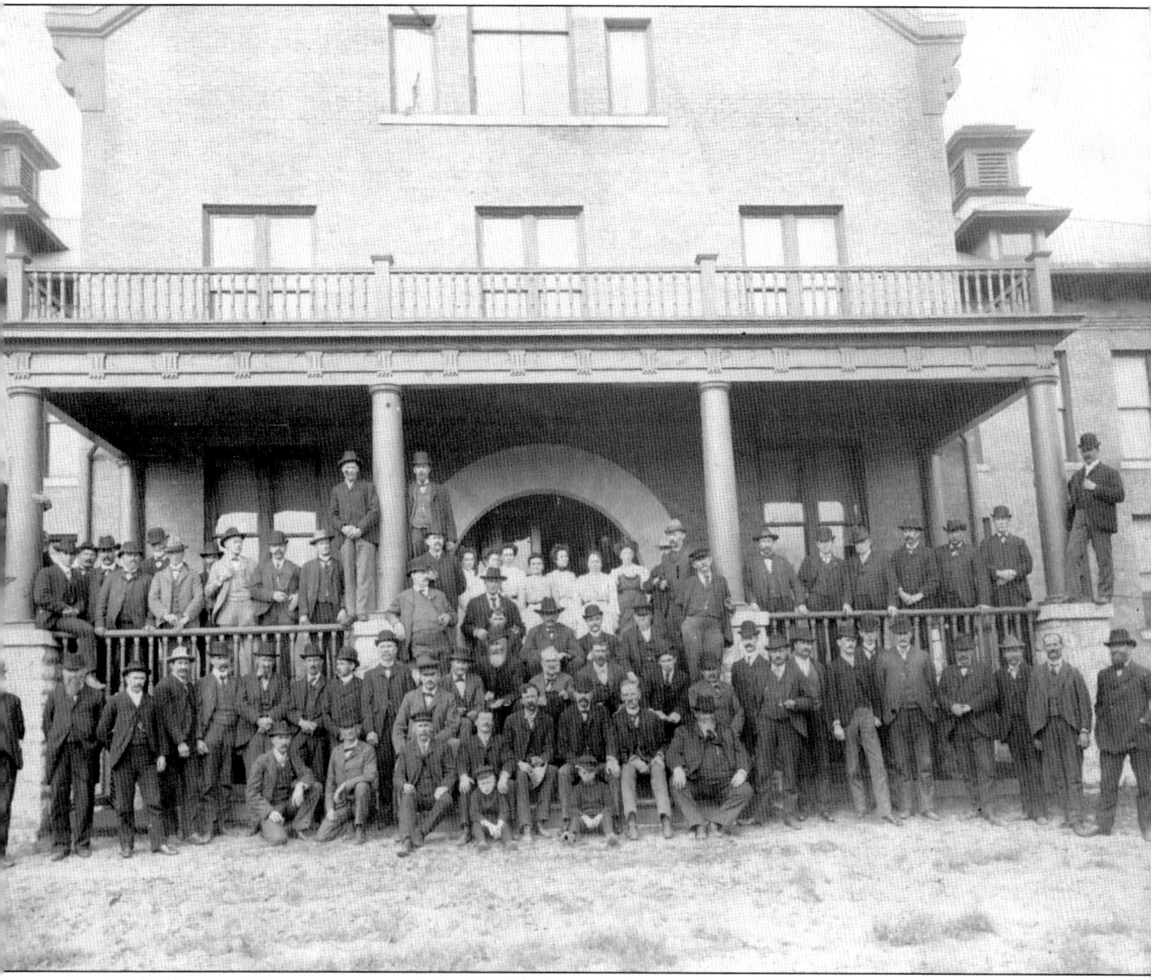

In 1885, Ottawa County acquired the Really farm to be used as a county poor farm. In January 1896, voters agreed to an expenditure of $9,000 for additions and improvements. By the end of the year, work was completed and the facility was ready for use. (Courtesy of the Tri-Cities Museum, Grand Haven.)

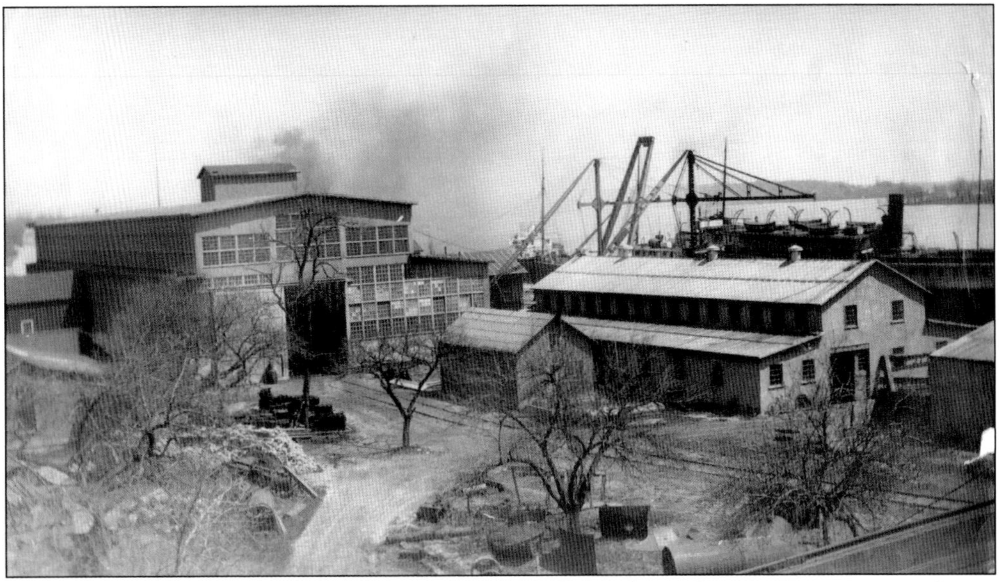

Johnston Boiler Works, founded by J.W. Johnston, a descendant of steam engine pioneer James Watt, began producing boilers in Ferrysburg in 1864. Johnston and his company became nationally prominent with the Scotch Marine fire tube boiler. The company is still going strong. (Courtesy of the Tri-Cities Museum, Grand Haven.)

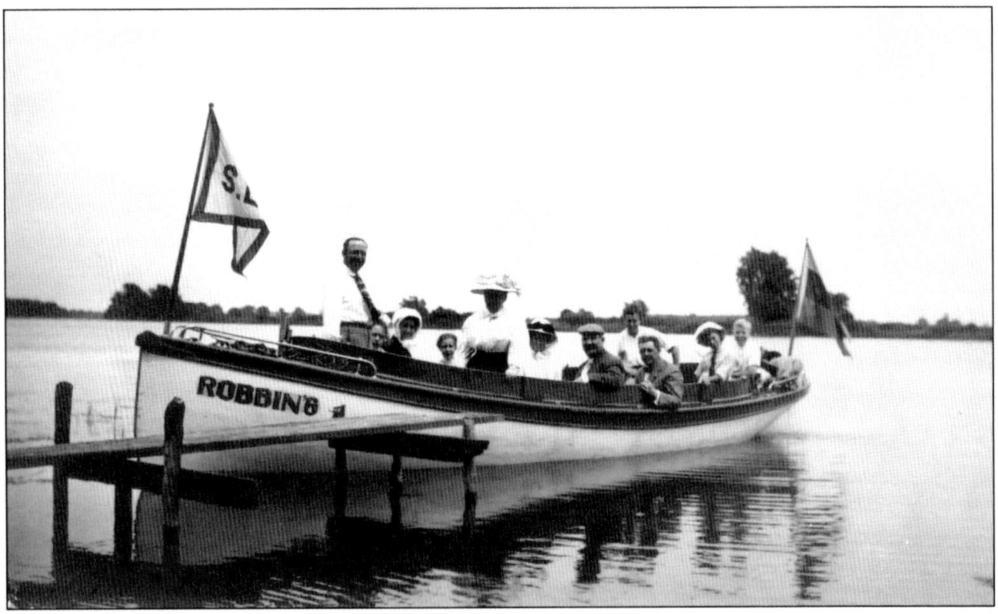

The Savidge family, among the early Spring Lake settlers, contributed greatly to the growth of the area. They were involved in lumber and other industries. William Savidge enjoyed boating and is shown here on the *Robbins II*, at Cross's Landing. Wearing a light-colored cap, he is seated amidships. (Courtesy of the Tri-Cities Museum, Grand Haven.)

Beginning in 1922, the annual Coast Guard Festival became Grand Haven's most important summer event. The group pictured here began the tradition when the men and their families shared a picnic. (Courtesy of the Loutit District Library, Grand Haven.)

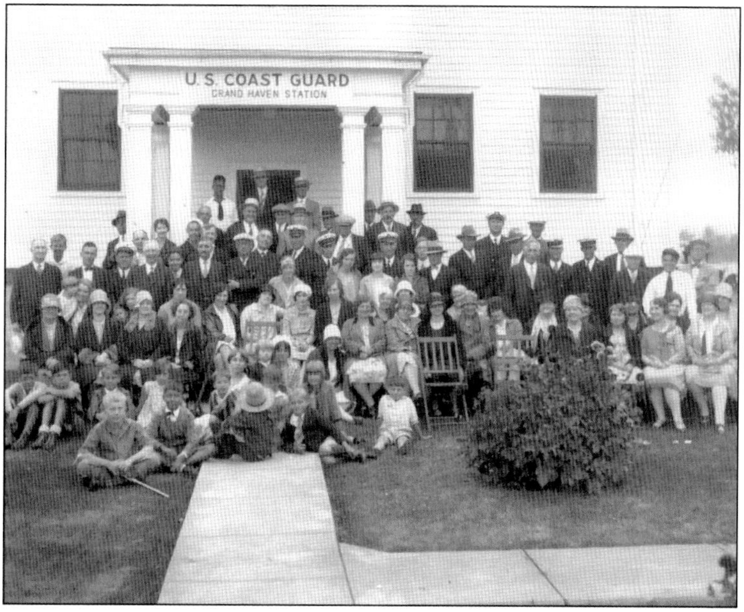

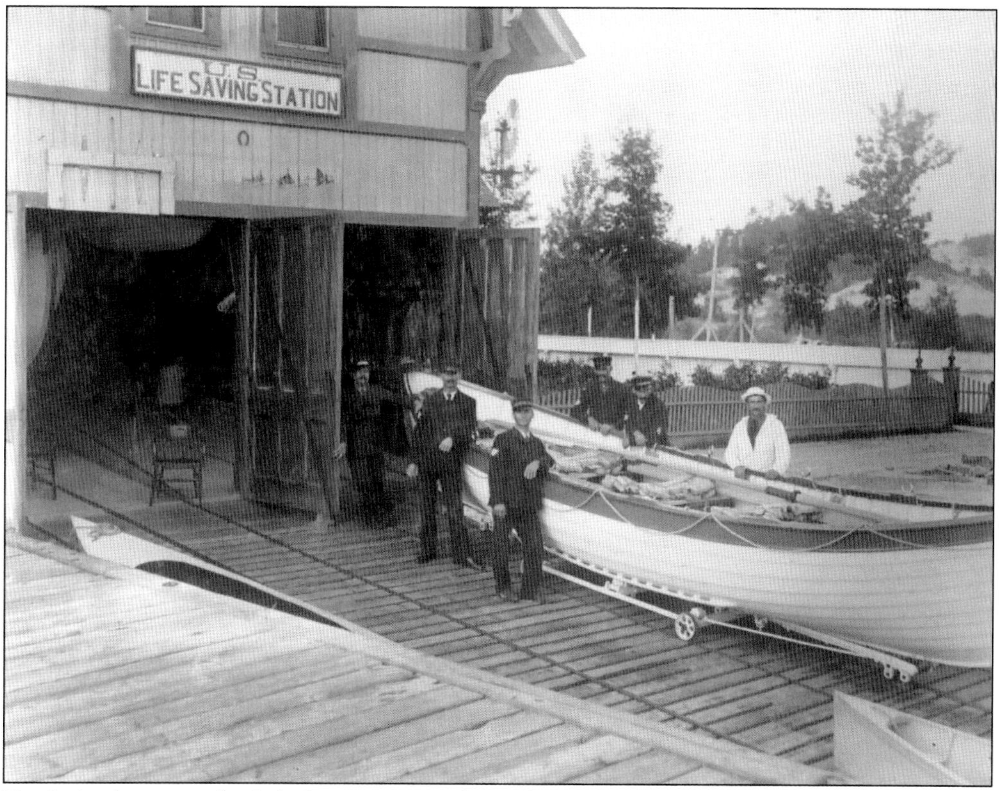

Tracks leading into the Life-Saving station, later the Coast Guard station, made it easier to get boats in and out of the water. Officers shown here on the left side of the vessel are, from left to right, Capt. William Walker, Jakob Van Weelden, and Frank Vogel. Pictured here on the right side are, from left to right, Heman Castle, Charles Peterson, and Charles Robinson. (Courtesy of the Loutit District Library, Grand Haven.)

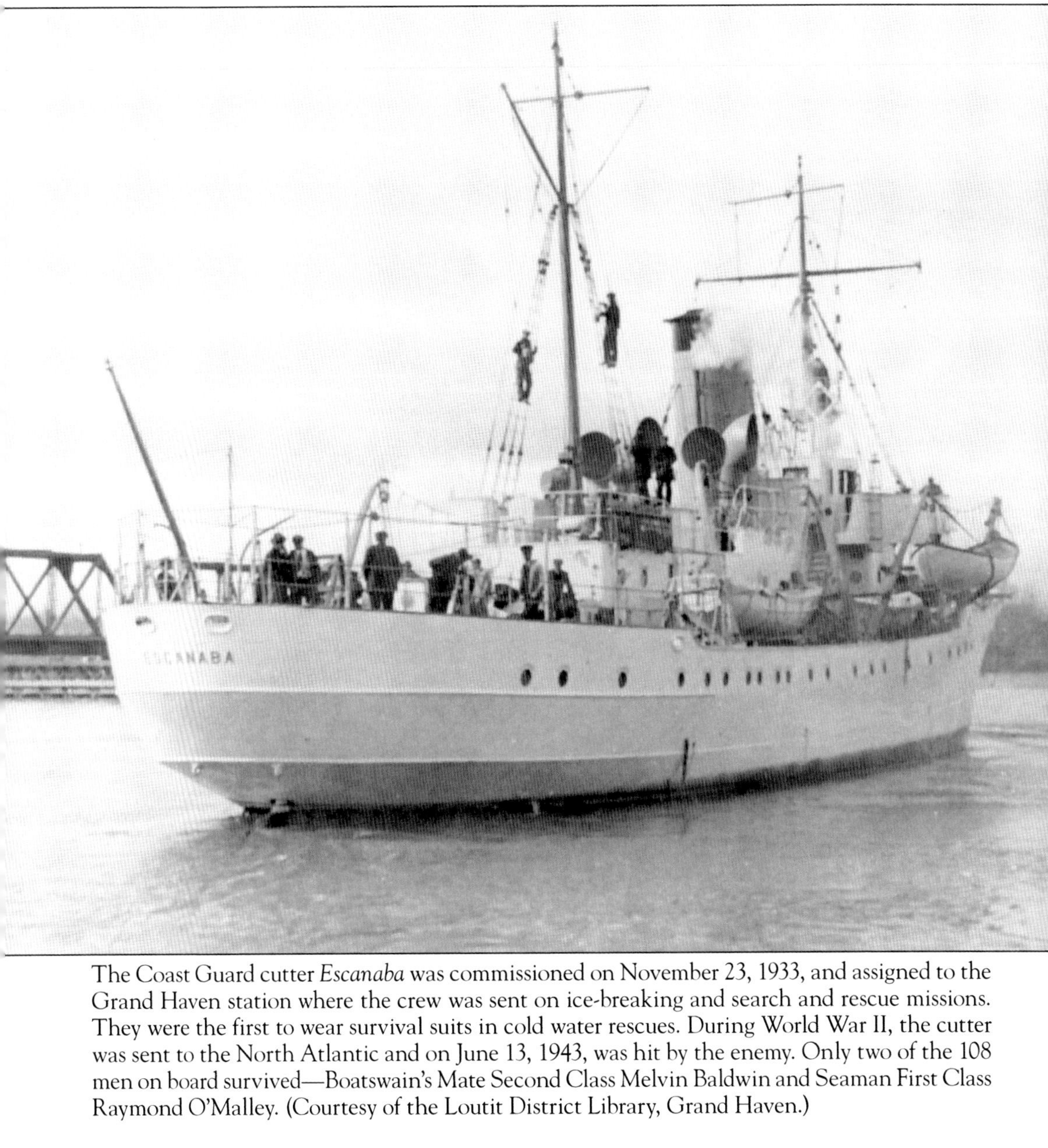

The Coast Guard cutter *Escanaba* was commissioned on November 23, 1933, and assigned to the Grand Haven station where the crew was sent on ice-breaking and search and rescue missions. They were the first to wear survival suits in cold water rescues. During World War II, the cutter was sent to the North Atlantic and on June 13, 1943, was hit by the enemy. Only two of the 108 men on board survived—Boatswain's Mate Second Class Melvin Baldwin and Seaman First Class Raymond O'Malley. (Courtesy of the Loutit District Library, Grand Haven.)

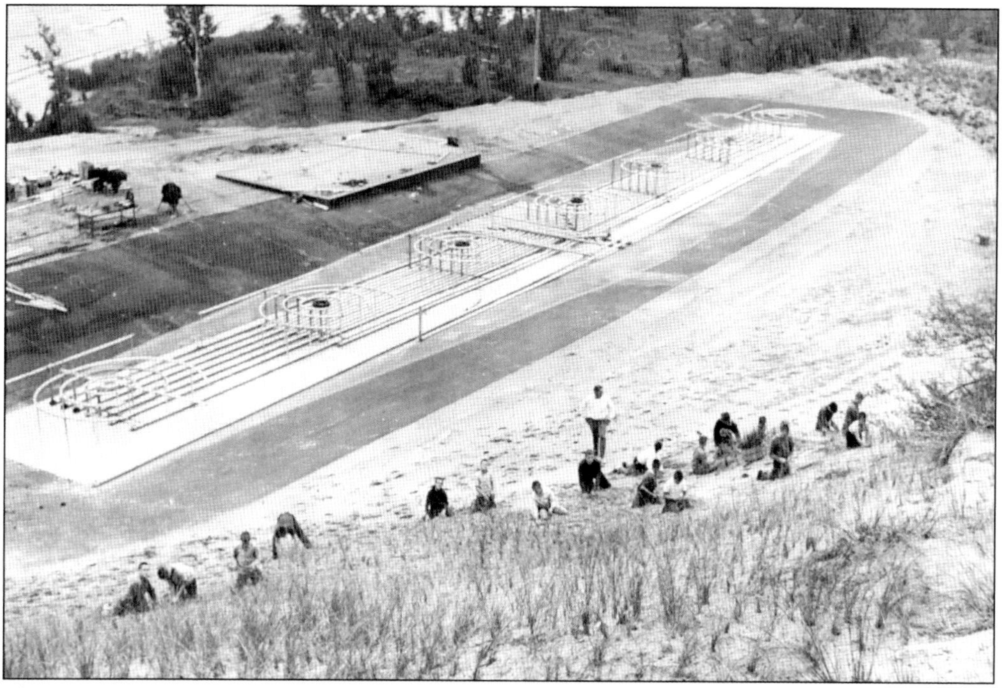

The musical fountain is one of Grand Haven's most popular attractions. Every night during the summer, locals and visitors flock to the waterfront for the light show and music of the 20-minute spectacle put on by the largest fountain of its kind. These 1963 images show its beginnings. Above, Boy Scouts plant sea grass on the Dewey Hill site. Below, cars lined up and boats stopped to take in the first performance. (Both, courtesy of the Loutit District Library, Grand Haven.)

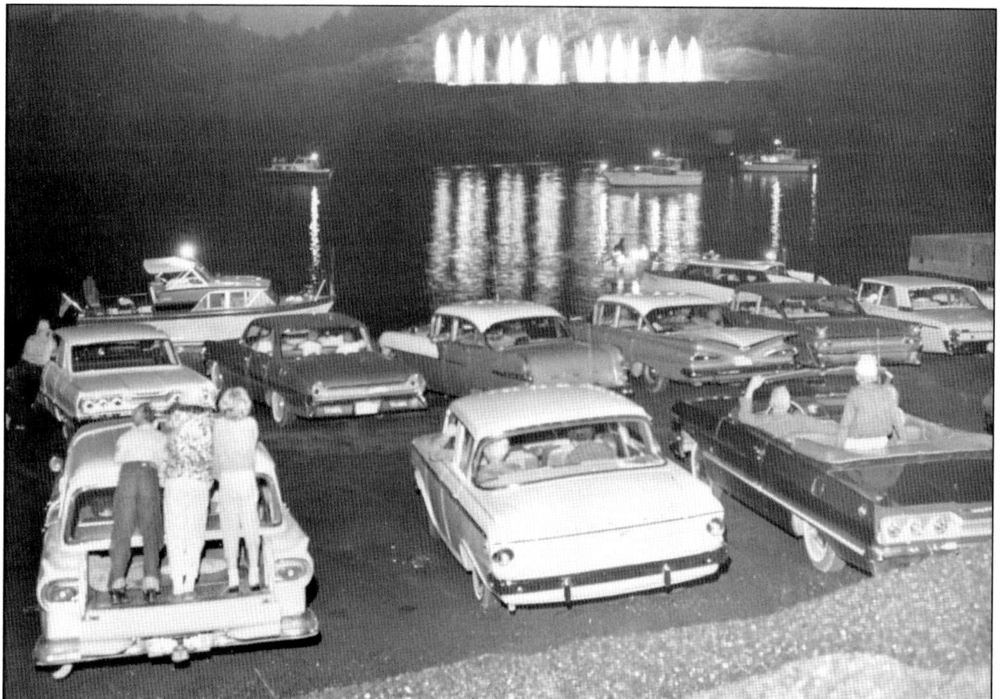

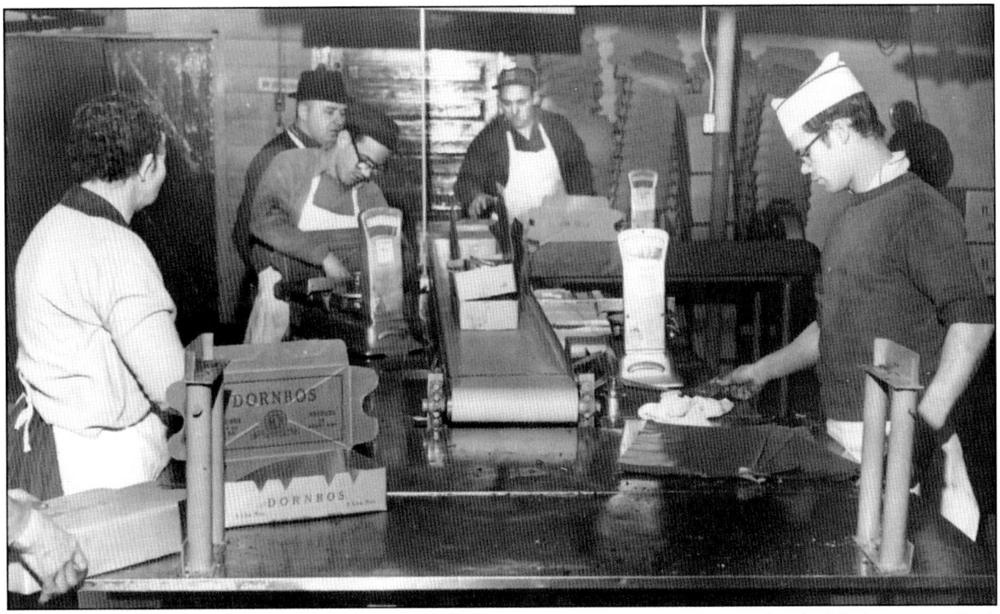

Henry Dornbos and Bros. had been selling fish for 74 years when the unthinkable happened. A botulism outbreak was traced back to the company after a load of smoked chubs was left in an unrefrigerated truck over a weekend. Though the company was not to blame, it closed in 1963. Some good came out of the tragedy, as it led to tighter regulations in the industry. (Courtesy of the Loutit District Library, Grand Haven.)

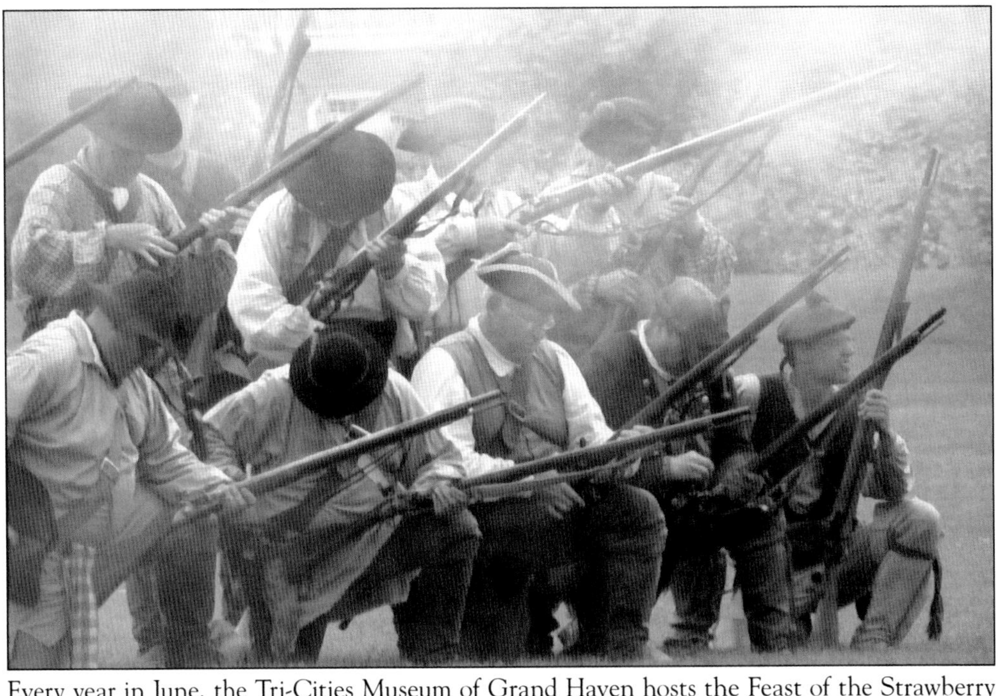

Every year in June, the Tri-Cities Museum of Grand Haven hosts the Feast of the Strawberry Moon on the riverbank. It is a fun-filled weekend celebrating life in the area during the 1700s. Reenactors representing fur traders, Native Americans, tradesmen of the days, and military units gather to show spectators what life was like in the old days. (Photograph by Jane Ladley.)

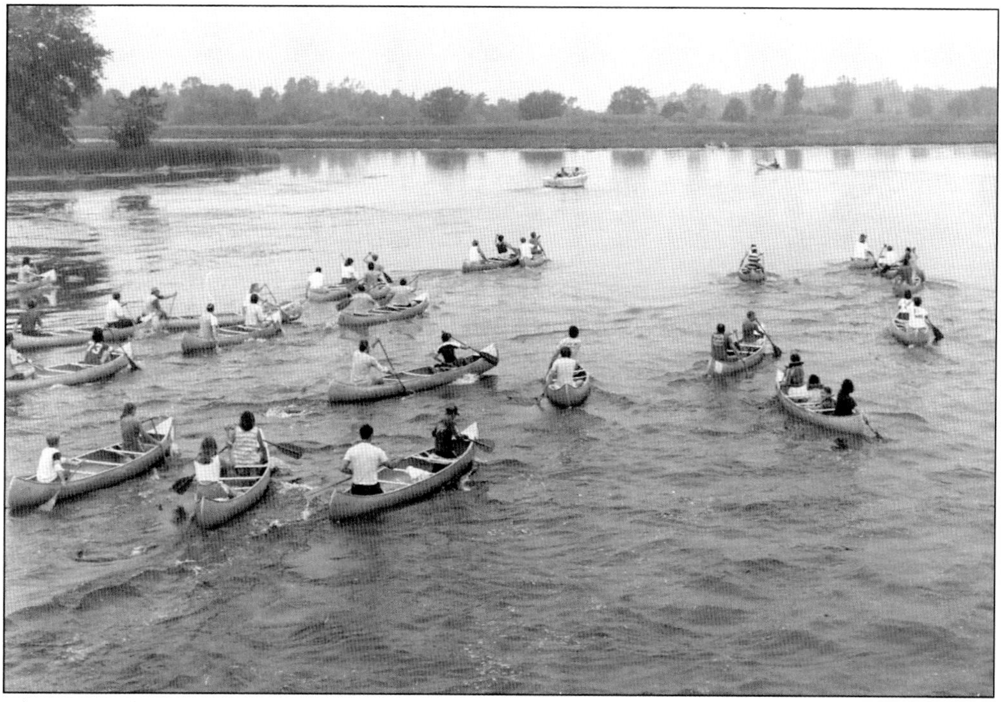

There is nothing better than a warm day spent canoeing on the river. With the river itself and Spring Lake with its many bayous, the possibilities are endless. By the late 20th century when this photograph was taken, the river was once again clean and safe for recreational use. (Courtesy of the Loutit District Library, Grand Haven.)

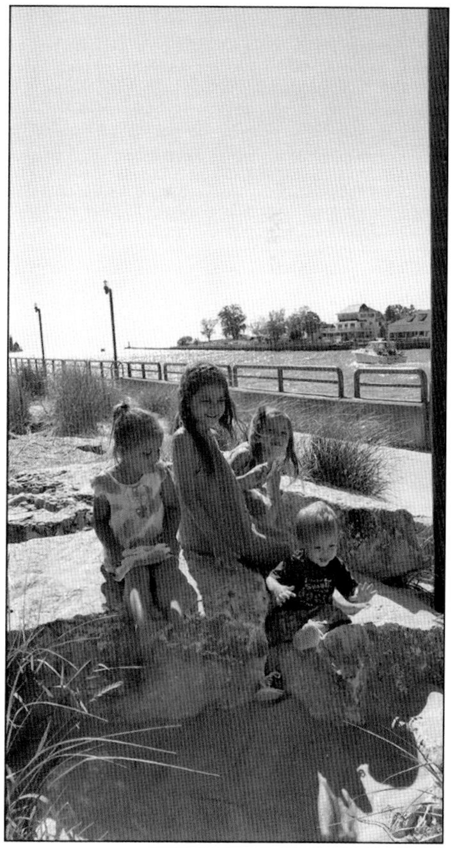

The Grand River ends here where the channel flows into Lake Michigan. Pictured, from left to right, are the De Vries sisters—Jasmine, Iris, and Lily—and their younger brother Joshua in front. They are enjoying time at the lake. Their parents are Daniel and Hazel De Vries of Shelbyville. (Courtesy of Daniel and Hazel De Vries.)